Beginning JavaFX™

■ ■ ■

LAWRENCE PREMKUMAR
PRAVEEN MOHAN

Apress®

Beginning JavaFX™

ISBN-13 (pbk): 978-1-4302-7199-4

ISBN-13 (electronic): 978-1-4302-7198-7

Printed and bound in the United States of America (POD)

President and Publisher: Paul Manning
Lead Editor: Steve Anglin
Development Editor: Tom Welsh
Technical Reviewer: Sten Anderson
Editorial Board: Clay Andres, Steve Anglin, Mark Beckner, Ewan Buckingham, Gary Cornell, Jonathan Gennick, Jonathan Hassell, Michelle Lowman, Matthew Moodie, Duncan Parkes, Jeffrey Pepper, Frank Pohlmann, Douglas Pundick, Ben Renow-Clarke, Dominic Shakeshaft, Matt Wade, Tom Welsh
Coordinating Editor: Kelly Moritz
Copy Editor: James A. Compton
Compositor: Kimberly Burton
Indexer: Toma Mulligan
Artist: April Milne
Cover Designer: Anna Ishchenko

Distributed to the book trade worldwide by Springer Science+Business Media, LLC., 233 Spring Street, 6th Floor, New York, NY 10013. Phone 1-800-SPRINGER, fax (201) 348-4505, e-mail orders-ny@springer-sbm.com, or visit www.springeronline.com.

For information on translations, please e-mail rights@apress.com, or visit www.apress.com.

Apress and friends of ED books may be purchased in bulk for academic, corporate, or promotional use. eBook versions and licenses are also available for most titles. For more information, reference our Special Bulk Sales–eBook Licensing web page at www.apress.com/info/bulksales.

The source code for this book is available to readers at www.apress.com. You will need to answer questions pertaining to this book in order to successfully download the code.

I dedicate this book to my beloved parents, Andrew and Jyothimani, brothers Bharath and Ranjith, wife Lavanya Lawrence, daughters Angel , Merlin and Bincy Lawrence and finally my friends Vimala Anne, Karkinath and Ravindra

— Lawrence PremKumar

I dedicate this book to my beloved parents, Dr. Prem Mohan and Sakunthala

—Praveen Mohan

Contents at a Glance

About the Authors xiv

About the Technical Reviewer xv

Acknowledgements xvi

Introduction xvii

Chapter 1: Introduction to RIA 1

Chapter 2: Introduction to JavaFX 9

Chapter 3: Data Types 33

Chapter 4: Operators and Expressions 47

Chapter 5: Functions 75

Chapter 6: Class Definitions 91

Chapter 7: Access Specifiers 109

Chapter 8: Inheritance 141

Chapter 9: Data Binding 155

Chapter 10: Sequences 175

Chapter 11: Triggers 189

Chapter 12: Introduction to JavaFX UI Elements 203

Chapter 13: Introduction to Animation 269

Index 303

Contents

About the Authors...xiv

About the Technical Reviewer xv

Acknowledgements xvi

Introduction xvii

Chapter 1: Introduction to RIA..1

   The History of RIA 1

   Key Characteristics of RIA 2

   RIA Workflow 2

   Why RIA..3

   Some RIA Examples 5

   Summary 7

Chapter 2: Introduction to JavaFX..9

   Why JavaFX 9

   Advantages of JavaFX...9

   History of JavaFX 10

   The JavaFX Platform 11

      The Developer Bundle.. 11

      The Designer Bundle 12

      Standalone... 12

   JavaFX Platform Integration: The Bigger Picture 13

   JavaFX Mobile: An Introduction 14

      Advantages of JavaFX Mobile.. 14

Deployment and Distribution 15

Getting Started 16

What to Download 16

Writing Your First JavaFX Application 16

Running Your Application Using NetBeans 21

Running the Application from the Command Line 27

Comments 30

Summary 31

Chapter 3: Data Types 33

Variable Declaration 33

var vs. def Declarations 34

Variable Naming 34

Variable Declaration Syntax 35

Data Types 36

Integer 39

Number 40

Boolean 41

Duration 42

Typecasting 43

Sequences 44

Default Values for Data Types 45

Summary 46

Chapter 4: Operators and Expressions 47

The Assignment Operator 48

The as Operator 49

Arithmetic Operators 50

The Modulus or Remainder Operator 51

The Arithmetic Assignment Operator 51

Operator Precedence 52

Unary Operators 52

The Increment and Decrement Operators: ++ and -- 53

The Unary + and − Operators 54

The not Operator 55

Relational Operators 55

Logical Operators 56

Range Expressions 59

Block Expressions 61

Looping Expressions 62

While Loops 66

Break Expressions 66

Continue Expressions 67

The if-else Expression 68

Exception Handling 70

The new Expression 71

Differentiating Expressions 72

Summary 73

Chapter 5: Functions 75

How a Function Works 77

A Function with Neither an Argument nor a Return Value 77

A Function with Arguments but Without a Return Value 78

A Function Without an Argument but with a Return Value 79

A Function with Arguments and a Return Value 80

Variable Access within a Function 81

Script-Level Variables 81

Local Variables 82

Function Overloading 82

Recursive Functions 83

Anonymous Functions...84

The run() Function...86

    Command-Line Arguments...87

Summary 89

Chapter 6: Class Definitions 91

Classes and Objects..91

    Classes 91

    Objects...92

Features of OOP 92

    Data Abstraction 92

    Encapsulation 92

    Inheritance...92

    Polymorphism...92

The Class Definition 93

    Creating Object Literals 94

    Initializing Class Attributes within an Object Literal 95

    Calling the Members of the Class 95

    Assigning Default Values to Data Members..97

    The init Block...97

    The postinit Block 99

Modifying Class Objects..99

Objects as Function Arguments 100

Non-Member Functions Accessing the Object...101

Static Members...102

Sharing a Function Name Between Script-Level and Member Functions 104

Calling a Java Method That Is a JavaFX Reserved Word 105

The abstract Class 106

Summary 107

■**Chapter 7: Access Specifiers**...**109**

The Script—The .fx File 110

The Script-Private Access Specifier 111

Packages 115

    Statics in JavaFX Script...117

    The package Access Specifier..118

    Package Access with Class Members 121

    Honoring Access Specifiers for Java Classes 123

The protected Access Specifier 124

The public Access Specifier 127

JavaFX Secondary Access Specifiers 131

    public-read 131

    public-init 134

    Secondary Specifiers and def 136

Access Specifiers for Class Definitions 136

    Script-private Classes 137

    Package-accessible Classes 137

    Protected Classes 138

    Public Classes 139

Summary 139

■**Chapter 8: Inheritance**..**141**

The Order of Initialization of Data Members 142

Overriding Data Members..143

Use of the super Keyword..144

Mixin Classes 145

   Creating a Subclass from Multiple Mixin Classes 148

   The Order of Initialization in Multiple Inheritance 149

Abstract Classes 150

   Using a JavaFX Class to Extend a Java Abstract Class 151

Anonymous Implementation of Java Interfaces 152

Summary 153

Chapter 9: Data Binding 155

What Does Binding Mean? 155

Recalculation of Expressions 157

Binding with Conditional Expressions 158

Binding with for Expressions 159

Binding Block Expressions 161

Binding Functions 162

Bound Functions 164

Binding with Object Literals 165

Bidirectional Binding 169

Lazy vs. Eager Binding 172

Summary 174

Chapter 10: Sequences 175

The sizeof Operator 176

Accessing the Elements of a Sequence 176

Nested Sequences 177

Creating a Sequence Using a Range Expression 178

Excluding the End Value in the Sequence 179

Sequence Slicing 179

Using a Predicate to Create a Subset of a Sequence 180

Working with Sequences 181

Inserting an Element into a Sequence.. 181

Deleting an Element from a Sequence.. 182

Reversing a Sequence... 184

Sequences as Function Parameters 184

Binding with Sequences 186

javafx.util.Sequences Utility Functions...187

Summary 188

Chapter 11: Triggers...189

Defining a Simple Trigger 189

A Trigger with Access to the Old Value..191

Using Triggers with bind 192

Implementing Binding Using Triggers..193

Validation Within the Trigger 195

Sequence Triggers...196

Nested Triggers 201

Summary 202

Chapter 12: Introduction to JavaFX UI Elements 203

Rendering Model: Immediate Mode vs. Retained Mode Rendering..................................204

Scene Graph 204

Scene... 205

Stage 206

Coordinate System...206

Graphical API Summary 207

Node – The Base UI Element 208

Geometries..210

    Stroke vs. Fill..210

Writing your First UI...212

Paints...220

    Solid Colors...220

    Gradients..222

Input Handling..230

    Keyboard Input..231

    Mouse Input..232

Text Rendering...234

Image Rendering..238

    Loading an Image..238

    Rendering an image...244

Transformations...246

    Translation..246

    Rotation...249

    Scaling & Shear...252

Controls & Layouts...255

StyleSheets..260

Charts..260

Effects..263

Bounds...263

    Bounds Class...263

    Node Bounds Variables...264

Summary..267

■ **Chapter 13: Introduction to Animation** **269**

What is Animation? 269

Animation in JavaFX 269

　　Play, Pause, or Stop a Timeline 274

　　KeyFrame Attributes 276

　　Simplified Syntax..282

　　Transitions 283

Summary 301

■ **Index**..**303**

About the Authors

 **Lawrence PremKumar** is a tech lead at Yahoo and has more than six years of experience in Java and J2EE technologies. He has spent 4more than four years with Sun Microsystems on Java client side quality team (AWT, Swing) since JDK6 to JDK 6u18. He is a hard-core and passionate client developer who has been associated with JavaFX for more than three years across various releases and has made significant contributions to JavaFX Graphics and Controls, in terms of development and quality. He has been actively evangelizing client JavaFX technologies across different universities and corporations.

 **Praveen Mohan** is a principal engineer at Yahoo and has more than eleven years of experience in Java and J2EE. He has spent more than nine years with Sun Microsystems, leading various Java Quality teams from the client side across multiple releases, starting from JDK 1.2.2 to JDK6. He has been specializing in various client Java technologies such as Swing, AWT, Java2D, Java3D, JavaFX, Media and Java Deployment, throughout his career. He has made significant contributions toward the development and quality of JavaFX and he has led the JavaFX graphics, controls, animation, and mobile compatibility quality teams at Sun across multiple releases of JavaFX. He has been actively evangelizing the JavaFX technology in various forums, universities, and conferences. He is passionate about 2D Graphics, Media, and Quality Engineering.

About the Technical Reviewer

■ **Sten Anderson** has been working with Java since the late 90s and is currently a Senior Consultant for the software consultancy, Citytech, in Chicago. Sten blogs about Java, JavaFX, Groovy, and any number of other things at `http://blogs.citytechinc.com/sanderson/`.

Acknowledgments

Writing a book is always a big effort, especially with such a rapid rate of change in the JavaFX technology. Making this book a reality has taken a lot of effort from many dedicated folks and it's our great pleasure to acknowledge their hard work.

First of all, we would like to thank our Manager, Rabi Cherian, who has constantly encouraged and motivated us to share our knowledge with rest of the world. He put a lot of special effort into adjusting project deadlines to give us enough time to focus on the book. We also want to acknowledge Elancheran, Girish, and Srinivas from the JavaFX Quality Team at Sun for taking up additional work so as to give us sufficient time to work on this book.

We would like to acknowledge the monumental efforts of our technical reviewers Sten Anderson and Tom Welsh for their conscientious technical guidance throughout the project and they have done a remarkable job in ensuring the contents of this book are of high quality. Our copy editor Jim Compton has an excellent eye for consistency. He has eliminated many embarrassing errors and has made lots of thoughtful suggestions for improvement throughout the project.

We also want to recognize the efforts of Kelly Moritz, who has been coordinating the project in an excellent manner, which helped us complete the book on time.

Introduction

This book covers all the essential features of JavaFX Platform and will teach you various aspects of the language and UI elements. It has been designed to proceed from less complex to more complex topics in a gradual manner so that you are not overwhelmed with myriad of concepts to learn and understand upfront. This book is for Flash, Silverlight, and other RIA developers looking to use and integrate JavaFX in their RIA, whether it is for desktop or mobile environments. However, our goal is to teach you JavaFX from the ground up, and you don't need prior programming expertise to use this book and hence this book is also suitable for those who are new to RIA development. Your time as a reader is extremely valuable, and you are likely waiting to read a pile of books besides this one. So we have made it concise by tightening things up and eliminating redundant examples.

We recommend that you be hands-on while reading this book, as it is mostly code-driven and will help you learn the concepts through practical exploration while reading. This way, you can actually get to program with JavaFX, rather than just reading the book, and you can also become comfortable and productive with it readily.

We have worked hard to keep pace with the changing syntax and architectures of the technology to ensure that the examples and explanations given in this book are both up-to-date and backward–compatible at least from JavaFX 1.1 to JavaFX 1.3.

Since this is a Java based technology, we have also highlighted the differences and collaborations between Java and JavaFX wherever appropriate so that even an existing Java application can be well integrated with JavaFX.

We hope this book helps you learn JavaFX quickly and makes you very hands-on and productive in coming up with a cool RIA.

—Lawrence PremKumar

—Praveen Mohan

CHAPTER 1

■■■

Introduction to RIA

Rich Internet Applications (RIAs) have always been about the user experience. RIAs, by (Wikipedia) definition, are web applications that have most of the characteristics of desktop applications, typically delivered through web-browser plug-ins or independently via sandboxes or virtual machines. The term *RIA* has many different definitions within the Internet development community, but all of those definitions boil down to enhancing the end-user experience in different ways. RIAs transfer the processing necessary for the user interface to the web client but keep the bulk of the data (maintaining the state of the program, its data, and so on) back in the application server, thus offering a better user experience with a lot more flare and pushing the boundaries of what we expect from the browser.

Many of us still remember the old days when we saw only static, plain text showing up on the browser. In recent times, we have come a long way, with dynamic content playing a vital role in the web application; this has definitely pushed the user experience way beyond the simple pages of old. Now RIA technology is bringing a similar revolution on the client side of computing that truly makes work easier, more accessible and more fun for everyone. One can view RIA as a convergence of user interface paradigms that exist for the desktop and the web and that facilitate the delivery of a uniform user experience across platforms, devices, and browsers. *Rich* in the context of RIA means a fluid, convenient, engaging, delightful user experience that works better than the halting, page-at-time, form-submission-dominated interaction model.

The History of RIA

The concept of RIA was introduced in March 2002 by vendors like Macromedia who were addressing limitations at that time in the richness of user interfaces, presentation of media content, and overall sophistication of the application from a user perspective. The primary emphasis was on the richness of the user experience and not actually on the technology, and the goal was to offer an enhanced user experience independent of the technology. However, RIA has taken many years to progress and mature, and it is only now reaching a stage where RIA tools are beginning to deliver on their long-held promise of easily developed and deployed cross-platform applications.

There are many players in the RIA arena currently, the biggest and prominent one being the Adobe Flash platform. However, recent developments—including the growth of powerful Web development technologies and improved standards support in the latest Web browsers—have boosted RIA's potential reach and capabilities, thus encouraging far more players, including AJAX (Asynchronous JavaScript and XML), Adobe Flex, Microsoft Silverlight, Mozilla Prism, Sun Microsystems JavaFX, and others to enter the market. But when we look at these technologies from a development platform perspective, only few of them, such as Flex, Silverlight, and JavaFX, would qualify as full-fledged development platforms for

RIA. Nevertheless, each of these products has its own unique strengths and weaknesses, which we will uncover as we go deep into the JavaFX technology in the following chapters.

Key Characteristics of RIA

The key characteristics expected of an RIA platform typically include the following:

Advanced Communications: Sophisticated communications with supporting servers through optimized network protocols can considerably enhance the user experience.

Minimize Complexity: RIA Frameworks come in handy when dealing with complex user interfaces that are normally difficult to design, develop, deploy, and debug while enhancing the end user experience.

Consistency: Consistency of user experience across multiple operating systems, devices, and browsers has become far more important in the user interface paradigm with today's wider connectivity to the Internet.

Installation and Maintenance: Most RIA frameworks operate within a plug-in or a sandbox, so the installation and maintenance of these plug-ins must be much more intuitive and should work without the user thinking about the complexities of how it's done.

Offline: An RIA platform needs the ability to let the user work with the application without connecting to the Internet and synchronizing it automatically when the user goes live.

Security: RIAs should be as secure as any other web application, and the framework should be well-equipped to enforce limitations appropriately when the user lacks the required privileges, especially when running within a constrained environment such as a sandbox.

Performance: Perceived performance in terms of UI responsiveness and smoother visual transitions and animations are key aspects of any RIA.

Richness: Richness can be defined in terms of responsiveness, immediacy, convenience, production values, and ease-of-use.

Standards: Adhering to standards becomes important in heterogeneous environments when multiple technologies hybridize together in providing a better user experience.

Ease-of-use: An RIA platform needs the ability to deliver enhanced ease-of-use for the end-users.

Rapid Development: An RIA Framework should facilitate rapid development of a rich user experience through its easy-to-use interfaces in ways that help developers and not scare them off.

RIA Workflow

Creating the rich user experience brought out by RIAs is normally a collaborative effort between designers providing rich graphical assets and developers integrating them appropriately with the business logic, refining the overall user experience through multiple iterations. Visual designers have always been able to create beautiful experiences, whether that's a painting, a sculpture, a web page, or some form of artwork, and they know how to evoke emotion and reach out to the people viewing the piece. The developers, on the other hand, are task-oriented and focus on making the business logic work in an optimized way. The success of an RIA framework depends on how it helps designers take their ideas and turn those into interfaces that developers can eventually code around. Hence it is important for the RIA framework to offer a solid designer-developer workflow to cater to the needs of two different categories of professionals, in order to be successful in the marketplace. Figure 1-1 shows this workflow.

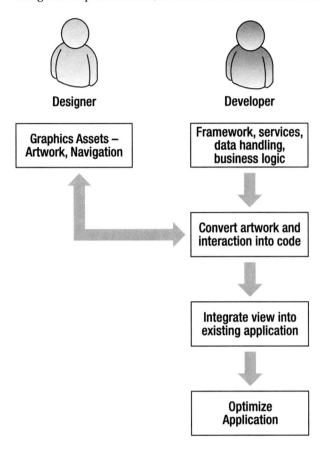

Figure 1-1. RIA workflow

Why RIA

Applications are the basis of all computing experiences, and we need them to do what we do. However, most of the headaches the average person faces while using computers come from the way applications have been developed and deployed over the years. Traditional applications are tied to your computer, your operating system, and perhaps the file system. The problem with all of this is that it forces us to develop an understanding of the underlying layer below the application. In order to get work done, or experience something great, we need to know about file types, codecs, drivers, and other things that really have nothing to do with the task we are trying to accomplish.

In contrast, the RIA has brought about a huge change in computing for the average person. We can have great digital experiences that are easy to find and easy to use on the Web. With the advent of standards that web browsers have been developed to comply with, and with the ability to connect to the Web from wherever you are with whatever device you have, people now expect to be able to experience content on the web consistently, anywhere, at any time. RIAs are a new breed of application that have emerged, bringing the best of the Web and the best of the traditional desktop application together.

A well designed RIA can be a truly engaging experience to the user. It will allow the user to flow to many areas of the application without the click-and-wait that was the norm when browsing the Internet since its inception. RIA can also seamlessly include multimedia (audio, video, screencasts, and so on) and third-party tools (maps, messengers) to enhance the user's experience.

An RIA moves the ability to do work to the Web. It makes the process that we use to do something available to us everywhere regardless of what operating system we may be using. Further, our data and the content we create are also always available to us, moving our entire workflow from the computer to the "Internet cloud." When applications and their associated data truly reside in the cloud, radical new possibilities emerge. Sharing data or collaborating with others becomes much easier. People can collaborate on tasks in real-time or asynchronously, and they can use streaming video, audio, and text to communicate with each other as they are working on something. A good RIA often exposes the pitfalls in a traditional web application through being able to interact with the server data in a more intuitive ways.

Great RIAs also abstract the idea of "files." Your data is stored contextually, and is usually searchable within that context. You never really deal with raw files when working with an RIA; you deal with your ideas instead. These workflows can be radically more productive, as they keep the focus on getting work done, and they require no knowledge of the underlying platform on the part of the end user.

The traditional Web relied heavily on a few interface controls we have all come to know well. Things like links, combo boxes, and forms are great for dealing with interactive "pages," but they aren't all that helpful when you are editing images, streaming video, mapping GPS data, or making phone calls. New user interface requirements have driven the aforementioned technologies to allow designers and developers to explore the possibilities of brand new ways to interact with these types of data and processes.

The laptop and desktop computer are hardly the only places where we expect rich experiences and want to access our data. Great RIA technologies must also stretch their presence to devices including the mobile world as well as home theater. Most of the technologies mentioned offer the ability to develop for a plethora of devices. This space is emerging, but it may likely be the most critical of all. The race for ubiquity here is on and far from decided.

For enterprise applications, you are not tied to any particular technology when moving to RIA. You are not limited to any specific application server or language. There are many enterprise RIAs that employ ColdFusion, Java/J2EE, .NET, and PHP, and there are numerous other options out there. As with your client-side interface technology, your back-end technology should be determined by the needs of your application, your resources, and your infrastructure. Are you serving dynamic data? Are you streaming media? Are you employing real-time messaging? Are you upgrading an existing system, or building one from the ground up? Does your organization support open-source initiatives? Does your organization prefer commercial products that have technical support? What is your budget for technology? There are many variables in the equation, and many solutions to the problem. RIA is not locked into any one specific technology, nor does anyone expect it to ever be. The term "rich" is an appropriate reference to the user experience, but an RIA seldom sacrifices the other key aspects of the application, such as security, performance, stability, reliability, and so on, that are integral parts of any enterprise application.

Some RIA Examples

There are innumerable RIAs on the web that people use on a day-to-day basis without realizing that they are working with an RIA. In general, an RIA is anything that provides an engaging and delightful experience to the end user without having him/her go through a complex interface, multiple page refreshes, and the like to get what he or she wants. Some of the classic RIAs that people find exciting to use are illustrated in Figures 1-2 through 1-4; in addition to these sites, many of the social networking sites that people use every day are also RIAs.

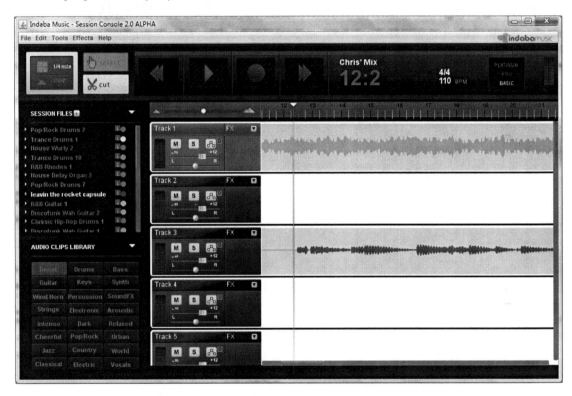

Figure 1-2. RIA from Indaba for mixing and managing music online (www.indabamusic.com)

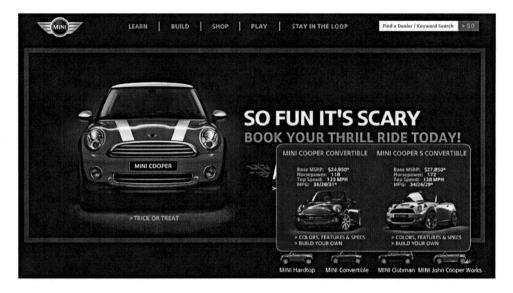

Figure 1-3. www.miniusa.com

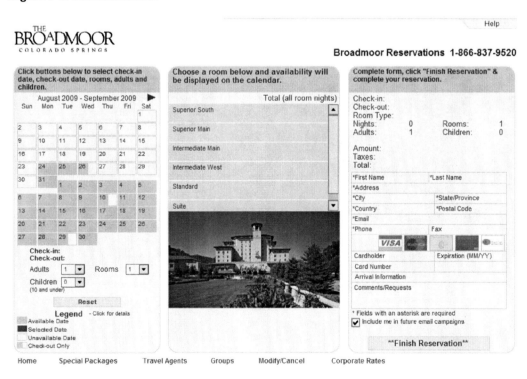

Figure 1-4. www.worldwidetelescope.org/webclient/

Summary

Rich Internet Applications are allowing designers to create web sites in original ways that could never be imagined before, some of which you have just seen. RIA technologies are offering a number of new options for designing a creative visual interface. Rich Internet Applications are starting to have a serious impact on the whole software industry. It is amazing to see how Rich Internet Applications are starting to move into some of the most common and coveted areas of application development, and it would be truly exciting to be involved in a revolution in computing that truly makes work easier and more enjoyable for developers as well as consumers. In the next chapter, you will learn more about the JavaFX technology and its benefits, applicability, and usage.

■ ■ ■

CHAPTER 2

Introduction to JavaFX

As described by Sun, JavaFX is an expressive and rich client platform for creating and delivering immersive Internet experiences across different screens. The main intention of this technology is to write Rich Internet Applications (RIAs) that run seamlessly across screens (desktop, mobile, or IP TV), providing a uniform user experience. JavaFX applications are written using a statically typed, declarative language called JavaFX Script that makes it easy to program in a visual context, enabling developers to create highly expressive and intuitive GUIs quickly and easily.

JavaFX is fully integrated with the Java Runtime Environment (JRE) and takes full advantage of the performance and ubiquity of the Java platform. JavaFX applications will run on any desktop and browser that runs the JRE and easily integrate with Java Platform, Mobile Edition (Java ME), opening the door to billions of mobile phones and other connected devices! JavaFX also leverages the other benefits of the Java platform, such as object-orientation, inheritance, polymorphism, a well-established security model, well-defined exception handling, memory management through garbage collection, and the mature Java Virtual Machine (JVM).

Why JavaFX

Developers are seeking the most efficient way of creating expressive content in applications that appear on desktops, on the Internet, and on mobile devices. They need to build high-fidelity GUIs that operate seamlessly on multiple web browsers, operating systems, and devices, without having to port or rewrite their applications for each screen. To meet this goal, developers need to work efficiently with team members such as graphic designers and media authors to exchange audio, video, and other rich media assets. The JavaFX platform contains an essential set of tools and technologies that enable developers and designers to collaborate, create, and deploy applications with expressive content.

Advantages of JavaFX

JavaFX is a full-fledged development platform for RIAs and has many advantages over other equivalent technologies in the market. Out of all, there are some key factors that differentiate JavaFX significantly.

> **RIAs for all screens**: JavaFX provides a unified development and deployment model for building expressive RIAs across desktop, browser, mobile, and TV.

> **Rich client platform:** JavaFX makes it easy and intuitive to integrate graphics, video, audio, animation, and rich text.

Ease of use: JavaFX Script is an easy-to-learn, easy-to-implement language that is statically typed, offering a declarative syntax that makes it easy to program in a visual context without worrying about the internals.

Powerful runtime: JavaFX leverages the extreme ubiquity, power, performance and security of the JRE.

Time-to-market: JavaFX offers a dramatically shortened production cycle for designers and developers through its designer–developer workflow. JavaFX allows you to incorporate multimedia assets from popular third-party design tools such as Adobe Illustrator and Photoshop using the JavaFX Production Suite.

Ready-made mass market: JavaFX allows you to distribute your RIAs widely, more quickly and easily across billions of Java-powered devices.

Preserve your investment: You can reuse your existing Java libraries in JavaFX and thus preserve the investment you've already made in Java.

Cross-browser functionality: JavaFX provides a uniform user experience across all browsers on multiple platforms.

Enterprise Integrations: With JavaFX you are ready to integrate a rich UI with a complex enterprise back-end.

Proven Security Model: You'll get broader system access with the proven Java security model.

History of JavaFX

JavaFX was originally known as F3 (Form Follows Function) and was a pet project of Christopher Oliver, a software engineer at Sun Microsystems who came onboard through Sun's acquisition of SeeBeyond. At the JavaOne 2007 conference, Sun officially launched F3 as the JavaFX platform, and it had an interpreter-based language by then. In July 2008, Sun launched its first preview version of JavaFX with its own compiler. JavaFX 1.0 was released in December 2008 with many more enhancements and optimizations to the platform.

JavaFX 1.1 was released in February 2009. Its primary focus was the mobile platform, and JavaFX was made fully functional on mobile devices, as demonstrated at the Mobile World Conference in February 2009.

Sun continued adding more features, optimizations, and performance improvements, and it released JavaFX 1.2 at the JavaOne 2009 conference. At press time, Sun is currently working on JavaFX 1.3, tentatively targeted to be released in early 2010.

The JavaFX Platform

The JavaFX 1.2.1 platform release includes various components, as illustrated in Figure 2-1. Let us see each one of them in detail.

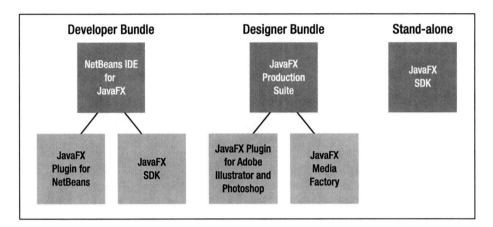

Figure 2-1. *The JavaFX platform: an overview*

The Developer Bundle

The developer bundle consists of the following elements:

>**NetBeans IDE 6.7.1 for JavaFX 1.2.1:** This provides a sophisticated integrated development environment for building, previewing, and debugging JavaFX applications. The editor features a drag-and-drop palette so you can quickly add JavaFX objects with transformations, effects, and animation. This IDE also comes with its own set of building block examples and the JavaFX Mobile Emulator, a mobile phone simulator.

>**JavaFX Plug-in for NetBeans IDE:** If you are already using the NetBeans IDE, you can add the JavaFX plug-in to include support for developing JavaFX applications.

>**JavaFX Plug-in for Eclipse IDE:** Sun also offers a JavaFX plug-in for the Eclipse IDE, which works with Eclipse IDE 3.4 or newer.

The Designer Bundle

The designer bundle consists of JavaFX Production Suite, a single download that contains the following tools to enable designers to exchange visual assets with developers:

Plug-ins for Adobe Illustrator and Adobe Photoshop: Plug-ins are available for popular designer tools such as Adobe Photoshop and Adobe Illustrator that allow designers to export the visual assets created by these tools to JavaFX applications. Developers can start building their applications based on mockups that the designer creates. As the visual design evolves, it is easy for the developer to incorporate changes in the artwork for the final version of their application. When a designer saves a graphic to the JavaFX format, they can compare how it will look in desktop and mobile applications, and they can view metrics that enable them to minimize resource demands on mobile devices.

JavaFX Media Factory: This contains two separate tools:

- **SVG Converter**: Converts SVG Content into JavaFX Format.

- **JavaFX Graphics Viewer**: Allows you to view graphic assets that were converted to the JavaFX format. It allows you to preview each graphic as it will appear in either desktop or mobile applications.

Standalone

If you prefer using other tools, or developing directly via the command line, you can download the stand-alone JavaFX 1.2.1 SDK. The SDK includes the following components (also included when you download NetBeans IDE for JavaFX):

JavaFX Desktop Runtime

JavaFX Mobile Emulator (for Windows)

JavaFX APIs

JavaFX Compiler

JavaFX API documentation

Examples

JavaFX Platform Integration: The Bigger Picture

Figure 2-2 illustrates the bigger picture of how the JavaFX platform integrates different platform elements, the runtime, tools, and frameworks to deliver applications, content, and services to consumers using multiple devices.

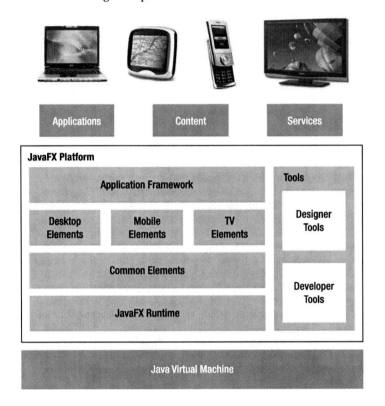

Figure 2-2. *The JavaFX Platform: the bigger picture*

Here is a brief introduction to each of the elements illustrated in Figure 2.2:

JavaFX Runtime: Contains cross-platform and platform-specific runtime environments and supporting libraries.

Common Elements: Contains APIs and other runtimes that work consistently across platforms.

Desktop Elements: Contains API extensions that are specific to the desktop platform.

Mobile Elements: Contains API extensions that are specific to the mobile platform.

TV Elements: Contains API extensions that are specific to the TV platform.

Application Framework: Forms the building block for application development.

Designer Tool: Allows visual designers and graphics experts to create graphic assets using popular content authoring tools such as Adobe Photoshop and Adobe Illustrator and bring those assets into the JavaFX application using the respective JavaFX plug-ins provided by Sun Microsystems. This shortens the production cycle of RIAs drastically. Sun is also working on its own content authoring tool, a preview of which was demonstrated at JavaOne 2009.

Developer Tool: Helps developers create JavaFX applications, services, and content.

JavaFX Mobile: An Introduction

With JavaFX Mobile, Sun is bringing expressiveness to the most powerful and pervasive mobile platform. On mobile devices, JavaFX runs directly on Java ME to take advantage of the platform's ubiquity, security, and highly capable feature-set. With JavaFX Mobile, developers and designers benefit from using the same JavaFX tools, such as the JavaFX SDK and the JavaFX Production Suite, that they have been using to create content for the desktop and browser. This makes it much easier to start creating mobile content, and it opens up the mobile device to a much wider pool of developers and designers.

Consumers today expect richer experiences on their mobile devices and also want their content to work well in bandwidth-constrained network environments and in offline modes. However, creating content for mobile devices typically requires highly specialized programming skills that many content and service providers may not have in-house. Moreover, as companies look to deliver their content and services to consumers across all of their devices (Mobile, Desktop, TV, and so on), they want to do so with a consistent and device appropriate user experience. Developers want an easier way to create rich and expressive content for mobile devices and want to be able to collaborate with team members such as graphics designers and media authors in an efficient manner that allows simple exchange of audio, video and other rich media assets. Device manufacturers want to enable richer experiences while leveraging their existing technology investments. Thus everyone from device manufacturers to service providers to developers to end consumers benefits from the combination of Java and JavaFX Mobile.

Advantages of JavaFX Mobile

Here are the advantages of using the JavaFX Mobile platform to develop and deliver expressive content:

- You can get your content in front of more users than with any other platform by cutting across multiple OEMs and platforms.

- JavaFX makes it easy to design dynamic interfaces that integrate audio, video, text, graphics, and animation!

- Java is backed by nearly all operators and OEMs, making it the strongest platform in the industry.

- JavaFX Mobile lets operators and OEMs build on their existing investment in Java to lower their implementation costs.

- JavaFX Mobile allows developers to build expressive interfaces while reusing existing Java code.

- JavaFX Mobile provides the broadest access to device-level capabilities of any cross-device platform.

- JavaFX Mobile protects the user through a proven security model that enables safe access to data and device capabilities

- JavaFX Mobile provides strong developer tools along with a better developer–designer workflow that leverages existing, popular tools.

- Developers can easily target their content across desktops and mobile devices with a single, unified SDK and a common API.

- JavaFX Mobile provides a full mobile emulator to prototype and optimize content directly on your desktop. As of JavaFX 1.2.1, the supported mobile devices are HTC Diamond and LG Incite.

Deployment and Distribution

At one time we used to think of computers as the center of the Internet. But of late, the reach of the Internet has become entirely global and has gone well beyond just computers as a delivery mechanism, extending to a world of devices such as mobile phones, Internet billboards, set-top boxes, car dashboards, and more. All these devices touch consumers on a daily basis in every aspect of their lives, and consumers obviously want to stay connected wherever they are with whatever devices they have. Java as a technology caters to the needs of these consumers, and Java is presently deployed on billions of devices globally and has a developer base of over 6 million. JavaFX leverages the ubiquity of Java and hence allows JavaFX developers to reach a wider audience over more devices than any other technology.

JavaFX applications can be deployed and distributed in the following ways:

Java Plug-in: A tool used for deploying Java applets that run inside a web browser.

Java Web Start: A tool used for deploying standalone Java applications on the desktop, using Java Network Launching Protocol (JNLP).

The Java Store: JavaFX applications can be submitted for distribution through the Java Store. End users can go to the Java Store and "drag to install" or perform a traditional installation directly to their desktops.

The JavaFX SDK contains a JavaFX Packager utility, which creates an application in a format that is specific for a target profile, either desktop or mobile. The NetBeans IDE incorporates this utility and is available to users when they choose an execution model.

Getting Started

This section will get you started using the NetBeans IDE to write a small "Hello World" program in JavaFX, compile it, and execute it on multiple platforms.

What to Download

First make sure that you meet the system and software requirements listed at
http://java.sun.com/javafx/1/reference/system-requirements-1-2.html. Check that you have the required hardware and available free disk space, and the correct version of the Java Software Development Kit (JDK) or Java Runtime Environment (JRE) before proceeding with any of the following installation instructions.

Application developers should download the following:

If you are new to the NetBeans IDE: Download and install NetBeans IDE for JavaFX 1.2.1. This version is available for Windows and Mac OS X platforms. A beta release is available for Ubuntu and OpenSolaris platforms. The NetBeans IDE for JavaFX 1.2.1 is a full-featured development environment that is packaged with the JavaFX Software Development Kit (SDK) and with best-practice examples that can help you build your software development project. The installation includes the JavaFX Mobile Emulator, which is currently available only on the Windows platform. (Future releases of JavaFX may also have an emulator available on the Mac platform.)

If you already have NetBeans IDE: Update your IDE with JavaFX 1.2.1 Plug-in for NetBeans. This version is available for Windows and Mac OS X platforms. A beta release is provided for the Ubuntu Linux and OpenSolaris platforms. The plug-ins provide the features that support the development of JavaFX applications in the NetBeans IDE. They also include the JavaFX SDK and best-practice examples. The installation includes the JavaFX Mobile Emulator, which is currently available on the Microsoft Windows platform only.

Now let's learn how to start a new project in NetBeans to create a "Hello World" program.

Writing Your First JavaFX Application

In this section, you will learn how to write a simple "Hello World" JavaFX application using NetBeans.

- Make sure you have installed and set up the NetBeans IDE along with the Java Development Kit.

- Start the NetBeans IDE.

- Click the File menu and choose the New Project menu item, as shown in Figure 2-3.

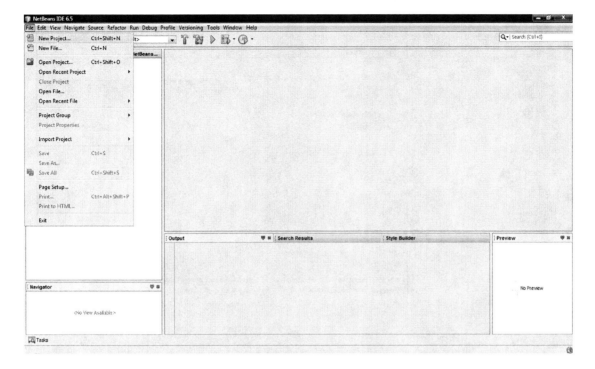

Figure 2-3. *The NetBeans main screen with the New Projects option*

- Select JavaFX from Categories. Click the Next button as shown in Figure 2-4.

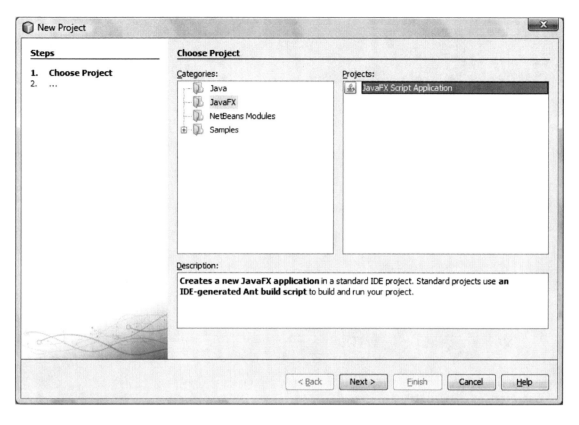

Figure 2-4. The NetBeans: New Project screen

- Enter the Name and Location of the JavaFX project as shown in Figure 2-5.

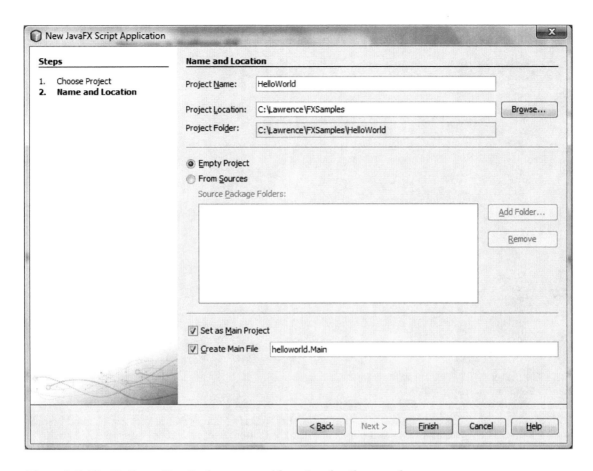

Figure 2-5. *The NetBeans New Project screen with project details entered*

- Click the Finish button.

- Now you'll see that a new JavaFX Project has been created; the screen looks as shown in Figure 2-6. You will see a `Main.fx` file; this is a default file that NetBeans has created. Modify the string "Application content" to read "Hello World from JavaFX." and change the content of the title to "Hello JavaFX" as shown in Figure 2-6.

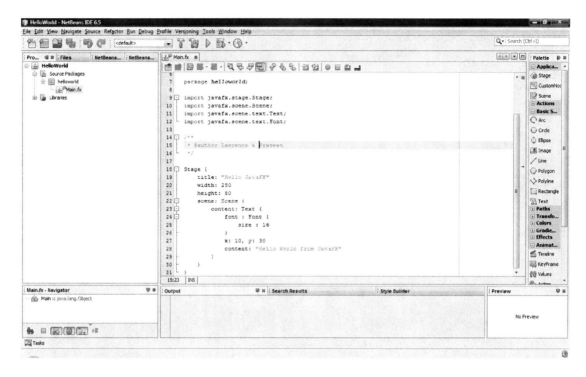

Figure 2-6. *The Main.fx file in NetBeans*

Notice that JavaFX Script code is included within the `Main.fx` file by default. This code, listed below, includes several `import` statements and object literals. These literals represent key concepts within the JavaFX application, and are described in detail after the code snippet.

```
/*
 * Main.fx
 *
 */

package helloworld;

import javafx.stage.Stage;
import javafx.scene.Scene;
import javafx.scene.text.Text;
import javafx.scene.text.Font;

/**
 * @author Lawrence & Praveen
 */
```

```
Stage {
title: "Hello JavaFX"
    width: 250
    height: 80
    scene: Scene {
        content: Text {
            font : Font {
                size : 16
            }
            x: 10, y: 30
            content: "Hello World from JavaFX"
        }
    }
}
```

The following object literals are created by default:

Stage: The top-level container required to display any visible JavaFX objects. This can be considered as an equivalent of a `java.awt.Frame` or `java.awt.Window` in Java. Default instance variables such as `title`, `width`, and `height` are attributes of the stage. Scene attribute defines the client area within the stage.

Scene: Similar to a drawing surface for the graphical content of your application. A scene instance variable has a `content` attribute that holds the actual graphical elements to be displayed.

Text: Displays textual information in the scene.

Font: Defines the font used to display the text in the scene.

The concepts of *stage* and *scene* can easily be related back to real-world scenarios in which a stage is normally a platform on which a scene would be presented, and a scene is normally created by various actors. So in this case, a scene is composed of actors such as text, and the scene is shown from within a stage. The JavaFX developers deliberately defined the APIs to be in sync with the real-world scenario to keep the platform simple, easy-to-understand, and intuitive to even nonprogrammers.

Running Your Application Using NetBeans

There are thee modes in which you can deploy this application using NetBeans: standalone, browser/Java Web Start, and Mobile Emulator. Let's see each one of them in detail.

Standalone Mode

The default mode set in NetBeans in the standalone mode, and running the project as-is without modifying any configuration parameters will run the application in standalone mode.

There are two ways to do this: First, you can just click the ▶ button on the toolbar if the application is the Main application. Alternatively, you can right-click on the project and select Run Project if this project is not set as the Main Project in NetBeans (Main Project should be highlighted in bold under the Projects tab on the left).

The output of our application run in standalone mode would look like Figure 2-7.

Figure 2-7. *The output of Main.fx*

Browser/Java Web Start Mode

To run our "Hello World" application on the browser, right-click on the project and go to Properties. As shown in Figure 2-8, choose Run option from the list on the left and click the Run In Browser radio button for Application Execution Model.

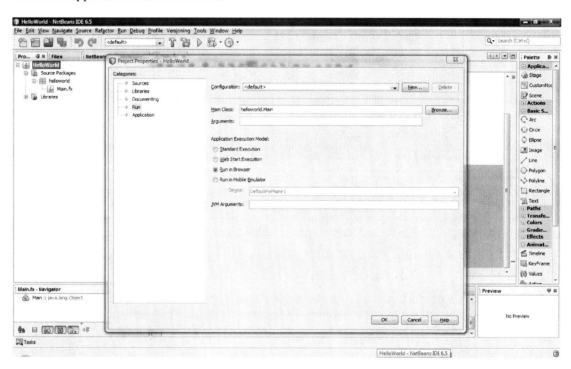

Figure 2-8. *NetBeans: Running in Browser mode*

To run it as a Java Web Start application, choose Web Start Execution as the Application Execution Model, as shown in Figure 2-9.

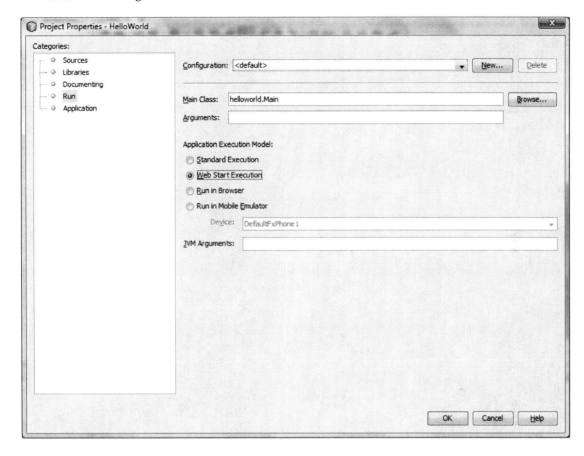

Figure 2-9. *NetBeans: Running in Web Start mode*

After choosing the application execution model, choose Application from the list on the left side and set the appropriate width and height for the applet, as shown in Figure 2-10.

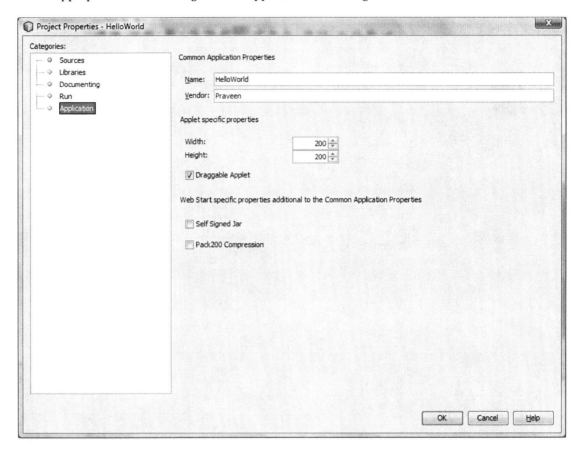

Figure 2-10. *NetBeans: Setting application properties*

The project is now all set for executing on the browser, so just right-click and select Run Project or press F6 if this is the Main project. NetBeans will automatically open up the default browser on your platform and run the application.

Mobile Emulator

To run the "Hello World" program on Mobile Emulator, choose Run in Mobile Emulator as the Application Execution Model, as shown in Figure 2-11.

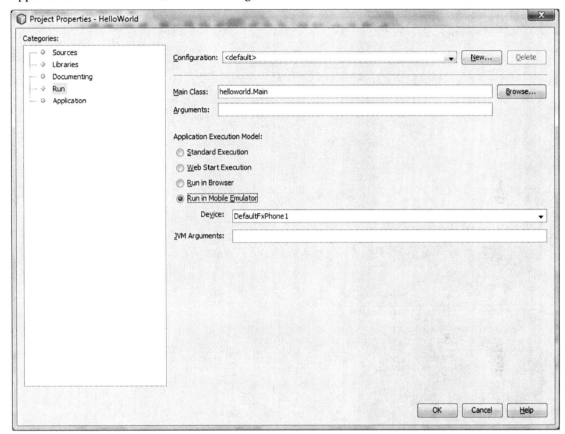

Figure 2-11. NetBeans: Running in Mobile Emulator mode

After choosing the execution model, just right-click and select Run Project or press F6 if this is the Main project. You will see the output shown in Figure 2-12.

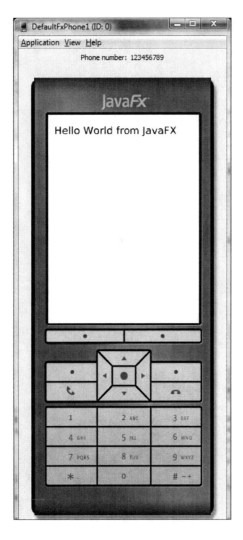

Figure 2-12. Output of Main.fx on Mobile Emulator (Windows)

■ **Note** fx is the file extension for a JavaFX program. JavaFX also has a compiler and an interpreter. javafxc is the JavaFX compiler, which converts a JavaFX program to .class files (byte code); javafx is the JavaFX interpreter, which takes the .class file and executes it.

At this point, you may compare our JavaFX Script program with a Java or C/C++ application and wonder where the entry point is. In JavaFX, there is no need to bother about the entry point; it is taken care by the JavaFX runtime engine, because JavaFX is a "declarative programming language" (one that determines its path of execution at runtime). However, in certain cases, you will need a `run()` method to be included in your application; you'll learn more about that in later chapters.

Running the Application from the Command Line

This section will outline how to build and run the application from the command line for people who do not use IDEs. Let's assume you have typed the code of `Main.fx` in a text editor and saved it in some location on the file system, such as `c:\helloworld\Main.fx`.

First take care of the following prerequisites:

`JAVA_HOME` must be set to the recommended JDK, namely `c:\jdk1.6.0_14`. Don't include the `bin` folder.

`JAVAFX_HOME` must be set to the JavaFX SDK, which you can download separately from `www.javafx.com`); for example, `c:\javafx-sdk1.2`. Don't include the `bin` folder.

`PATH` must be set to `%JAVAFX_HOME%\bin`. This is more of a convenience, as it allows you to use JavaFX and JavaFXC executables directly without specifying the full path.

Compiling the Application for Standalone Execution

To run in standalone mode from the command line, the application must be first compiled for execution. Take the following steps to compile the JavaFX program:

1. Make sure you create a folder to store the class files, called, say, `classes`, at the same level as the `helloworld` folder; for example, `c:\classes` if you have the source code under `c:\helloworld`.

2. Give the following command:

   ```
   javafxc -d classes helloworld/Main.fx
   ```

   where `-d` specifies where to store the class files. This will compile `Main.fx` and store all the class files under `c:\classes`.

3. To run the application, give the following command:

   ```
   javafx -classpath classes helloworld.Main
   ```

This will display the output shown earlier, in Figure 2.7.

Compiling the Application for Browser/Java Web Start Execution with JavaFX Packager

In order to build the application to run on a browser or in Java Web Start, we need to use the JavaFX Packager. Let's examine this tool in detail.

JavaFX Packager is a command-line utility that comes with the JavaFX SDK and helps developers build applications seamlessly for whatever profile they want to deploy on. It is a single utility that you use to build your application for standalone, browser, Web Start, or mobile. NetBeans IDE internally uses this utility to build your application.

JavaFXPackager requires the following mandatory input parameters:

> `-src:` The directory where source files are available

> `-profile`: The target profile (such as `MOBILE` or `DESKTOP`)

> `-appClass:` The main class for your application, the entry point

JavaFXPackager also allows the following optional parameters:

> `-appWidth:` Required for Web Start/browser mode, specifies the application width. The default value is 200.

> `-appHeight:` Required for Web Start/browser mode, specifies the application height. The default value is 200.

> `-sign:` Specifies whether the application must be signed; required for browser/Web Start mode. The default value is unsigned. An application must be signed if it accesses any local resources or remote resources from a server that is different from the one where the application will be hosted.

> `-draggable:` Specifies whether the applet must be draggable from browser on to the desktop. By default, applets are not draggable.

> `-res:` Any resources used by the application, such as images, media, and so on.

Building and Running the Application Using JavaFX Packager for the DESKTOP Profile

To build the application for running on browser, give the following command (note that a dot can be used to represent the current directory):

```
<JAVAFX_HOME>/bin/javafxpackager -src c:\helloworld -appClass helloworld.Main -profile
DESKTOP -appWidth 250  -appHeight 80  -draggable
```

This will create a folder `dist` in the current directory, which will contain the following:

> `Main.jar`: This contains the classes and resources.

> `Main.jnlp`: This is a `jnlp` file that can be launched using Java Web Start.

`Main_browser.jnlp`: This helper `jnlp` file facilitates running the application on the browser.

`Main.html`: This is an HTML file embedding the JavaFX applet.

Now to run the application on a browser, just load the HTML file in the browser and the applet will be loaded.

To run it on Java Web Start, you can open the `Main.jnlp` file from the browser. You can also double-click it if the JNLP mime type is configured properly on your native side and on the browser. If configured properly, Java Web Start will show the download progress dialog.

Alternatively, you can run the application from the command line, as follows:

```
<JAVA_HOME>/bin/javaws Main.jnlp
```

To run it as a plain standalone application, you can use the following command:

```
<JAVAFX_HOME>/bin/javafx -classpath Main.jar helloworld.Main
```

Building and Running the Application Using JavaFXPackager for the MOBILE Profile

To build the application to run on Mobile Emulator, give the following command:

```
<JAVAFX_HOME>/bin/javafxpackager -src "c:\helloword" -appClass helloworld.Main -profile
MOBILE
```

This creates a `dist` folder with two files in the current directory:

`Main.jar`: A `jar` file containing the classes and resources.

`Main.jad`: The descriptor file that the emulator platform can decode.

To launch the application on Mobile Emulator, give the following command from within the `dist` folder:

```
<JAVAFX_HOME>/emulator/bin/emulator -Xdescriptor:Main.jad
```

This will open up the Emulator and load the application as well. There are additional parameters for Emulator, such as the device type, memory, and so on, but those are optional.

■ **Note** Executing the application on the browser or Java Web Start requires an Internet connection the first time, since the JavaFX runtime will be downloaded from the web dynamically when the application is launched. However, subsequent executions will use the locally cached runtime unless the user has explicitly cleared the cache or the contents of the cache have gone past the time-out period.

Comments

When writing code in any language, it is important to remember to include written comments about what each line or group of statements is doing. To keep the JavaFX interpreter from trying to execute this text, you must hide it between comment characters. Table 2-1 shows the two types of comments available in JavaFX.

Table 2-1. *Comment Markers in JavaFX*

Comment Type	Description
// comment	All characters after the // to the end of the line are ignored.
/* comment */	All characters between /* and */ are ignored. These comments can extend onto multiple lines.

■ **Note** Comment syntax in JavaFX is the same as in Java. If a line of code does something important, it is useful to call attention to it with a short comment. It is always considered "good programming" to provide comments for all your code to help future programmers (including yourself) understand what's happening.

The type of comment you use and the purpose you use it for are entirely up to you, the programmer. Two styles of commenting programs are the Sun Microsystems and Microsoft styles. Most of the Sun documentation uses the following style for multiple lines, because it is useful with the automatic document generator that comes with the Java Development Kit:

```
JavaDoc Style
/**
    *   this is a multi-lined comment
    *   for the following class
    *
    */
```

The `JavaDoc Style` tag tells the document generator to use the comments as text in the resulting HTML file that is created automatically from source code. It is nice to get into the habit of using it.

Summary

In this chapter, we have introduced what JavaFX technology is all about, including its advantages, platform components, and the bigger picture of where this technology fits in. We have also taken you through a tour of how to use the technology to develop a simple "Hello World" application through the NetBeans IDE as well as in standalone mode, and you learned how to deploy the application for the desktop, browser, Java Web Start and emulator. In the next chapter, we will dive into the JavaFX Script language to explore the data types it offers to programmers.

CHAPTER 3

■ ■ ■

Data Types

JavaFX Script is a statically typed language, in which the type is associated with the variable and not the value. Hence it is capable of detecting type errors at compile time and thus allows many type errors to be caught early in the development cycle. Static type checkers evaluate only the type information that can be determined at compile time, but they are able to verify that the checked conditions hold for all possible executions of the program, which eliminates the need to repeat type checks every time the program is executed. This makes execution and storage more efficient and optimized.

Variable Declaration

Variable declarations in JavaFX Script are similar to those in Java itself. JavaFX Script is a *case-sensitive* language, which means that an identifier written in uppercase is not equivalent to another one with the same name but written in lowercase.

In JavaFX Script every variable, function, and expression (if statement, loop, and so on) has a type, which is determined from the context of how it has been used. JavaFX Script data types consist of an element specifier and a cardinality.

The element specifier tells what type of data a variable holds. Listing 3-1 presents two examples.

Listing 3-1. Examples of variable declarations

```
var x = 10;
var pi = 3.142;
```

Here the variable x holds a value of the Integer type, and the variable pi holds a value of the Number (or floating-point) type of data.

■ **Note** The cardinality of a data type determines how many elements can be held in a JavaFX Script type. Cardinality will be covered later in this chapter.

---

var vs. def Declarations

We can also define a variable using def as well. With def, variables are defined once and never assigned to again during their lifetime. Variables declared using var, however, can be assigned a new definition anytime. Listing 3-2 shows an example.

Listing 3-2. Examples of def declarations

```
def pi = 3.14;
def v1 = bind (x + y); //  bind is a keyword and it will be covered in detail in the Binding
chapter.
```

■ **Note** Bind is a keyword and will be covered in detail in Chapter 11, "Binding."

In this example, the value of pi is a going to be a constant, so it is wise to declare it as def. Similarly, the value of v1 is derived from x, y and cannot be assigned directly, since it is bound. Hence it is a better programming practice to declare v1 as def instead of var. Remember that the value of v1 will change when the x or y value changes, but the definition of v1 never changes (the summation of x + y, in this case).

It is important for the programmer to choose between var and def when declaring variables, and using def at appropriate places will reap huge benefits in memory and performance because the compiler knows in advance that the value defined by def is to remain constant, and it optimizes the way that value will be stored and used during the program lifecycle.

Variable Naming

A valid variable name is a sequence of one or more letters, digits, or underscore characters (_). JavaFX Script uses the same rules as Java to name the variables:

- No special character can be part of a variable name. Only letters, digits, and single underscore characters are valid.

- A variable name must always begin with a letter or an underline character (_).

- A variable name can't be a reserved word or keyword.

■ **Note** When choosing a name for your variables, use full words instead of cryptic abbreviations. Doing so will make your code easier to read and understand.

Reserved Keywords in JavaFX Script

Table 3-1 lists the standard JavaFX Script reserved keywords.

Table 3-1. *JavaFX Script Reserved Keywords*

abstract	after	and	as	assert	at	attribute	bind	bound	break
by	catch	class	continue	delete	do	else	exclusive	extends	false
finally	first	for	from	function	if	import	in	indexof	init
insert	into	inverse	last	lazy	let	new	not	null	on
or	override	package	postinit	private	protected	public	readonly	replace	return
reverse	sizeof	static	step	super	then	this	throw	true	try
tween	typeof	var	where	while	with				

Variable Declaration Syntax

Use one of the following syntax forms to declare a variable:

```
var variableName : <data type>;
```

or

```
var variableName : <data type> = initialization;
```

or

```
var variableName - initialization;
```

var is a keyword, which is used to declaring a variable. A variable's type declaration is optional. If the type is omitted from a variable declaration statement, the compiler infers or derives the data type of that variable from the value assigned to it; this is called *type inference*. A variable that is not assigned an initial value will be assigned a default value that varies based on the data type. See "Default Values for Data Types" later in this chapter for a complete list of default values.

■ **Note** Once the compiler derives the type from the given data, the data type for that variable is set permanently and cannot be changed later, because JavaFX Script is a statically typed language. By contrast, in a dynamically typed language like JavaScript, the type can change over a variable's lifetime.

Data Types

There are five data types available in JavaFX Script:

> String
>
> Integer
>
> Number
>
> Boolean
>
> Duration

String

A String is a set of characters enclosed within either single or double quotes. You declare it with one of the following syntax forms:

```
var variableName : String;
var variableName : String = "initial Value";  // a string is initialized with double quotes
var variableName = 'initial Value'; // string is initialized with single quotes or double
quotes, type is inferred
```

Listing 3-3 shows examples of each type.

Listing 3-3. *Examples of String declarations*

```
var str1 :  String ='JavaFX';                  //  String data type declaration
var str2 :  String = "JavaFX";                 //  String data type declaration
var str3  =   "JavaFX";                  //  String inferred type
println("  str1 =  { str1 } ");
println('  str2 = { str2 }");
println(" str3  = {str3 } ");
```

The `println` statements produce the following output:

```
JavaFX
JavaFX
JavaFX
```

The code in Listing 3-3 demonstrates String data type declarations, along with the declaration of a string inferred type. The first three lines all declare a string data type and initialize its value. The first two examples explicitly define the data type; in the third, the compiler will infer it automatically from the value assigned to the variable.

The String data type in JavaFX Script maps to the String class in Java. This means that we call the methods of Java's String class in JavaFX Script. Listing 3-4 demonstrates how this works.

Listing 3-4.*Calling methods of the Java String class*

```
var str : String = "Scripting 'JavaFX' Language";
println("str {str}");      // ostr = Scripting 'JavaFX' Language
// find the length of the string.
println("str length = {str.length() }"); // str length = 18
// convert the string to uppercase
var upperCaseString = str.toUpperCase(); // UpperCase = SCRIPTING LANGUAGE
println("UpperCase = {upperCaseString}");
// convert the string to lowercase.
var lowerCaseString = upperCaseString.toLowerCase();    // lowerCase = scripting language
println("lowerCase = {lowerCaseString}");
// get the substring
var subString = str.substring(10); // subString = Language
println(" subString = {subString}");
```

This code produces the following output:

```
str = Scripting 'JavaFX' Language
str length = 18
UpperCase = SCRIPTING LANGUAGE
lowerCase = scripting language
subString = Language
```

Listing 3-4 demonstrates that the JavaFX Script String data type can be used to invoke Java String class methods. Substring, length, toLowerCase(), and toUpperCase() are methods from the Java.lang.String class that are accessed using JavaFX Script String types.

Strings in JavaFX Script are immutable, as in Java; this means you cannot change the characters in the string. For example, the method str.toLowercase() appears to modify the string, but it actually returns a new string object, leaving the original one unchanged.

One notable difference in JavaFX Script is that you can include two single quotes with a double-quoted string and two double quotes within a single-quoted string as follows:

```
var s: String = "JavaFX is a 'cool' technology";
var s1: String = 'JavaFX is a "cool" technology';
```

The single and double quoted text used within the string will be treated as-is and you will see quote characters when printing the values as well. Another pair of special characters that are treated differently within the string are the curly braces. Anything specified between curly braces within a string is treated as an expression. Listing 3-5 presents an example.

Listing 3-5. Examples of quotes and braces with strings

```
var i: Integer = 10;
var j: Integer = 10;
println("Value of  'i + j' is: {i + j}");
```

This code displays the following output:

```
Value of  'i + j' is: 20
```

In this example, {i + j} is treated as an expression and evaluated, and the result of the evaluation is converted to String and replaces {i + j}.

However, these are special cases, and to include other special characters, such as the backslash or line feed, you will have to use the escape character, discussed next.

Escape Sequences

The character and string escape sequences allow for the representation of some nonprinting characters. Table 3-2 lists some of the common escape characters.

Table 3-2. Common Escape Sequences

\t	tab
\n	new line
\b	backspace
\f	form feed
\r	carriage return
\"	double quote
\'	single quote
\\	backslash

As an example, the code in Listing 3-6 will include a new line in the given string.

Listing 3-6. Using the escape character for a new line

```
var escStr: String = "JavaFX \n is cool";
println("String with esc character: {escStr}");
```

This code produces the following output:

```
String with esc character: JavaFX
 is cool
```

Integer

An Integer value represents a number with no decimal or fractional part—a whole number. An Integer can be either positive or negative.

The following snippet shows how to get the minimum and maximum value that an Integer primitive data type can hold.

```
var intMin: Integer =  java.lang.Integer.MIN_VALUE;
println("intMin = {intMin}");
var intMax: Integer =  java.lang.Integer.MAX_VALUE;
println("intMax = {intMax}");
```

It produces the following output:

```
intMin = -2147483648
intMax =  2147483647
```

From this example, it is clear that the JavaFX Script Integer primitive data type maps to the `java.lang.Integer` class in Java, which means that we can use the methods in `java.lang.Integer` on the JavaFX Script Integer data type. An Integer literal may be expressed in decimal (base 10), hexadecimal (base 16), or octal (base 8). Let us see each of these numeric representations in detail.

Decimal Number

A decimal number is either the single ASCII character 0, representing the integer zero, or an ASCII digit from 1 to 9, optionally followed by one or more ASCII digits from 0 to 9, representing a positive integer.

Following are the decimal numbers:

0 1 2 3 4 5 6 7 8 9

Here are two examples:

```
var width : Integer = 150;
var translat
eX: Integer = -15;
```

Hexadecimal Number

A hexadecimal number consists of the leading ASCII characters 0x or 0X followed by one or more ASCII hexadecimal digits. It may be positive, zero, or negative. Hexadecimal digits with values 10 through 15 are represented by the ASCII letters a through f or A through F. The letters may be uppercase or lowercase.

Following are the hexadecimal numerals:

0 1 2 3 4 5 6 7 8 9 A B C D E F

or

0 1 2 3 4 5 6 7 8 9 a b c d e f

Here is an example:

```
var xValue : Integer = 0X12A;
```

Octal Number

An octal number consists of the ASCII digit 0 followed by one or more of the ASCII digits 0 through 7 and can represent a positive, zero, or negative integer.
Following are the hexadecimal numbers:

0 1 2 3 4 5 6 7

Here is an example:

```
var no : Number = 05;
```

■ **Note** Octal numerals always consist of two or more digits. 0 is always considered to be a decimal number; but in practice, the numbers 0 , 00, and 0x0 all represent exactly the same integer value.

Number

Values of the Number data type are also known as real or floating-point numbers. This data type is used when evaluating any expression that requires fractional precision. A Number can contain either a decimal point, an *e* (uppercase or lowercase), which is used to represent "ten to the power of" in scientific notation, or both. The exponent part is an e or E followed by an integer, which can be signed (preceded by either + or –). Listing 3-7 presents an example.

Listing 3-7. Examples of floating-point numbers

```
var pi : Number = 3.142;        // pi is a floating point no.
var num : Number = 10; // 10 will be promoted to 10.0
var num1 = 10; // Type inferred as Integer
```

The first statement declares a Number variable pi, which holds the decimal number 3.142. The second statement declares a Number variable num, which holds the number 10. But after executing the second statement the variable value becomes 10.0, since the data is promoted from Integer to Number. The third line does not specify the data type but assigns a value of 10. Hence the data type for num1 will be automatically inferred by the compiler as Integer.

Listing 3-8 demonstrates different ways of declaring a Number.

Listing 3-8. *Examples of Number declarations*

```
// declare a variable with out initial value
var a : Number ;
println("a {a}");              // a 0.0
// declare a variable with the inital value
var pi = 3.142;
println("pi = {pi}");              // pi = 3.142
// declare a variable with intial value expressed in scientific notation or expontential
form.
var b : Number = 10e2;
println("b = {b}");              // b = 1000.0
```

These declarations produce the following output:

```
a 0.0
pi = 3.142
b = 1000.0
```

The code in Listing 3-8 demonstrates different ways of declaring a Number variable. The first example declares a variable of Number type but does not initialize it. Hence a default value of 0.0 would be assigned. The second example initializes the variable but does not define the data type. The compiler would in this case automatically infer the type as Number. Finally, the third example declares a Number variable and initializes it with an exponent decimal value.

Listing 3-9 demonstrates the range of the Number data type.

Listing 3-9. *Example to print the minimum and maximum value of Number data type*

```
var numMin: Number =  java.lang.Double.MIN_VALUE;
println("Minimum value of Number data type  = {numMin}");
var numMax: Number =  java.lang.Double.MAX_VALUE;
println("Maximum value of Number data type = {numMax}");
```

This code produces the following output:

```
Minimum value of Number data type  = 4.9E-324
Maximum value of Number data type = 1.7976931348623157E308
```

Boolean

A Boolean variable has two states, true and false, which are appropriately represented by the keywords true and false. The Boolean variable, therefore, represents the state of something that can have only one of two values. These values are typically used as checkpoints for determining whether to take a certain action. Listing 3-10 demonstrates how to use the Boolean data type.

Listing 3-10. Examples of Boolean variables

```
var flag : Boolean = true;
if(flag) {
    println(This line will be printed on the console);
}
```

The `if` conditional statement is covered in depth in Chapter 4, "Expressions, Conditional Statements and Loops." For now, all you need to know is that the `if` statement checks to see whether the statement in the parentheses is true or false. If the statement is true, it executes the statements between the curly braces.

■ **Note** All data types are subclasses of `java.lang.Object`. However, unlike Java, JavaFX Script doesn't require you to initialize the variable when it is declared. If a variable is not initialized, the compiler will initialize it automatically using the default value for its data type.

Duration

A Duration value represents data in terms of time. It is typically used in animation applications, to work with timelines, transitions, keyframes, and so on. As an example, Listing 3-11 demonstrates different ways to represent 3.5 minutes.

Listing 3-11. Examples of representing the value 3.5 minutes

```
var d1 = 3.5m;
var d2 = 3m + 30s;
var d3 = 3500ms;
var d4 = 3m + 0.5s;
var d5 = Duration.valueOf(3500);
```

Listing 3-12 demonstrates Duration's usage in a timeline.

Listing 3-12. Using Duration in a timeline

```
var x: Number = 0;
Timeline {
    at (0s) {x => 0 tween Interpolate.LINEAR},
    at (3s) {x => 2.0 tween Interpolate.LINEAR}
    repeatCount: Timeline.INDEFINITE
}
```

This example changes the x value from 0 to 2.0 within a timeframe of 3 seconds. To represent indefinite time, we can use `Duration.INDEFINITE`.

■ **Note** Timelines are covered in detail in Chapter 13, "Introduction to Animation."

The Duration class provides numerous convenient methods for converting data to and from Duration time. Listing 3-13 shows some examples.

Listing 3-13. *Converting data to and from Duration values*

```
var d = 4h;
var noOfHours = d.toHours();
var noOfMinutes = d.toMinutes();
var noOfSeconds = d.toSeconds();
var noOfMillis = d.toMillis();
var d1 = d.add(10m); // d1 = 250m
var d2 = d.sub(1h); // d2 = 3h
var d3 = d.mul(10); // d3 = 2400m
var d4 = d.div(10); // d4 = 24m
```

Listing 3-13 demonstrates the build-in functions of the Duration data type. In the third statement, variable d of Duration data type is converted to minutes using the **toMinutes()** function. Likewise, the **toSeconds()** and **toMillis()** functions are used in the fourth and fifth statements. In addition to the conversion functions, Duration values can be added, subtracted , multiplied and divided using built-in functions as shown in the last four statements.

■ **Note** You will learn more about the Duration data type in Chapter 13.

Typecasting

Type conversion or *typecasting* refers to changing the value of a variable from one data type into another. This is done to take advantage of certain features of type hierarchies. For instance, values from a more limited set, such as integers, can be stored in a more compact format and later converted to a different format, enabling operations that would not otherwise be possible, such as division with several decimal places of accuracy when there is a need for that.

Casting can be implicit or explicit. Implicit casting are safe and handled by the compiler itself. Normally, upcasting is implicit whereas downcasting requires explicit notation in the code. Listing 3-14 shows an example.

Listing 3-14. *An example of typecasting*

```
var d: Number = 10.0;
var l:Integer = 2;
d = l; // This is implicit casting
```

In this code, casting is implicitly done by the compiler since we are assigning a subtype to a supertype. However, the following code will give a warning:

```
var d: Number = 10.0;
var l:Integer = 2;
l = d;
```

Here is the output:

```
<src.fx>: warning: possible loss of precision
found   : Number
required: Integer
```

To avoid this warning, downcasting has to be specified explicitly, using as keyword:

```
l = d as Integer;
```

We will discuss casting in more detail when we deal with objects in Chapter 9, "Inheritance."

Sequences

Sequences in JavaFX Script are similar to arrays in Java, which hold a set of value of similar data type under a single variable name. As shown in Listing 3-15, sequences can be constructed explicitly.

Listing 3-15. *Sequences constructed explicitly*

```
[ 76, 9, 34, 2]
['red', 'green', 'blue']
```

However, they can also be specified as ranges:

```
[100 .. 200]
```

Listing 3-16 shows some examples of how sequence variables are declared.

Listing 3-16. *Some variables of the Sequence type*

```
var nodes : CustomNode[];
var numbers : Number[];
def primes = [2, 3, 5, 7, 11];
```

■ **Note** Sequences in JavaFX Script are far more powerful and hence will be covered in detail in Chapter 10. This section is just an introduction.

Default Values for Data Types

As noted when we discussed data type declarations earlier in the chapter, each data type has its own default value that will be used when no initial value is provided. Table 3-3 summarizes the default values for different data types.

Table 3-3. *Default Values for Data Types*

Type	Declaration	Default Value	Element Specifier	Literal or Creation Examples
String	`: String`	`""`	`java.lang.String`	`"Brownian"`
Integer	`: Integer`	0	`java.lang.Integer`	`1956`
Number	`: Number`	0.0	`java.lang.Double`	`1.4142`
Boolean	`: Boolean`	false	`java.lang.Boolean`	`true`
Duration	`: Duration`	0ms	`javafx.lang.Duration`	`47s`
Other class types	`: ClassName`	null	`ClassName`	`Point {x: 3 y: 9}`
Function types	`: function(name : ParamType, ...) : ReturnType`	null	`function(name : ParamType, ...) : ReturnType`	`function(x:Integer):String { " {x} "}`
Sequence types	`: ElementSpec[]`	[]	`ElementSpec`	`[9, 14, 21, 4]`

> ▓ **Note** Class types are covered in Chapter 6, " Class Definitions," and function types are covered in Chapter 5, "Functions."

Summary

In this chapter, you have seen what data types JavaFX offers and how to use them. The primitive data types that are supported by JavaFX are String, Integer, Number, Boolean, and Duration. A String is a set of characters enclosed by either single or double quotes. The Integer data type holds only whole numbers, not fractions or floating point numbers. Integers can be expressed in decimal, octal, or hexadecimal form. A Number can either contain a decimal point, an *e* (uppercase or lowercase), which is used to represent an exponent in scientific notation, or both. The Boolean data type can hold either true or false. The Duration data type represents values in terms of time such as seconds, milliseconds, and so on.

In the next chapter, you will learn about the operators and expressions available in JavaFX Script.

CHAPTER 4

■ ■ ■

Operators and Expressions

An *expression* in a programming language is a combination of values, operators, variables and functions that are evaluated in a particular order of precedence to produce a value. An *operator* performs an operation on one or more operands to produce a value. In JavaFX Script, everything that is not a definition is an expression. This chapter describes the syntax, meaning, and the use of various expressions and operators in JavaFX Script.

Most of the operators in JavaFX Script are the same as in Java, with a very few exceptions. In this chapter, you will see the following operators in detail:

- The assignment operator

- Arithmetic operators

- Unary operators

- Relational operators

- Logical operators

Operators combine multiple operands together to form an expression, and JavaFX Script supports different types of expressions. You will learn about the following expressions in this chapter:

- Range expressions

- Block expressions

- Looping expressions

  - while

  - for

- Conditional expressions

  - if-else

- Error-handling expressions

  - try, catch, finally, throw

- New expressions

The operators and expressions that are omitted from this chapter will be covered in subsequent chapters when we deal with the topics related to them. See the Summary of this chapter for more about expressions and operators not covered here.

The Assignment Operator

Many of the examples that you have seen so far in previous chapters have used the assignment operator. Lets' take a close look at this operator. The assignment operator works just as in any other language—the value of the expression or the variable on the right side value is assigned to the variable on the left side. Listing 4-1 shows the syntax formats for an assignment operator.

Listing 4-1. Assignment operator syntax

```
variable name = value;
```

or

```
variable name = expression ;
```

Following is a simple example of a variable being initialized with a value while it is defined:

```
var width : Integer = 10;
```

This can be considered two statements merged into one—first a declaration statement and then the assignment statement. You can split it as follows:

```
var width  : Integer;
width =10;
```

Similarly, def variables are assigned with a constant definition when they are created, as shown next:

```
def PI = 3.142;
```

Here, PI is a def (constant definition) and holds a value, 3.142. Note that the data type of PI is derived automatically from the value assigned to it through the assignment operator. In this case, it is of type Number.

Now let us see an expression with an assignment operator.

```
var area : Number = 3.142 * r * r;
```

In this example, the arithmetic expression on the right side is evaluated first and then assigned to the variable on the left.

Assignments are not restricted to evaluating a simple expression and assigning its result to the variable on the left; they can also be used for creating an instance of a class, as shown in the following example.

```
var button : Button = Button {
    text : "Click Me"
}
```

Here, an instance of a `Button class` (JavaFX class) is created and assigned to a variable named `button`. In the next example, an instance of a `java.io.File` class is created and assigned to a variable named `File`.

```
var file : java.io.File = new File("HelloWorld.java");
```

You will learn more about class definitions and objects in Chapter 6,"Class Definitions."
In Listing 4-2, different datatype values are assigned to different variables and are printed on the console using the `println` output statement.

Listing 4-2. *A simple program using the assignment operator*

```
var a : Integer = 10;
var b : Boolean = true;
var pi : Number = 22.0/7.0;
var dur : Duration = 10ms;
var name : String = "JavaFX is cool..! ";
println("a  = {a}");
println("b = {b}");
println("pi =  {pi}");
println("dur ={ dur}");
println("name = {name}");
```

   Output
```
a  = 10
b = true
pi =  3.142
dur =10ms
name = JavaFX is cool..!
```

Sometimes you may need to assign the same value to multiple variables. Instead of using multiple assignment statements, you can do that in a single assignment statement, as follows:

```
a = b = c;
```

The value of c is first assigned to b, and then the b value to a.

The as Operator

The `as` operator is used to convert one data type to another. In JavaFX Script ,`as` is a keyword and is used to do type casting. You learned about type casting in Chapter 3, "Data Types," so the following is just a refresher. Listing 4-3 shows a simple example of how `as` can be used.

Listing 4-3. *Example of the as operator*

```
def PI : Number = 22.0/7.0;
println("PI =  { PI } ");
var x : Integer = PI as Integer ;
println("x = {x}");
```

Output
```
PI = 3.142
x = 3
```

In Listing 4-3, the value of the variable PI has been assigned to an Integer variable, x. Since PI is of type Number and we are narrowing its precision to Integer, the compiler will show a warning that there is a loss of precision if you don't use the as operator. Using as, indicates to the compiler that the programmer knows what he or she is doing and hence the compiler need not worry. So in this example, the compiler does not display any warning.

Casting is not just limited to numeric data types but can be extended to user-defined data types as well. You will learn more about this in Chapter 6, "Class Definitions" and Chapter 8, "Inheritance," when we deal with the concept of superclasses and subclasses.

Arithmetic Operators

The arithmetic operators are binary operators and are used in arithmetic expressions. The arithmetic operators can be combined with the assignment operator to perform arithmetic and assignment operations both together. The usage of these operators is pretty much the same as in any other language.

Table 4-1 shows the arithmetic operators with their precedence; the Example column demonstrates how they can be used.

Table 4-1. *Operator Precedence for Arithmetic Operators*

Operator	Meaning	Precedence	Example
*	Multiplication	1	a * b
/	Division	2	a /b
mod	Modulus	3	a mod b
+	Addition	4	a + b
−	Subtraction	5	a − b

The Modulus or Remainder Operator

In JavaFX Script the modulus or remainder operator is represented by the keyword mod. The mod operator returns the remainder of a division operation. It can be applied to the Number and Integer data types. Listing 4-4 demonstrates the use of the modulus operator, and the code is self-explanatory.

Listing 4-4. *Using the modulus operator*

```
var numMod  = 22.0  mod 7.0;
println("numMod = {numMod}");
var intMod = 22 mod 7;
println("intMod = {intMod}");
```

   Output
```
numMod = 1.0
intMod = 1
```

■ **Note** In Java, the mod operator is represented by the '% symbol.

The Arithmetic Assignment Operator

When an arithmetic operator is combined with an assignment operator, it is called an *arithmetic assignment operator*. This operator allows you to do the arithmetic and assignment operation in a single statement. The arithmetic assignment operators have the following syntax:

```
variable = variable arithmetic operator expression;
```

Using an arithmetic assignment operator is best suited for cases when a variable is used in an expression and the same variable is used to store the result of the expression. Here is a simple example:

```
x = x + 2;
```

The variable x is used in an arithmetic operation, and the same variable is used to store the value of the expression as well. So we are using the variable x twice. Using an arithmetic assignment operator, the same expression can be simplified as follows:

```
x+=2;
```

Both statements perform the same operation; that is, they increment the value of the variable x by 2.
Similarly, other arithmetic operators can also be combined with the assignment operator to perform the respective arithmetic and assignment operations in a single statement.

Operator Precedence

Each operator is assigned a *precedence* or priority, which determines the order in which the operator operates on the operand. As in an ordinary arithmetic expression, multiplication and division have a higher precedence than addition and subtraction. If two operators have the same precedence, they are executed according to the order in which they appear in the statement. For most operators (except the assignment operator), the order is from left to right.

Let's look at an example to see how an expression is evaluated and in what order:

```
x = 20 + 50.0 * 7 / 2;
```

Since the multiplication (*) and division (/) operators have the highest precedence, they are executed first, followed by the addition (+) operation.

```
50.0 * 7             // since both * and / operators have the same precedence
                     and multiplication(*) is on the left side,
                     multiplication is done first, yielding the result 350.0.

350.0 / 2            // the next highest precedence is the / operator, so division is
                     done next, yielding the result 175.0.

20 + 175.0           // the final operator left in the expression is
                     addition (+), which yields the value 195.0, which
                     is the final value of the expression that is
                     assigned to 'x'
```

If you want to change the order of the execution, enclose the respective operator and the operands in parentheses. Let us rewrite the previous example as follows:

```
x =(20 + 50.0) * 7 / 2;
```

Now the operation (20 + 50.0) is evaluated first, since the parentheses take precedence over multiplication. You can see the operator precedence across all the JavaFX Script operators in Table 4.4, at the end of the "Operators" section.

Unary Operators

A single operator operating on a single value is called a *unary operator*. The following unary operators are available in JavaFX Script:

- Increment and Decrement
- Unary – and +
- Unary not

The Increment and Decrement Operators: ++ and --

The increment (++) and decrement (--) operators perform a simple task. The first increments (increases) the value of its operand by 1 and the second decrements (decreases) the value of its operand by 1. There are two variants of each of these operators: prefix mode and postfix mode. Listing 4-5 shows the prefix and suffix syntax for unary increment operators and Listing 4-6 shows the prefix and suffix syntax for unary decrement operators.

Listing 4-5. *Syntax of the unary increment operator*

```
++ variable;   // prefix form of Increment operator
variable ++;   // postfix form of Increment operator
```

Listing 4-6. *Syntax of the unary decrement operator*

```
-- variable;   // prefix form of decrement operator
variable -- // postfix form of decrement operator
```

In prefix mode the operator comes before the affected variable, and in postfix mode it comes after the variable. As demonstrated in the examples in Listing 4-7, the two modes differ in the timing at which the incrementing/ decrementing takes place.

Listing 4-7. *Unary increment/decrement operators*

```
1.    var x  : Integer = 10;
2.    var y = x++;
3.    var z = ++x;
4.    println("x = {x}  y = {y}   z = {z}");     // x = 12 y = 10   z = 12
5.    var p = x--;
6.    var q = --x;
7.    println("x = {x}   p = {p}   q = {q}");     // x = 10  p = 12  q = 10
```

```
    Output
x = 12   y = 10   z = 12
x = 10   p = 12   q = 10
```

In line 1, we declare a variable x and initialize its value to 10. In line 2, we are incrementing x using the postfix ++ operator and at the same time assigning the value of this expression to y. Looking at the line, you may assume that the value of y will be 11. But that is not correct because the value of the expression before the increment is assigned to y and x value is incremented afterward. Hence y will take the value of 10 and after this assignment; x will be incremented to 11.

Similarly, in line 3, we are assigning ++x to a variable z. Here x will be incremented first and then assigned to z. Hence, x increments from 11 to 12, and this value is assigned to z. This is the exact difference between prefix and postfix mode. In postfix mode, the expression is evaluated first and incremented or decremented after, whereas in postfix mode, the value is incremented/decremented first and then the expression is evaluated. Now you can apply the same logic to variables p and q as well.

Listing 4-8 provides another example of how prefix and postfix modes differ from each other.

Listing 4-8. Prefix and postfix operators

```
1.    var x : Integer  = 7;
2.    println("initial value x = {x}");
3    println("postfix variant incrementng the value of x = {x++}");
4.    println("value x = {x}");
5.    println("prefix variant incrementng the value of x = {++x}");
6.    println("value x = {x}");
```

Output
```
initial value x = 7
postfix variant incrementng the value of x = 7
value x = 8
prefix variant incrementng the value of x = 9
value x = 9
```

If you understood the example in Listing 4-7, you can easily predict the results for Listing 4-8 without looking at the output.

In line 1, we are declaring a variable x and initializing it with 7. In line 2, we are printing the value of x, which is 7. In line 3, we are incrementing x with the postfix increment operator and printing its value. Since postfix incrementing happens after the evaluation of the expression in which it is involved, `println()` is executed first, printing the actual value of x, which is **7.** After the `print` operation, the value of x is incremented to 8. In line 4, we print the incremented value of x, which is 8. In line 5, we are again printing the x value and at the same time incrementing it using the prefix increment operator. Here the incrementing happens before the `print()` operation, so `println()` prints the incremented value of x, which is 9.

The same evaluation logic applies to the prefix and postfix decrement operator as well.

Hence, the choice between using prefix and postfix operators depends on the context—the actual expression in which the operator is involved and the expected value of the respective expression.

The Unary + and – Operators

JavaFX Script variables can hold either positive numbers (by default all number are positive) or negative numbers. If you need to specify a number as negative, then you need to put a minus (–) sign in front of the value or the variable. The minus sign can be used to change the algebraic sign of a value or a variable:

```
var c = -10 ;
```

This example states that –10 is assigned to a variable c. In the same way, the value of an expression can be made negative by applying the minus sign in front of the expression, as in the following example:

```
var d  = - ( x * x  );
```

Here, the variable d will hold the negative value of the square of x.

As mentioned at the beginning of this section, there is also a unary + operator. Its use is implicit, since all numbers are positive by default.

The not Operator

The not operator is a unary operator used to complement either a relational or a logical expression. Listing 4-9 shows its syntax.

Listing 4-9. *Syntax of the not operator*

```
not logical or relational expression
```

The not operator negates the value of the logical or relational expression that follows it. If the expression evaluates to True, the not operator will change that to False and vice-versa. Listing 4-10 shows an example.

Listing 4-10. *Using the not operator*

```
var a = 10;
var b = 5;
var x : Boolean = not ( a > b );
println(x);
```

Output
```
false
```

As you see in the example, the actual value of the relational expression is true since a is greater than b. But the not operator changes that to false while assigning it to variable x.

▨ **Note** In Java, the negation operator is represented by ! (the exclamation symbol).

Relational Operators

Relational operators are used to compare the relationship between two operands. Relational expressions involving these operators always produce Boolean results and are often used in conditional expressions, as you will see later in this chapter. Table 4-2 shows the relational operators available in JavaFX Script.

Table 4-2. Relational Operators

Operator	Meaning	Example
<	Less than	`Operand1 < Operand2`
<=	Less than or equal to	`Operand1 <= Operand2`
>	Greater than	`Operand1 > Operand2`
>=	Greater than or equal to	`Operand1 >= Operand2`
==	Equal to	`Operand1 == Operand 2`
!=	Not equal	`Operand1 != Operand2`

Note: All relational operators except equal (==) and not equal (!=) can be applied only to simple data types like Integer or Number. Equal to and Not Equal To can be applied to objects as well.

```
var x  = 10 > 5;
```

Here we are comparing whether 10 is greater than 5. Since 10 is greater than 5, the value of x after executing the statement will be True. Since relational expressions fetch a Boolean result, the data type of x would automatically be inferred as Boolean by the compiler.

Logical Operators

Logical operators are binary operators used to combine the value of two or more relational expressions. Similar to relational expressions, logical expressions also produce only Boolean results.

Table 4-3 shows the logical operators available in JavaFX Script.

Table 4-3. Logical Operators

Operator	Meaning	Syntax
and	Logical AND operator	`Relational expression1` `and` `Relational expression 2`
or	Logical OR operator	`Relational expression1` `or` `Relational expression 2`

Logical operators work as cutoff or short-circuit operators. For example, if an **and** operator combines two relational expressions to form a logical expression, and the relational expression on the left side evaluates to False, then the value of the whole logical expression evaluates to False and the right- side relational expression is not evaluated at all. In the same way, if an **or** logical operator combines two relational expressions and the left- side relational expression evaluates to True, then the right expression is ignored and the value of the whole logical expression becomes True.

Here is an example of how two relational expressions are combined with a logical operator:

```
var x = ( 10 > 5 and 2 < 5 );
var firstGrade = ( totalMark => 60 or totalMarks <= 80 );
```

Besides using variables or data values as you've seen, the relational expressions combined by the logical operators can also include complex expressions as well.

▨ **Note** In Java, the logical operators are represented by different symbols - && for AND and || for OR. In JavaFX Script, they have been deliberately named in plain English for convenience.

Table 4-4 summarizes the operator precedence for all the operators available in JavaFX Script.

Table 4-4. *Operator Precedence in JavaFX Script*

Operator	Description	Precedence
()	Parentheses	1
++	Post increment	2
--	Post decrement	
++	Pre increment	3
--	Post decrement	
not	Logical complement	
sizeof	Size of a sequence	
indexof	Index of a sequence element	
reverse	Reversing a sequence order	
=>	Tween operator	*Continued*

Operator	Description	Precedence
*	Multiplication	4
/	Division	
mod	modulus	
+	Addition	5
-	Subtraction	
==	Equal	6
!=	Not equal	
<	Less than	
<=	Less than or equal to	
>	Greater than	
>=	Greater than or equal to	
instanceof	Type checking	7
as	Cast	
and	Logical AND	8
or	Logical OR	9
+=	Addition and assignment	10
-=	subtraction and assignment	
*=	multiplication and assignment	
/=	Division and assignment	
%=	Modulus and assignment	
=	Assignment	11

Range Expressions

A *range expression* defines a sequence of numeric values forming an arithmetic series, using the syntax shown in Listing 4-11.

Listing 4-11. *Syntax of a range expression*

```
[number1..number2]
```

A range expression defines a sequence whose elements consist of the integers from number1 to number2 inclusive. The following example shows a simple range expression.

```
var nums = [0..3];
println (nums);
```

Output
```
[ 0, 1, 2, 3 ]
```

A range expression must have a starting and an ending value and may optionally specify a step value, to define the number by which the sequence must be incremented. The default step value of 1 is used if none is specified. The following example would redefine the previous range with a step value of 2.

```
var nums = [0..3 step 2];
println (nums);
```

Output
```
[ 0,  2]
```

Here, the resulting sequence just includes 0, 2 and not the final value. When there is a step value, first the starting value is included in the sequence and then the step factor is applied repeatedly until the end value is reached. Note that the end value 3 is not included here since it does not meet the step criteria.

The range expression can be pictorially represented as shown in Figure 4-1.

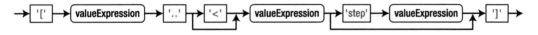

Figure 4-1. *The range expression*

In this diagram, the three valueExpressions must be of either type Integer or Number. If any of them is of type Number, the rangeExpression will become a sequence of Numbers.

Table 4-5 shows examples of range expressions with corresponding output values.

Table 4-5. *Range Expressions*

Range Expression	Value	Comments
[1..5]	[1, 2, 3, 4, 5]	Uses the default step value of 1.
[1..<5]	[1, 2, 3, 4]	All values between 1 and 5, inclusive of 1 but exclusive of 5.
[1..5.0]	[1.0, 2.0, 3.0, 4.0, 5.0]	A number sequence of values between 1.0 and 5.0.
[3.6..7]	[3.6, 4.6, 5.6, 6.6]	3.6, then 3.6 + 1, and so on until the end value is reached.
[1..9 step 2]	[1, 3, 5, 7, 9]	All values between 1 and 9 with an explicit step of 2
[100..90 step -3]	[100, 97, 94, 91]	Negative step. Values decrease.
[0.0..1.0 step 0.25]	[0.0, 0.25, 0.5, 0.75, 1]	Fractional step value.
[0.0..<1.0 step 0.25]	[0.0, 0.25, 0.5, 0.75]	Fractional step value, excluding the end value in the range.
[5..1]	[]	Compiler Warning: "empty sequence range literal, probably not what you meant." For descending sequences, step value must be negative.
var y = 2; [y * 2..y*5]	[4, 5, 6, 7, 8, 9, 10]	Expressions as start/end values.
var y = 2; [y * 2..y*5 step y]	[4, 6, 8, 10]	Start/End/Step values as expressions.
[1..10 step -1]	[]	Compiler Warning: "Empty sequence range literal, probably not what you meant." For ascending sequences, step value must be positive.

■ **Note** Range expressions are unique to JavaFX in the sense that they are not available in Java. Range expressions have varied applications in JavaFX Script in places such as sequences, for loops, and so on. Because range expressions can be defined by using other expressions to define their start, end, and step values, these expressions can become very powerful and can greatly simplify the way for loops and sequences are defined.

Block Expressions

A *block* is a collection of definitions and/or expressions surrounded by curly braces and separated by semicolons. The value of the block expression is the value of the last expression in the block. If the last statement is not an expression, then the value of the block is Void. Listing 4-12 shows an example.

Listing 4-12. Example of a block expression

```
println( {
var sum = 0;
    var counter = 10;
    while (counter > 0) {
            sum += counter;
            --counter;
    }
     "Sum is {sum}"
} );
```

Output
Sum is 55

As you can see, the value of the block enclosed within the println() is the value of the last expression, which is Sum is {sum}.

Listing 4-13 illustrates a conditional block expression.

Listing 4-13. Example of a conditional block expression

```
var flag: Boolean = true;
var x = if (flag) {
45 * 2 + 10;
} else {
90 * 2 + 20;
}
println(x);
```

Output
100 (if flag value is true as given in the code)
200 (if flag value is changed to false)

Here, the value of the if and else blocks takes the value of the arithmetic expression defined within the block since that is the last (only) expression in the block. Please note that the variables declared within a block can be used only in that block or in its child blocks, since they are local to the block.

■ **Tip** Using the type and value of the last expression as the type/value of the block comes handy in many places. One good example is in functions where you don't have to have a return expression explicitly at the end of the block, and the last expression's value would be returned automatically. Similarly, the function need not explicitly declare a return type; the return type would be inferred automatically from the last expression of the function block. You will learn more about this in Chapter 5, "Functions."

Looping Expressions

Loops are an integral part of any programming language; they are used to control the flow of execution. Looping expressions are *iterative*; they repeat until the Boolean expression that controls the loop evaluates to False. JavaFX Script offers two types of looping constructs: `for` and `while`. You will examine each of them in detail in this section.

The `for` expression iterates over one or more sequences. The value of the `for` expression comes from its body. If the body is of type `Void`, the value of the `for` expression would also be `Void`. The body of the `for` loop is executed for each valid value specified by the range (which you specify within square brackets [ ]).

■ **Note** The Void type indicates that an expression does not have a value. Examples of Void expressions are the while expression and calls to functions that have no return value. The only time Void can be used to declare a type explicitly is to declare the return type of a function that does not return a value. You will see this in detail in Chapter 5. For now, Void can be considered to be equivalent of an expression having "no value."

Listing 4-14 is a simple example of a `for` expression.

Listing 4-14. Example of a for loop

```
for (i in [1..5]) {
    print ("{i} ");
}
```

Output
1 2 3 4 5

In this example, the syntax [x..y] is a range expression representing a range of values. Here the loop repeats for five times, with i taking values from 1 to 5 (inclusive). No need to declare the variable i explicitly outside the `for` loop, as it will be implicitly created when the loop begins and discarded when the loop is terminated. The value of the `for`-expression is considered to be `Void` since the body of the `for`-expression (`println`) does not have a valid return value.

Listing 4-15 demonstrates a **for** expression that returns a valid value.

Listing 4-15. *Example of a for expression with a valid value*

```
var seq = for (i in [1..3]) 2 * i;
println(seq);
```

Output
```
[2, 4, 6]
```

Here, i takes the value of 1 to 3, and the body of the **for**-expression returns a valid value of i multiplied by 2. Since the **for**-expression yields a valid value, it can be assigned to a variable of type Sequence. Though we have not explicitly defined **seq** to be of type Sequence, the compiler will infer the type automatically to be Integer[ ], since the **for** expression returns multiple values. Hence the code shown in Listing 4-15 would yield the same result as this:

```
var seq: Integer [] = [2, 4, 6];
```

■ **Note** A for expression is always expected to return a sequence, even if it just returns a single value. The compiler will always try to infer the data type as a sequence when the result of the for expression is assigned to a variable.

The **for** expression can be pictorially represented as shown in Figure 4-2.

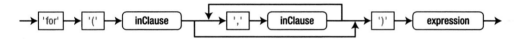

Figure 4-2. *The for expression*

As you can see, a **for** expression can have multiple **in** clauses; an **in** clause can be defined pictorially as shown in Figure 4-3.

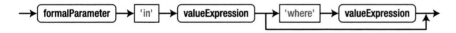

Figure 4-3. *The in-clause*

An **in** clause typically returns a range of values for which the loop has to repeat, and both a **for**-Expression and an **in** clause can optionally include a **where** clause to validate the values from the given range conditionally.

The **for** examples that you have seen so far have used a single **in**-clause within the **for**-expression. Now let us see a **for** expression with multiple **in** clauses.

```
var seq = for (x in [1..2], word in ["Richard", "Brian"]) "{x} {word}";
```

Having multiple in clauses can be considered like having a nested for-loop in Java. When we have more than one in clause, the rightmost in clause acts as the innermost loop.

The output of the previous example is as follows:

```
seq = [ 1 Richard, 1 Brian, 2 Richard, 2 Brian ]
```

The same code can be replicated in a conventional way as shown in Listing 4-16.

Listing 4-16. *Example of a conventional for expression with multiple in clauses*

```
var seq: String[];
for (x in [1..2]) {
    for (word in ["Richard", "Brian"]) {
        insert "{x} {word}" into seq;
    }
}
println(seq);
```

Output
```
[ 1 Richard, 1 Brian, 2 Richard, 2 Brian ]
```

As you see, this code has yielded the same result as that of the for expression with multiple in clauses shown previously. Here the insert statement just inserts a new element into the sequence; you will learn more about this in Chapter 10, "Sequences."

So far, we have only seen plain in clauses that do not validate the range values conditionally. In Listing 4-17, you can see how to validate the range values conditionally within an in clause using where.

Listing 4-17. *Example of a for expression with conditional validation*

```
var words = for (length in [3..6], word in ['moose', 'wolf', 'turkey', 'bee'] where
word.length() >= length) word;
```

In this example, the inner in clause validates if a specific range value size actually exceeds the length (specified by the outer in clause), and this range value would be used only if the condition is met.

Now let's see iteratively how the sequence is built when the value of length changes from 3 to 6:

```
    Iteration 1
length = 3   seq = ['moose', 'wolf', 'turkey', 'bee']
    Iteration 2
length = 4    seq = ['moose', 'wolf', 'turkey', 'bee', 'moose', 'wolf', 'turkey']
    Iteration 3
length = 5    seq = ['moose', 'wolf', 'turkey', 'bee', 'moose', 'wolf', 'turkey', 'moose',
'turkey']
    Iteration 4
length = 6    seq = ['moose', 'wolf', 'turkey', 'bee', 'moose', 'wolf', 'turkey', 'moose',
'turkey', 'turkey']
```

As you see in the output, in the second iteration bee is dropped from the range of word since the condition defined by the where clause is not satisfied. Similarly wolf is dropped for iteration 3 and moose is dropped for iteration 4.

The same example can also be written in the conventional way as shown in Listing 4-18.

Listing 4-18. Example of the conventional way of using conditional validations in a for expression

```
var words = for (length in [3..6]) {
for (word in ['moose', 'wolf', 'turkey', 'bee']) {
        if (word.length() >= length)  {
        word
        } else {
            null
        }
    }
};
```

The output of Listing 4-18 is the same as that of Listing 4-17.

■ **Note** The else part in Listing 4-18 generates a null value but unlike in Java, null values are ignored and not inserted into the sequence.

The range expressions in a for loop can themselves contain expressions and can also depend on the range value of the previous in clause, such as the one shown in Listing 4-19.

Listing 4-19. Example of an expression within a range expression

```
var seq = for (x in [1..5], y in [1..(x-1)]) {
println("X Val: {x}, Y Val: {y}, Mod Val: {x mod y}");
x mod y;
}
println(seq);
```

```
    Output
X Val: 2, Y Val: 1, Mod Val: 0
X Val: 3, Y Val: 1, Mod Val: 0
X Val: 3, Y Val: 2, Mod Val: 1
X Val: 4, Y Val: 1, Mod Val: 0
X Val: 4, Y Val: 2, Mod Val: 0
X Val: 4, Y Val: 3, Mod Val: 1
X Val: 5, Y Val: 1, Mod Val: 0
X Val: 5, Y Val: 2, Mod Val: 1
X Val: 5, Y Val: 3, Mod Val: 2
X Val: 5, Y Val: 4, Mod Val: 1
[ 0, 0, 1, 0, 0, 1, 0, 1, 2, 1 ]
```

In this example note that the first iteration of x value, with a value of 1, is skipped because it does not fetch a valid y value. The rest of the output is self-explanatory.

With the combination of range expression, multiple **in** clauses, and conditional validation of the range values, the **for** expression in JavaFX Script makes looping code much simpler, less verbose, and very powerful.

While Loops

While expressions are the same in JavaFX Script as in Java. The expression specified after the close parenthesis repeats as long as the Boolean expression controlling the while loop evaluates to True. Listing 4-20 shows a simple example of a while loop, and the code is self-explanatory.

Listing 4-20. *Example of a while loop*

```
var i = 0;
while (i < 5) {
println(i);
i ++;
}
```
   Output
```
0
1
2
3
4
```

A while *expression can be pictorially represented as shown in Figure 4-4.*

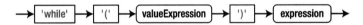

Figure 4-4. *The while expression*

In Figure 4-4, `valueExpression` yields a binary value (True or False), based on which the execution of the while loop is repeated. Unlike a **for** expression, the value of the **while** expression is always **Void** and hence it cannot be used in assignments like **for** expressions.

Break Expressions

A **break** expression is used to terminate (abruptly) a loop in which it is lexically contained and needs to be used with **while** or **for** expressions. The value of the **break** expression is always **Void** since it abruptly ends the execution of a loop. Usage of **break** in JavaFX Script is same as in Java. Listing 4-21 shows an example.

Listing 4-21. *Example of using break within a while loop*

```
var x = 0;
while (x <= 5.0) {
x++;
println(x);
if (x > 2.5 ) {
    break;
}
}
```

Output

```
1
2
3
```

This example uses a **break** expression to break the **while** loop conditionally.
Now let us see how to use this from within a **for** expression, as shown in Listing 4-22.

Listing 4-22. *Example of using break within a for expression*

```
var words: String[];
for (length in [3..6]) {
for (word in ['moose', 'wolf', 'turkey', 'bee']) {
    if (word.length() >= length)  {
        insert word into words;
    } else {
        break;
    }
}
};
```

Output

```
words = [ moose, wolf, turkey, bee, moose, wolf, turkey, moose ]
```

The code in Listing 4-22 breaks the inner loop whenever the length of **word** does not meet the length specified by the outer loop.

Continue Expressions

The **continue** expression is the same in JavaScript as in Java. It abruptly completes the current iteration of the loop in which it is lexically contained and attempts to start the next iteration. The statements that follow **continue** won't be executed and control is transferred to the top of the loop. Listing 4-23 demonstrates a **continue** expression.

Listing 4-23. *Example of a continue expression*

```
var notPrime = false;

for (x in [2..100]) {

    for (y in [2..(x-1)]) {

        if (x mod y == 0) {

            notPrime = true;

            break;

        }

    }

    if (notPrime) {

notPrime = false;
continue;
    } else {

        print("{x} ");

    }

}
```

Output
2 3 5 7 11S 13 17 19 23 29 31 37 41 43 47 53 59 61 67 71 73 79 83 89 97

This example is self-explanatory. However, note that the value of `continue` is also always `Void`.

The if-else Expression

The `if-else` expression in JavaFX Script is pretty much the same as in Java. `If-else` is probably the most basic way of controlling program flow. The `if-else` expression in JavaFX Script uses the truth or falsehood of the associated conditional expression to decide the program flow. If the conditional expression evaluates to True, the first block of code or the expression following the conditional expression is executed. If the conditional expression evaluates to false, the else block is executed.

The if-else expression can be pictorially represented as shown in Figure 4-5.

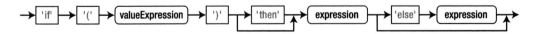

Figure 4-5. *The if-else expression*

As described in Figure 4-5, the else and then parts of the if-else expression are optional.

The value of an `if` expression can either be a valid value or `Void` depending on the value that the first and second expressions evaluate to. If the else part is present and if neither of the expressions are of the `Void` type, then the `if` expression will have a valid value. The value will be that of the first expression if `valueExpression` evaluates to True and will be that of the second if `valueExpression` is False. If the `valueExpression` is False and if there is no else block, the value of the `if` expression would be `Void`.

▓ **Note** The Java language has the if-else statement as well as the ternary operator, such as a > b? a: b. In JavaFX Script, the same if statement is used for both, thanks to block expressions. You will find both usages in the examples given in this chapter.

Listing 4-24 shows a simple *if-else* expression.

Listing 4-24. *Example of an if-else expression*

```
var mark: Integer = 60;
if (mark >= 50) {
println("PASS");
} else {
println ("FAIL");
}
```

Output
```
PASS
```

The same expression can alternatively be specified in one statement, as shown in the following example. Here we omit the braces since there is only one statement in each of the blocks.

```
If (mark >= 50) println("PASS") else println("FAIL");
```

Since the value of `mark` is 60, this will print `PASS`. If the `mark` value is changed to anything less than 50, then the `else` block will be executed, printing FAIL. The value of the `if` expression as such would be `Void` since neither of the expressions have a valid value here.

Since the if-else expression can bear a value, it can be used to assign a value to a variable conditionally, as shown in Listing 4-25.

Listing 4-25. *Example of if-else with a value*

```
var flag = true;
var x = if (flag) "JavaFX" else 3.14;
println(x);
```

Output
```
JavaFX
```

This result occurs because `flag` is set to True. If the) `flag` value is changed to false, the output would be 3.14.

In Listing 4-25, the type of the variable x would be an Object here as there is no more specific type that has String and Number as sub-types.

When using `if-else` expressions for assignments, you have to ensure there is an `else` part and both the expressions given under `if` and `else` yield valid values. If not, this would result in a compilation error.

■ **Note** Neither Java nor JavaFX Script allows you to use a number as a Boolean the way C and C++ do, where truth is non-zero and falsehood is zero. So, If you need to use a number a, you should first change it to Boolean through a conditional expression such as (a != 0) or (a > 0).

Exception Handling

Exception handling in JavaFX Script is almost the same as in Java. The same `try-catch-finally` blocks used in Java are applicable to JavaFX Script as well but need to be written with JavaFX Script variable declaration syntax.

Listing 4-26 shows a simple example of how the `try-catch-finally` is written in JavaFX Script.

Listing 4-26. *Example of a try-catch-finally block*

```
    try {
    throw new Exception("Demonstrating try-catch-finally");
} catch (e:Exception) {
    println("Exception thrown {e}");
        } finally {
        println("finally reached");
        }
```

Listing 4-26 could also be written as follows:
```
    try {
    throw new Exception("Demonstrating try-catch-finally");
} catch (any) {
    println("Exception thrown {any}");
        } finally {
        println("finally reached");
        }
```

Output
```
Exception thrown java.lang.Exception: Demonstrating try-catch-finally
finally reached
```

Listing 4-26 throws an exception intentionally from within the **try** block to see if it is caught by the respective **catch** block. As you see in the output, the respective **catch** block as well as the **finally** block are called when the exception is thrown. Now let us see in detail how this works in JavaFX Script.

The typical **try-catch-finally** and **throw** clauses in JavaFX Script are pictorially described in Figures 4-6 through 4-8. First, Figure 4-6 shows the complete **try-catch-finally** structure.

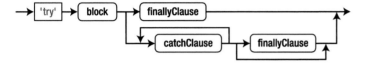

Figure 4-6. *The try expression*

The **try** block (Figure 4-6) is executed until either an exception is thrown or it finishes successfully. When there is an exception, each **catch** clause is inspected to see which of the **catch** block's **formalParameter**s matches that of the exception thrown. Figure 4-7 represents the **catch** block pictorially.

Figure 4-7. *The catch expression*

If any of the catch blocks is tuned to receive the exception thrown, the respective block is executed, with **formalParameter** replaced with the exception object. No further **catch** blocks will be executed. If none of the **catch** blocks match the exception thrown, then the exception propagates out of the **try-catch-finally** blocks.

A **finally** block, if present, will always be executed after the **try** block regardless of whether any exception is thrown.

The **throw** expression in JavaFX Script (Figure 4-8) is same as in Java and causes an exception to be thrown. Since it completes abruptly, it does not have any value.

Figure 4-8. *The throw expression*

A **try** expression does not have any value and hence it is of type **Void**.

The new Expression

A **new** expression is used to create instance of a Java class. It allows us to specify the parameters required by the constructor of the respective Java class. Figure 4-9 is a diagram of its syntax, and listing 4-27 shows some examples of the **new** operator to create instances of Java classes.

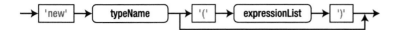

Figure 4-9. *The new expression*

Listing 4-27. *Examples of the new expression*

```
var f = new java.io.File("JavaFX.txt");
var fis: java.io.FileInputStream = new java.io.FileInputStream("Sun.doc");
var str = new java.lang.String("JavaFX is cool");
```

Instances of JavaFX classes can also be created with the new operator, but it is recommended to use object literals for JavaFX class instances. You will see more about object literals when we deal with class definitions in JavaFX Script.

Differentiating Expressions

In JavaFX Script, one expression must be differentiated from another by a semicolon, without which there will be a compilation error. Listing 4-28 shows good and bad examples.

Listing 4-28. *Correctly and incorrectly differentiating expressions*

```
println(n) // This line would show a compilation error for missing semicolon
var xx = 9; // Correct
var yy = 100 // This will not show a compilation error since there are no expressions
following this one.
```

   Output
```
You have forgotten the ';', which is needed to separate one expression from the next.
println(n)
        ^
```

Hence it is important to close an expression with a semicolon (;) when there are further expressions following it.

Summary

JavaFX Script operators operate on one or more operands or values and produce either a Boolean or Numeric value or a reference. Arithmetic, Relational and logical operators are binary operators. The mod, increment/decrement, not, –, and + are unary operators. Each operator is assigned a precedence or priority which determines the order in which the operator operates on the operand.

Some operators are not covered in this chapter; they are as follows:

- indexof
- instanceof
- sizeof
- reverse

In this chapter, you have also learned about various expressions such as `for`, `while`, `break`, `continue`, `if-else`, `range`, `block`, `try-catch-finally`, and so on, its syntax and usage. There are still more expressions that are not covered here, such as

- Object literals
- Qualified names
- PostFix expressions
    - Member access
    - Function invocation
    - This
- Sequence
    - Selection
    - Indexing
    - Slice
- Function expressions
- Timeline expressions

The operators and expressions not covered in this chapter will be covered in later chapters when we go in-depth into topics such as class definitions, access modifiers, functions, timelines, and so on. In the next chapter, you will learn more about functions in JavaFX Script and their usage.

CHAPTER 5

■■■

Functions

A *function* is a block of statements enclosed within curly braces. This block is given a name and is invoked using the specified name.

One of the important reasons to use functions is that they help organize the code conceptually and logically, avoiding redundancy within your program. Functions help break the bulk of code into smaller chunks by logically grouping the statements. Typically the code that is called frequently within your program is moved to a function that is then invoked from multiple places instead of duplicating the same code in all the places. Sometimes this is referred to as the "divide and conquer" approach.

In JavaFX Script, functions can be classified into two types based on where they are located within your program; there are script-level functions and member functions of a class definition. Script-level functions are written directly within the script (an .fx file) and not inside any class definition present in the script. Functions of this type are visible to the entire script and within any class definitions that may exist in the script. It is also possible to make these functions visible outside the script, by specifying appropriate access specifiers; you will learn more about this in Chapter 7, "Access Specifiers."

Member functions (also known as *instance functions*) are functions defined within a class as a member of the class and are accessible within the class by default. To access these functions outside the class, you will have to create an instance of the class. Here also it is possible to make these members visible outside of the script by specifying appropriate access specifiers.

■ **Note** All the examples in this chapter are script-private functions, meaning they will not have any access specifiers defined and would be accessible only within the script.

Functions are normally defined by the application developer depending on the requirement of the application. In addition to that, you can find many functions available in the JavaFX APIs that you can use within your application. For instance, you have seen many examples using `println`, which is a function offered by the JavaFX APIs that is implicitly available within any JavaFX application (no import required).

Let us see the syntax for defining a function:

```
[modifiers] function function-name([parameterName : parameterType , .. ] ) : [ return type ]
{
    // statements
}
```

The access modifiers that can be specified while declaring a function in JavaFX Script are package, protected and public. These modifiers are reserved words in JavaFX Script, and you will learn more about them in Chapter 7. Specifying an access modifier is optional; if nothing is specified, the default will be "script-private" access and will make the function visible only within the script where it is declared.

In addition to the access modifiers, you can also specify certain other modifiers such as bound, abstract and override in the function definition. Bound functions are explained in detail in Chapter 9, "Data Binding." You will learn more about abstract and overridden functions in Chapter 8, "Inheritance." They have been listed here in the syntax just for completeness. These modifiers are additive in nature and hence can be combined with the access modifiers.

Every function requires an identifier, which is the function name. The rules for naming variables that you have already learned apply to function naming as well. *Arguments* (or *parameters*) are the inputs for the function, and they are separated by commas. Arguments are enclosed within the parentheses. It is not mandatory that a function have an argument; you can define a function with no arguments. Similarly, even if you define an argument, it is not necessary to define the data type for the argument, as it will be inferred automatically by the compiler. Nevertheless, there are circumstances where you will declare the data type while defining the function arguments, as you will see later in this chapter. If the function returns a value, you specify the return type after the closing parenthesis separated by a colon. The return type of the function is optional as well; if it is not specified, the compiler tries to infer a valid return type automatically from the last statement in the function body. If the last statement is an expression that does not yield a value (such as a println statement), then the default return type of Void is assumed. The executable block of code that is enclosed with the curly braces forms the body of the function.

Let us see how to write a simple function. Listing 5-1 is our first example.

Listing 5-1. *Example of a simple function*

```
1.    function sayHello ( name )  {
2.        println("Hello {name} ..!");
3.    }
4.    println("My team Members");
5.    sayHello("praveen");    // function call
6.    sayHello("lawrence");
```

Output
```
My team Members
praveen
lawrence
```

Listing 5-1 is a very simple program that demonstrates how to write a function. The aim of the function is just to print some names with a welcome message. In this example the function is defined above the function call (the statement that calls the function). But it is not mandatory to define the function above the statement that calls it in JavaFX Script; we can define the function anywhere within the script.

This rule is similar to that for the main() function in Java, which can appear anywhere within the class definition.

How a Function Works

Let us analyze how the function shown in Listing 5-1 works. When the function **sayHello** is invoked at line 5 with an argument of **praveen**, control goes to line 1, taking the value **praveen** and copying it to the variable **name** specified in the parameter list of the function. The value **praveen** in line 5 is called an *actual argument*, since it is the actual value that is passed to the function. The variable **name** in line 1 is called a *formal argument*, since it just collects the value passed from the function call. Formal arguments are also called *formal parameters*. The scope of the formal parameter is restricted to the body of the function. They are created when the function is called and destroyed when the function ends.

As you have seen in the syntax, specifying arguments and return types is optional in JavaFX Script. With this in mind, let us see the following combinations of function definitions in detail:

- Functions with neither an argument nor a return value

- Functions with an argument but without a return value

- Functions without an argument but with a return value

- Functions with both an argument and a return value

A Function with Neither an Argument nor a Return Value

Let us see how to define a function that does not take any arguments and does not return anything. Listing 5-2 shows an example.

Syntax
```
modifiers function-name( ) {
    // statements
}
```

or

```
modifiers function-name( ) : Void {
    // statements
}
```

Listing 5-2. Example of a function with neither an argument nor a return value

```
1.    for(i in [1..5])  {
2.        sayHello();
3.    }
4.
5.    function sayHello(){
6.        println("This is a function without an argument and a return value");
7.    }
```

Output
```
This is a function without an argument and a return value
This is a function without an argument and a return value
This is a function without an argument and a return value
```

```
This is a function without an argument and a return value
This is a function without an argument and a return value
```

In Listing 5-2, we have defined a function called sayHello() from line 5 to line 7. This function doesn't take any argument (the parentheses are empty) and there is no return type as well. We are calling the same function five times in line 2 using a for loop. For each function call, the output statement is printed on the console as shown in the output section. Since the block expression that forms the body of the function does not have a valid value, the compiler would automatically infer a return type of Void.

A Function with Arguments but Without a Return Value

Let us see how to write a function with some arguments (or parameters) but without a return value.

Syntax
```
modifiers function-name(parameterName : parameterType , .. ) {
    // statements
}
```

or

```
modifiers function-name( parameterName : parameterType , ..) : Void {
    // statements
}
```

Listing 5-3 shows an example of a function that takes an argument but does not have a return value.

Listing 5-3. *Example of a function with arguments but no return value*

```
1.    function factorial( num : Integer) : Void {
2.        var i : Integer = 1;
3.        var fact : Integer = 1;
4.        while(i <= num ){
5.            fact = fact * i++;
6.        }
7.        println("factorial of {num} is {fact}");
8.    }
9.
11.   var n2 : Integer = 6;
12.   factorial(5);
13.   factorial(n2);
```

Output
```
factorial of 5 is 120
factorial of 6 is 720
```

The aim of the function defined in Listing 5-3 is to find the factorial of a given number. From line 1 to line 8, we define the function named factorial, and in lines 12 and 13 we call the function. When the function is called, its body of the function is executed, accepting the argument passed. In this function body, a block expression calculates the factorial of the given number and prints it out. Please note that the value of this block expression is Void because the value of the last expression in the block is a println, which does not yield any value. Hence the return type of the function is considered to be Void.

■ **Note** In JavaFX Script, unlike in Java, the arguments passed to a function are read-only and cannot be modified by the function. Trying to modify the parameters will result in a compilation error.

A Function Without an Argument but with a Return Value

Let us see how to write a function that does not accept any arguments but returns a valid value.

Syntax
```
modifiers function-name( ) : [return type] {
    // statements
    return expression ;
}
```
or
```
modifiers function-name( )   {

    // statements
    return expression;
}
```
or
```
modifiers function-name( ) : [return type]{
    // statements
}
```

As you can see, there are three ways of declaring a function that does not accept an argument but returns a valid value. The first syntax shows a function declaration with its return type specified explicitly and a return statement within the body of the function. The second syntax shows a function declaration where the return type is not specified in the first line of the function declaration, but the function body specifies a return statement explicitly. In this case, the compiler will automatically infer the return type from the return statement. The third syntax shows a function declaration where we have specified the return type in the first line of the function declaration, but we have not specified anything within the function body. In this case the return type of the function is determined by the last statement of the function.

Now let us see a simple example (Listing 5-4).

Listing 5-4. Example of a function without an argument but with a return value

```
1.    function getPI( ) {
2.        return 22.0/7.0;
3.    }
4.
5.    function getOddsLessThanTen( ) {
6.        [1..10 step 2];
```

```
7.     }
8.
9.     function printName() : String{
10.
11.
12.             "Jack and Jill";
13.    }
14.
15.    var pi = getPI();
16.    println("pi value = {pi}");
17.    var nos : Integer [] = getOddsLessThanTen( );
18.    println(" Odd numbers = {nos}");
19.    println(printName());
```

Output
```
pi value = 3.142857
 Odd numbers = 13579
Jack and Jill
```

This example has three different functions that show how functions return their values. The first function, **getPI()**, returns the value of Pi. We have explicitly specified the **return** statement.

The second function, **getOddsLessThanTen()**, returns a range from 1 to 9 with a step of 2. We have not specified any **return** statement or the return type for this function, so in this case the compiler automatically infers that the function **getOddsLessThanTen()** returns a Sequence by looking at the last statement of the function.

The third function, **printName()**, returns a String depending upon the **if** expression. In this function we have specified both the return type and the **return** statement.

A Function with Arguments and a Return Value

Let us see how to write a function that accepts some arguments and returns a valid value.

Syntax
```
modifiers function-name( parameterName : parameterType ,.. ) : [return type] {
    // statements
    return expression;
}
```

Listing 5-5 shows an example.

Listing 5-5. *Example of a function that has arguments and a return value*

```
1.     function functionExpression(a:Integer, b:Integer):Number {
2.         var x = a + b;
3.         var y = a - b;
4.         return squareOfNumber(x) / squareOfNumber (y);
5.     }
6.
7.     function squareOfNumber(n:Integer): Number {
8.         n * n;
```

```
9.     }
10.    println("{ functionExpression(5,8) }");
```

Output
18.777779

This example demonstrates how one function calls another within the body of the function and, at the same time, plays the role of the expression that decides the return value.

▨ **Note** A function can take any number of arguments of any data type, but it can return only one return value. If you need to return multiple values, use a Sequence as the return type of the function.

Variable Access within a Function

A function can access script-level variables, parameters, and local variables. Let's see each of them in detail.

Script-Level Variables

A variable defined within the script is called a *script-level* variable. Such a variable can be accessed anywhere within the script: within the script functions, within the blocks, within the class member functions, and so on. The value of this variable can be changed anywhere within the script. Script-level variables are like static variables in Java. Listing 5-6 shows an example.

Listing 5-6. *Using a script-level variable*

```
1.     var scriptLevelVar  : Number = 10;
2.
3.     public  function simpleFunction(  ) {
4.         println("Accessing scriptLevelVar with in the simple function =
{scriptLevelVar}");
5.         // modifing the value of scriptLevelVar
6.         scriptLevelVar = 45.34;
7.         println("Modified value of scriptLevelVar in simple function = {scriptLevelVar}");
8.     }
9.
10.    function run (){
11.        println("Accessing the scriptLevelVar in run function \nscriptLevelVar =
{scriptLevelVar}");
12.        simpleFunction(  ) ;
13.        ;  scriptLevelVar++;
14.        println("Modified value in run function scriptLevelVar = {scriptLevelVar}");
15.    }
```

Output
```
Accessing the scriptLevelVar in run function
scriptLevelVar = 10.0
Accessing scriptLevelVar with in the function = 10.0
Modified value of scriptLevelVar in function = 45.34
Modified value in run function scriptLevelVar = 46.34
```

This example demonstrates how a script-level variable can be accessed and modified from within a function.

▓ **Note** Script-level variables are created before the run() function is invoked.

Local Variables

Local variables are variables that are defined within the function and can only be accessed within it. The life-span of such variables is same as that of the function in which they are declared. These variables are created when the function is called and are destroyed when the function completes execution. Their value can be changed any number of times within the body of the function.

Function Overloading

Function overloading is typically about a set of functions sharing the same function name, but accepting different arguments and performing different activities depending on the kind of parameters sent to them. This is also known as *polymorphism* in OOP (Object Oriented Programming). When an overloaded function is called, the JavaFX Script checks the number and type of parameter(s) of all the functions defined with the same name and calls the one whose parameters exactly match the calling statement. Listing 5-7 shows an example.

Listing 5-7. *Example of an overloaded function*

```
1.     function fun() {
2.         println("Function Overloaded without any argument.");
3.     }
4.
5.     function fun(a : Integer , b : Integer) {
6.         println("Function Overloaded with  Integer argument a ={ a } , b = {b}");
7.     }
8.
9.     function fun(n : Number ) {
10.        println("Function Overloaded with  Number argument n = {n}");
11.    }
12.
13.    fun();
14.    fun(5, 10);
```

```
15.    fun(22.0/7.0);
16.    fun(40);
```

Output
```
Function Overloaded without any argument.
Function Overloaded with Integer argument a = 5 , b = 10
Function Overloaded with Number argument n = 3.142857
Function Overloaded with Number argument n = 40.0
```

The example in Listing 5-7 has different functions sharing the same function name. Each function has a different set of arguments. The first function doesn't take any argument, the second function takes two Integer arguments, and the third function takes one Number argument. When the function is called from line 13 to line 16, the JavaFX Script compiler checks the number and type of parameters and calls the corresponding function.

Line 16 is a special type of function call. The function argument doesn't match any of the function declarations directly. When this situation arises, JavaFX Script's automatic type conversion plays an important role in solving the issue. At Line 16, the function call has an Integer value, but none of the function declarations match. However, the last function matches in the number of arguments but differs in data type. Nevertheless, the function expects a Number type, which has a greater precision than the Integer, so it is actually safe to promote an Integer to a Number data type without any data loss. Hence the compiler converts 40 to a Number and calls the **fun()** function, which accepts a Number. You can easily see from the output that a plain 40 is converted into 40.0.

Recursive Functions

A function that calls itself either directly or indirectly until a condition is satisfied is called a *recursive* function. Let us take the most common example of the recursive function that calculates the factorial of a given number and the Fibonacci series. You have already seen the factorial example in this chapter. Listing 5-8 illustrates how the same problem can be solved using a recursive function.

Listing 5-8. *Example of a recursive function*

```
1.     function factorial( n : Integer ) : Integer{
2.         if( ( n==0) or ( n == 1 ) ) {
3.             return n;
4.         }
5.         else {
6.             return n * factorial(n - 1 );
7.         }
8.     }
9.
10.    println("factorial of 5 = {factorial(5) }");
11.    var fact = factorial(8);
12.    println("factorial of 8 = {fact}");
```

Output
```
factorial of 5 = 120
factorial of 8 = 40320
```

In Listing 5-8, the function factorial() takes an Integer as the argument and returns an Integer as output. In line 2 we are checking whether the argument n value is either 0 or 1. If the value of n is 1, then we are just returning the value of n. if the value is more than 1, the else part is executed. It calls the same function, passing n - 1. This recursion continues until the condition given in line 2 is satisfied.

▓ **Note** It is mandatory to declare the return type of a recursive function explicitly. Failing to do so will result in a compilation error.

Listing 5-9 shows another example of a recursive function.

Listing 5-9. *Example of a recursive function with multiple invocations*

```
1.       function fibonacciFun(n:Integer):Integer {
2.       if (n<2) {
3.           return n
4.       }
5.       else {
6.            (fibonacciFun(n-1) + fibonacciFun(n-2));
7.        }
8.    }
9.
10.   println(" fibonacci of 10 = { fibonacciFun(10) }");
11.   println(" fibonacci of 1 = { fibonacciFun(1) }");
```

Output
```
fibonacci of 10 = 55
```

Anonymous Functions

An *anonymous function* is one that doesn't have a function name. Using anonymous functions, we can convert a function in an expression, called a *function expression.*
    The first step to write an anonymous function is to define a variable of type Function.

Syntax
```
var function_variable_name : function ( : parameter , : parameter ) : [return type];
```

Example
```
var x  : function( : Integer,  : Integer) : Integer;
```

This section is very simple; it's just providing the signature of the function, without specifying the function name. It is similar to declaring a variable, but instead of the data type, we are specifying the function type.
    Here, *function_variable_name* is the variable that holds the function expression ,followed by the function keyword, which specifies that this is a variable of Function type. A Function type must also

define the parameters within a pair of parentheses. If there is no parameter, then it could just be the opening and closing parentheses. Following the parameters is the return type of the function.

Syntax
```
function_variable_name = function(argument name1 , argument name2 ) : [return type] {
        // statements
}
```

From this syntax, you see that an anonymous function is similar to a normal function, except that the function name is missing and we are assigning the function to a variable of the Function type.

Now let us see how to call the function variable that refers to an anonymous function expression, a step called *closure*. This is similar to calling the function using the function name and passing values to the arguments. But instead of a function name we are calling the anonymous function with the function variable name to which we have assigned the function expression.

Let's put it all together to make a complete script, as shown in Listing 5-10.

Listing 5-10. Example of an anonymous function

```
1.    var x : function(   : Integer ,   : Integer ) : Integer ;
2.
3.    x = function(a,b ) {
4.        if(a > b ) {
5.            a;
6.        }
7.        else {
8.            b;
9.        }
10.   };
11.
12.   println("greatest number of 5 and 10 = { x(5,10) }");
```

Output
```
greatest no of 5 and 10 = 10
```

In line 1, we have declared the variable **x** of type Function, which takes two Integers as arguments and whose return type is Integer. From line 3 to line 10 we have defined the function expression assigned to variable x. In line 12 we have an output statement which calls the anonymous function through the **x** variable (of Function type) by passing the values 5 and 10, and finally the return value of the function expression is printed.

Listing 5-11 shows another example of an anonymous function.

Listing 5-11. Example of a variable of type function with automatic type inference

```
1.    var fact = function (num : Integer )  {
2.        var i : Integer = 1;
3.        var fact : Integer = 1;
4.        while(i <= num ){
5.            fact = fact * i++;
6.        }
7.        return fact;
8.    }
9.    println("Factorial of 5 = { fact(5) } ");
```

Output
```
Factorial of 5 = 10
```

In Listing 5-10, we had declared function variable separately and function expression separately, but in Listing 5-11 we have combined the statements.

Now we know that in JavaFX Script, a variable can be of the Function type. Functions are described as *first-class objects* in JavaFX Script, which allows the programmers not only to create variables of type functions but also to pass such a variable arguments to other functions and return it as a return type from other functions.

The run() Function

The run() function is a special function in JavaFX Script that acts as the entry point to your application, similar to the main() function in Java. This function is implicitly created by the compiler internally as long as you do not have a public member (a variable, or a class, or a function) defined in your main script. However, if you have defined a public member, then the compiler lets you create the run() function as well and no longer generates it implicitly. If you fail to specify one despite having some public member, the compiler will throw a compilation error.

This function will be automatically called when you execute your application through the javafx executable, and any command-line arguments that the user may pass will be given to this function. Listing 5-12 shows a simple example of the run() function.

Listing 5-12. Example of the run() function

```
1.    function run (){
2.        println("This is the entry point for JavaFX Scripting..!");
3.    }
```

Let's call this script EntryPoint.fx. When this script is executed, we see the following output on the console. This run() function is called by the JavaFX runtime automatically.

Output
```
This is the entry point for JavaFX Scripting..!
```

Let's see another of the run() function (Listing 5-13).

Listing 5-13. Example that enforces addition of a run() function

```
1.    public  function areaOfCircle(radius :Number):Number {
2.        return  3.142 * radius * radius;
3.    }
4.
5.    function run(){
6.    println("This is the entry point for JavaFX Scripting..!");
7.    println("Area of the circle = {areaOfCircle( 7) } " );
8.    }
```

Output
```
This is the entry point for JavaFX Scripting..!
Area of the circle = 153.958
```

In this example we have defined a function called **areaOfCircle** and implemented the **run()** function. When the script is executed, the output shown is printed on the console. Notice that the function **areaOfCircle** is called within the **run()** function. Since the **run()** function is the entry point of the script, it will be called first, before **areaOfCircle**. If we move the function call **areaOfCircle** from line 7 to outside the **run()** function, say line 4, we will get a compilation error. This is because we have a public member in the script **areaOfCircle** and if there is a public member, JavaFX Script compiler enforces you to move all the loose expressions in to a run() function. In such a case, the **run()** function become mandatory. If you want to try this yourself, do the following in Listing 5-13.

1. Move the function call at line 7 to line 4.

2. Comment out the run() function entirely.

3. Remove the **public** keyword from the function **areaOfCircle**.

Now you will be able to compile and run the example without any errors.

■ **Note** When there is a public member in the script, a run() function becomes mandatory, and all the loose expressions in the script must be moved to that function. Otherwise, the compiler will throw an error.

Command-Line Arguments

The **run()** function can be defined with or without parameters. We have seen the function without parameter in the previous examples; let's see how to get the command-line arguments within the **run** function.

Syntax
```
function run( sequence of String ) {
                              // statements
                             }
```

Listing 5-14. ModifiedRun.fx, an example of a function with command-line arguments

```
1.    function run (cmdLine : String[]){
2.        println("Printing Command-line arguments");
3.        for( arg in cmdLine ){
4.            println(arg);
5.        }
6.    }
```

Run the script as follows:

```
D:\javafx-sdk1.3\bin\javafx ModifiedRun Learning JavaFX Script Command-line argument
```

Output
```
Printing Command-line arguments
Learning
JavaFX
Script
Command-line
argument
```

There is also another way of accessing the command-line attributes. The JavaFX API contains a class, named **FX** in the **javafx.lang** package that is implicitly imported into any JavaFX script (just like **java.lang** classes). There is a method **getArguments()** in the FX class that returns a sequence of strings representing the command-line arguments. If no arguments are passed, this method returns a null value. Listing 5-15 shows an example.

Listing 5-15. CommandLineArgsDemo.fx, an example using the getArguments() method

```
1.    public  function area_of_circle( radius :Number):Number {
2.        return 2 * 3.142 * radius ;
3.    }
4.
5.    function run (){
6.        println("Learning FX.getArguments() ..!");
7.        var args : String [] = FX.getArguments();
8.        println(area_of_circle (java.lang.Integer.parseInt(args[0])));
9.    }
```

Output
```
D:\javafx-sdk1.3\bin\javafx  CommandLineArgsDemo 20
Learning FX.getArguments() ..!
125.68
```

There is also another variant of **getArguments()** that accepts a string parameter, and this can be used when the incoming values are represented as key-value pairs. You would find this variant very useful typically when dealing with the browser version of the JavaFX Application (Applets). You can get more information about this from the JavaFX API documentation.

Summary

In this chapter you have learned about functions in detail. A function is a set of statements that are enclosed in curly braces. A function is accessed by its name, called a *function name*. A function definition may optionally include one or more modifiers, parameters and the return type. *Overloaded functions* are functions that share the same function name but differ in their number and type of arguments. Function parameters are read-only and hence cannot be modified. A function can be made anonymous by omitting a function name and instead assigning it to a variable of type Function. Anonymous functions can be invoked using the corresponding variable name, and such variables can be passed as parameters to other functions as well. The `run()` function acts as the entry point to any FX application, and the programmer has to define it if there is a public member declared within the script. Using this `run()` function and the `Javafx.lang.FX` class, you can get access to the command-line arguments.

In the next chapter, you will learn more about class definitions and how to go about defining and using classes and object literals within JavaFX Script.

■ ■ ■

CHAPTER 6

Class Definitions

JavaFX Script is an *object-oriented programming (OOP)* language. Because it is built on the Java platform, JavaFX Script inherits almost all the features of Java, including those that support object orientation. We will start this chapter by examining some basic concepts of OOP, and later you will learn how to implement your own class in JavaFX Script.

Object-oriented programming languages were developed to correct some of the flaws programmers found with procedural languages; for example, typically they are not very flexible. In OOP data is treated as a critical element and not allowed to flow unrestrictedly. OOP binds data closely to the functions that operate on it and protects it from accidental modification by outside functions. OOP allows the decomposition of a problem into a number of entities called *objects* and then builds data and functions around these objects. Thanks to the use of objects, one of the advantages of using OOP is its reusability of code. OOP also has these basic advantages:

- OOP provides a clear modular structure for programs, which makes it good for defining abstract data types in which implementation details are hidden and the unit has a clearly defined interface.

- OOP makes it easy to maintain and modify existing code, as new objects can be created with small differences from existing ones.

- Data is hidden and cannot be accessed by non-member functions.

Classes and Objects

Classes and objects are the two most important concepts of OOP, so we'll begin with a brief definition of each.

Classes

A *class* is a user-defined data type. It's a blueprint or prototype from which objects are created. A well-defined class demonstrates all or at least few of the features of OOP: data abstraction, encapsulation, polymorphism, and inheritance. We'll discuss these defining features shortly.

Objects

An *object* is an instance of a class, which replicates the real world object. For example, consider a computer. You see the computer as one unit, but it is built from many individual components —the motherboard, RAM, processor, hard disk, SMPS, and so on. Instead of looking at these individual components, you tend to look the whole. In the same a way, an object is made up of data members of the class.

Features of OOP

The object-oriented programming approach is defined by the following four features:

- Data abstraction
- Encapsulation
- Polymorphism
- Inheritance

Data Abstraction

Abstraction refers to the act of representing essential features without including the underlying details or explanations. Classes use the concept of abstraction and are defined as lists of abstract attributes.

Encapsulation

Encapsulation is the process of storing data and functions in a single unit and is achieved by declaring a class. It can also be called *data hiding*, since data cannot be accessible to the outside world, only those functions that reside within the class can access it. Encapsulation can be achieved by declaring packages and modules as well as classes.

Inheritance

Inheritance is the process by which an object belonging to one class can acquire the properties of another class. This is an important feature facilitating the reusability of code. It is achieved by deriving a new class from an existing class (base class). The new class (derived class) will have combined features of both the classes. In Chapter 8, "Inheritance," you will learn the types of inheritance and its implementation.

Polymorphism

Polymorphism is the ability of something to take more than one form. In OOP, the concept is exhibited in different behaviors in different instances, depending on the data types used in the operation (functions). Polymorphism is extensively used in implementing inheritance. It is also called *function overloading*, which you learned about in Chapter 5, "Functions."

The Class Definition

Now that you know what a class is, you can move on to learn how to define one. Figure 6-1 shows the structure of a class. As you can see, a class consists of data members and member functions. It may also contain optional `init()` and `postinit()` blocks, which we'll examine later in this chapter.

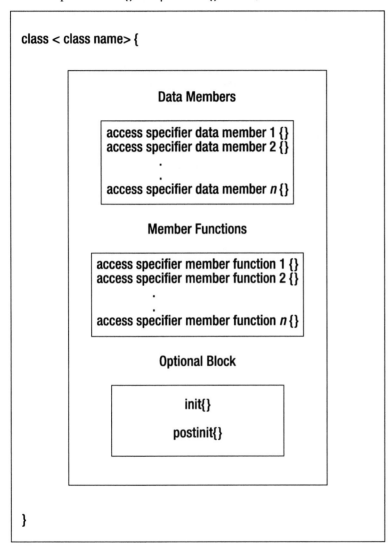

Figure 6-1. Classes contain data members and member functions

Class is a keyword, which tells the compiler that you are going to create a user-defined data type. Class-name is the name given to identify the class. The rules that applies to name a variable applies even for naming a class. The Opening and closing curly braces of the class contains the data members and the member functions

The access specifiers or modifiers that can be applied to a class declaration are package, protected, and public. You will learn all about access modifiers in Chapter 7, "Access Modifiers". Access to classes, data members, and member functions is regulated using access modifiers—a class can control what information or data can be accessible by other classes. To take advantage of encapsulation, you should minimize access whenever possible.

Data members are the attributes of the object and can have the access modifier package, protected, public, public-read or public-init. If you don't specify an access modifier, then such data members of the class will have script-level access and can be accessed in other classes in the same file.

Member functions are the functions that reside within the class. Member functions have the ability to access any data members and other member functions of the class. You can specify the access modifiers package, protected, and public for member functions.

Finally, the init and postinit blocks shown in Figure 6-1 are optional. You will learn about these two optional parts of a class definition later in this chapter. Listing 6-1 demonstrates a class definition.

Listing 6-1. *A simple class definition*

```
class Account {
    var accountNumber : Integer ;
    var accountHolderName : String;
    var balance : Number;

    function printAccountHolderInformation( ) {
        println("Account Number = {accountNumber}  Account Holder Name = {accountHolderName}
                Balance : {balance} ");
    }
}
```

This example declares a class called Account, which contains three data members, accountNumber, accountHolderName, and balance, along with a single member function called printAccountHolderInformation(), which prints the data members of the class. With this we have defined the blueprint of the object or defined the user-defined data type.

Creating Object Literals

Creating an *instance* of our new class means allocating memory for the object in RAM (main memory). An instance of a class can be created in two ways; here's the first:

Syntax
    var *object_name* : *class_name* = *class_name*{ };

This first syntax for creating a class instance is known as the JavaFX style. It is similar to declaring an ordinary variable. In this method, you specify that the object belongs to a particular class and then you create the instance.

The second method of creating the instance of the class is to use the Java style, creating the object using the new operator.

Syntax
```
var object_name : class_name = new class_name( );
```

Here, you are specifying that the object belongs to a particular class and then creating the object using the new operator.

■ **Note** When creating an object of a class using JavaFX style, use curly braces after the class name (class_name{ }). By contrast, when you use Java style to create an object of a class, you'll use parentheses after the class name (class_name( )).

Now let us create the objects of the class Account in both JavaFX style and Java style:

```
var account1 : Account = Account{ };    // JavaFX style
var account2 : Account = new Account( ) ; // Java style
```

Both statements create instances of the class Account. Object account1 is created using JavaFX style and account2 is created using Java style. Note that we have not initialized the attributes explicitly, which means that all the attributes will take their default values, depending on the data type.

Initializing Class Attributes within an Object Literal

So far, you have learned how to declare a class and create objects that are instances of the class. Now let's initialize an object. Listing 6-2 shows the code.

Listing 6-2. Initializing the attributes of the Account class

```
var account1 = Account{
    accountNumber : 121     //  initializing the data member
    accountHolderName : "Praveen"    //  initializing the data member
    balance : 56434.34     //  initializing the data member
};
```

In the above expression, we are creating the object account1 of class Account and initializing it. The data member of the object are initialized by the colon operator (:) followed by the value.

Calling the Members of the Class

Members of the class, which as you saw earlier may be either data members or member functions, are accessed using the dot (.) operator.

```
account1.name     // accessing datamember
account1.printAccountHolderInformation( ); // accessing member function
```

In these statements, you are accessing the name data member of class Account through its object account1, and you are accessing member function printAccountHolderInformation() of the same Account class.

Assume you have created four objects. Memory is allocated for four objects, but the member functions are loaded only once in memory. All the objects share the member functions. Figure 6-2 illustrates this structure.

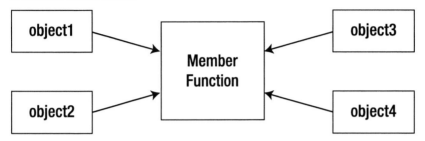

Figure 6-2. Data members of the class sharing the member function

Now let's access the member function of the class Account using the objects account1 and account2:

```
account1.printAccountHolderInformation( );     //  calling the member function
account2.printAccountHolderInformation( );     //  calling the member function
```

Finally, let's put all the pieces together—class definition, object creation, and initialization—to form a complete JavaFX class. Listing 6-3 shows the code.

▓ **Note** In JavaFX Script, unlike Java, it is not mandatory that a public class name should be same as the filename; the class and filename can be different.

Listing 6-3. The complete Account class

```
class Account {
    var accountNumber : Integer ;
    var accountHolderName : String;
    var balance : Number;
    function printAccountHolderInformation( ) {
        println("Account Number = {accountNumber} Account Holder Name = {accountHolderName}
                Balance : {balance} ");
    }
}
var account1 : Account = Account{ /*create an instance and initialize the object */
    accountNumber : 121
    accountHolderName : "Praveen"
    balance : 56434.34
```

```
};
var account2 = Account{} ; // create an instance
account1.printAccountHolderInformation( ); // calling the member function
account2.printAccountHolderInformation( ); // calling the member function
```

After executing Listing 6-3 you'll see the following output.

Output

```
account number = 121 Account Holder Name = Praveen  Balance : 56434.34
account number = 0 Account Holder Name =    Balance : 0.0
```

The output statement prints the details of the objects account1 and account2. In the output of account2, you can see that the value of account number is zero, the value of accountHolderName is null "", and balance is 0.0. This is because we have not initialized the data members of the object.

Assigning Default Values to Data Members

It is possible to set a default value for the data members of the class, if you don't initialize the object. If you initialize the object, then the default value is overridden.

```
var balance : Number = 500.0;    // 500.0 can be either dollars or any currency
```

In this assignment statement the data member balance of the Account class is initialized with 500.0. This is because the minimum balance of the newly opened account should have 500.0, whether rupees or dollars. If you modify the Account class example, Listing 6-3, by initializing the balance data member with the default value as shown in the assignment statement, executing the code will display the following output.

Output

```
Details of the account2       // just to denote that you are seeing the details of account2
account number = 0 Account Holder Name =    Balance : 500.0
```

The init Block

init is a keyword. It's an optional block; if present it is used to initialize the data member of the class, or you can add any initialization statements. You can consider the init block to be the constructor of the class. It is executed as the final step of instance initialization. The following init block shows how to initialize the balance data member of the class Account.

```
init {
    balance = 500.0;
}
```

Listing 6-4. A class definition that includes an init block

```
1.    class Distance {
2.         var feet : Integer = 1;      // default value is 1
3.         var inches : Number = 0.0;
4.
5.         init {
6.              println("within init block..");
7.              println("Default value is overridden by object initialization");
8.              println("feet = {feet}  inches = {inches}");
9.              println("Overriding the default value printing the ");
10.              feet = 10;
11.              inches = 4.5;
12.              println("feet = {feet}  inches = {inches}");
13.         }
14.
15.        function showdist() : Void {
16.             println("feet = {feet } inches = {inches } ");
17.        }
18.    }
19.
20.    var dist1 : Distance = Distance {
21.         feet : 5
22.         inches : 10.5
23.    }
24.    println("calling the member function to print the value of data member");
25.    dist1.showdist() ;
```

Output

```
within init block..
Default value is overridden by object initialization
feet = 5  inches = 10.5
Overriding the default value printing the
feet = 10  inches = 4.5
calling the member function to print the value of data member
feet = 10 inches = 4.5
```

In Listing 6-4, we declare a Distance class, which has two data members, feet and inches (which have default values of 1 and 0.0, respectively), and a member function named showdist() to display the value of feet and inches. In line 20, the object dist1 is created and initialized. We assign feet a value of 5 and inches a value of 10.5. Because we have initialized the object dist1, the default values of feet and inches are overridden. Now feet holds the value of 5 and inches holds the value of 10.5. Next the JavaFX script runtime will execute the init block. The first statement of the init block is line 6, which is an output statement announcing that now you are in the init block. In line 8, the values of feet and inches are printed, 5 and 10.5. Next we modify the feet and inches values by 10 and 4.5, and then print the overridden value of the object initialization. When object dist1 calls the showDist() function, the modified value in the init block is printed.

Order of Instance Initialization

Based on the previous example, we can summarize the sequence in which instances of a class are initialized:

1. Objects are created. If a default value is set, data member are initialized with it.

2. If the object is initialized, then any default value is overridden.

3. The init block is executed. If data members are set to a new value, then object initialization is overridden.

The postinit Block

As noted earlier, the postinit block is optional .It is executed after instance initialization has completed. Usually, you'll place code in postinit that has to be executed after the object is initialized. One of the best uses of a postinit block is to add event-handling code, such as keyevent() and mouseEvent() functions.

Syntax
```
postinit {
       //statements that is required after creation and initialization of the object.
    }
```

Modifying Class Objects

Now that you've seen what's included in a class definition, let's move on to working with class objects elsewhere in the code.

You can modify the objects of a class just like modifying any variable. The following two assignment statements show how to assign the value to data members of the class:

```
dist.feet = 6;
dist.inches =  7.11;
```

Let's modify the Distance class to modify the value of data member outside the class; Listing 6-5 shows the code.

Listing 6-5. *Modifying the value of a data member outside the class*

```
1.     class Distance {
2.          var feet : Integer = 1;     // default value is 1
3.          var inches : Number = 0.0;
4.
5.          function showdist() : Void {
6.                println("feet = {feet } inches = {inches } ");
7.          }
8.     }
9.
10.    var dist1 : Distance = Distance {  // creating the object and initializing it
```

```
11.          feet : 5
12.          inches : 10.5
13.      }
14.      println("dist1 object value");
15.      dist1.showdist() ;
16.       dist1.feet = 8;          // modifying the feet data member
17.      dist1.inches = 11.5;      // modifying the inches data member
18.      println("dist1 object value after changing the data member");
19.      dist1.showdist() ;
```

Output

```
dist1 object value
feet = 5 inches = 10.5
dist1 object value after changing the data member
feet = 8 inches = 11.5
```

Here, the `Distance` class is modified from the previous example to demonstrate how to change a data member of an object. In line 10 we create the instance `dist1` and it is initialized. In lines 16 and 17 the data members of the `dist1` instance are modified. To verify that the data member of `dist1` have been modified, we call the `dist1.showdist()` function, and the output shows the result.

Objects as Function Arguments

Not only is it common to have either simple variables or the data members of a class as arguments of the member function, it is also common to have the object itself as the function argument.

Let's modify the `Distance` class of the previous example to add a member function that takes the object as its argument. Listing 6-6 shows the code.

Listing 6-6. A member function that takes an object as its argument

```
1.     class Distance {
2.         var feet : Integer = 0;
3.         var inches : Number = 0.0;
4.
5.         function showdist() : Void {
6.             println("feet = {feet } inches = {inches } ");
7.         }
8.
9.         public function addDistance(tempDist1:Distance,tempDist2:Distance ) : Void {
10.             inches = tempDist1.inches + tempDist2.inches;
11.             if(inches >= 12.0 ) {
12.                 feet++;
13.                 inches -= 12.0;
14.             }
15.             feet  = feet + tempDist1.feet + tempDist2.feet;
16.         }
17.     }
18.     var dist1 : Distance = Distance {
```

```
19.         feet : 5
20.         inches : 10.5
21.     }
22.     var dist2 : Distance = Distance {
23.         feet : 7
24.         inches : 6.65
25.     }
26.     println("The value of dist1 object ");
27.     dist1.showdist() ;
28.     println("The value of dist2 object ");
29.     dist2.showdist() ;
30.     var dist3 = Distance {};
31.     dist3.addDistance(dist1 , dist2);
32.     println("The value of dist3 object ");
33.     dist3.showdist() ;
```

In this example, we first create three objects, dist1, dist2 and dist3. Notice that dist1 and dist2 are initialized, so they have the default value. The dist3 object is not initialized. In line 31, dist3 calls the addDistance(dist1 , dist2) member function, which takes dist1 and dist2 as its arguments. When execution control goes to line 9, the dist1 and dist2 object values are passed to the formal parameters tempDist1 and tempDist2. We add the inches values of the formal parameters and assign the result to the variable inches, which is the data member of dist3. Since the dist3 object calls addDistance(dist1 , dist2), there is no need to specify dist3 to access the data member, as we do for tempDist1 to access its data member.

Non-Member Functions Accessing the Object

It is not mandatory that only a member function of a class can access its objects. In some situations, even functions that are not members can access the object. Listing 6-7 demonstrates how a non member function can access the objects of the class and return the object.

Listing 6-7. A non-member function accessing class objects

```
1.      class Distance {
2.          var feet : Integer = 0;
3.          var inches : Number = 0.0;
4.          function showdist() : Void {
5.          println("feet = {feet } inches = {inches } ");
6.          }
7.      } //  end class
8.      /*  Non-member function */
9.      function addDistance(dist1: Distance , dist2 : Distance): Distance {
10.         var feet : Integer = dist1.feet + dist2.feet;
11.         var inches : Number = dist1.inches + dist2.inches;
12.         if(inches >= 12.0 ) {
13.             feet++;
14.             inches -= 12.0;
15.         }
16.         return Distance{ feet : feet  inches : inches }
```

```
17.    }
18.
19.    var dist1 : Distance = Distance {
20.        feet : 5
21.        inches : 10.5
22    }
23.    var dist2 : Distance = Distance {
24.        feet : 7
25.        inches : 6.65
26.    }
27.    println("The value of the dist1 object ");
28.    dist1.showdist() ;
29.    println("The value of the dist2 object ");
30.    dist2.showdist() ;
31.    var dist3 = addDistance(dist1 , dist2);
32.    println("The value of the dist3 object ");
33.    dist3.showdist() ;
```

Output

```
------
The value of the dist1 object
feet = 5 inches = 10.5
The value of the dist2 object
feet = 7 inches = 6.65
The value of the dist3 object
feet = 13 inches = 5.1499996
```

Listing 6-7 is a modified version of the previous example, Listing 6-6. Here we have pulled the addDistance function outside the class and make the member function return the object as the return value of the function.

Static Members

When you use script-level variables and script-level functions along with a class, the class can access those variables and functions as its own data members and member functions. This is because the script-level variables and functions become *static* within the class, and the instance of the class can also script variables and functions. Listing 6-8 shows an example; save the code as StaticMember.fx.

Listing 6-8. Using script-level variables and functions as static members of a class

```
1.    var x : Integer = 14;
2.    function square() {
3.        x * x;
4.    }
5.
6.    class StaticMember {
7.        var dataMem : Integer = x;
8.
```

```
9.        function memberFunction(){
10.            println("square of {x} = {square()}");
11.          println(x);
12.            }
13.     }
14.
15.     var st = StaticMember{}; // instance of the class
16.     println("{st.x}, {st.dataMem }");     // 14,14
17.     StaticMember.x = 3;
18.     println("{st.x}, square: {st.square() }");    //9, square:  9
19.     st.memberFunction();
20.     st. dataMem = 99;
21.     println("{StaticMember.x}, {st.dataMem }");    //3, 99
22.     st = StaticMember {
23.         dataMem : 71717
24.     };
25.     println("{StaticMember.x},  {st.dataMem }");    //3, 71717
```

Output

```
14,  14
3, square: 9
square of 3 = 9
3
3, 99
3,  71717
```

In this example, you can see a script-level variable x and a script-level function named square() that returns the square of x. A class StaticMember has a data member dataMem, which contains the value of x (that is, the default value , which is the script-level variable's value). This indicates that that x is accessed inside the class as a static variable of the script. In the same code, the member function callingScrptLevelFunction() calls the square() function in line 10. Another interesting statement in this example is that the object or instance of the StaticMember class can access the x and dataMem variables in line 16 also in other places in the example.

Function Overloading Within a Class

Chapter 5, "Functions," introduced the concept of function overloading. This concept can also be applied to member functions. Since you already know about function overloading, let's go straight to an example of how it works with member functions. Listing 6-9 shows an example.

Listing 6-9. Overloading a member function

```
class Circle {
    function draw(){
        println("Drawing a circle with the fixed x,y and the radius value");
    }
```

```
    function draw(radius : Number){
        println("Drawing a circle with the fixed x,y value with the given radius of
            {radius}");
    }

    function draw(x : Number , y : Number){
        println("Drawing a circle with the given x = {x } ,y = { y} value with default value
            radius");
    }

    function draw(x : Number , y : Number , radius : Number){
        println("Drawing a circle with the given x = {x } ,y = { y} value with the given
            radius of {radius}");
    }
}
var fo : Circle = Circle{};
fo.draw();
fo.draw(10.0);
fo.draw(35.0,55.5);
fo.draw(35.0 , 55.0 , 10.25);
```

Output
```
------
Drawing a circle with the fixed x,y and the radius value
Drawing a circle with the fixed x,y value with the given radius of 10.0
Drawing a circle with the given x = 35.0 ,y = 55.5 value with default value radius
Drawing a circle with the given x = 35.0 ,y = 55.0 value with the given radius o
f 10.25
```

In this example, you can see that the class `Circle` has four member functions with the same function name, but they differ in their parameters; this is the function overloading. When you invoke each function JavaFX looks for the corresponding function name whose parameters match. If the match is found, it calls that function.

Sharing a Function Name Between Script-Level and Member Functions

It is possible for a script-level function and the member function of the class to share the same name. JavaFX Script determines which function to call by the context in which it is called.

if you want to call the member function, you need to call it through an instance or object of the class. By contrast, you call a script-level function directly by its name within the script. If you need to call a member function outside its class, you must call it using the script name or the file name. Listing 6-10 shows an example.

■ **Note** Although it's possible for a Script-level function and a member function to share a name, you should avoid this practice, as it may be confusing.

Listing 6-10. A script-level function and a main function with the same name

```
1.    function sayHello( ){
2.        println("i am a script-level function..!");
3.    }
4.
5.    class MyClass {
6.        function sayHello( ){
7.            println("i am class member function..!");
8.        }
9.    }
10.   sayHello();
11.   var obj : MyClass = MyClass{}
12.   obj.sayHello( );
13    MyClass{}.sayHello();    // anonymous object calling the member function
```

Output

```
i am a script-level function..!
i am a class member function..!
i am class member function..!
```

In Listing 6-10, you can see that the script-level function and the member function have the same name, **sayHello()**. The script-level function is called directly by its name, as specified line 10. In line 12, the member function is called by an instance of the class. In line13, the member function is called using the anonymous object.

■ **Note** An anonymous object is one that doesn't have a name. You can see the anonymous object calling the member function in line 13.

Calling a Java Method That Is a JavaFX Reserved Word

How do you call a method on a Java object whose name happens to be the same as a JavaFX Script reserved word? You learned about JavaFX Script reserved words, or keywords, in Chapter 3, "Data Types." You cannot directly use a reserved word to name a variable (as in **var while;**), class (such as **class true {}**), or other user-defined entity. You could, however, indiscriminately use reserved words to name your classes, functions, variables, and so on; but this would be unwise. Instead, the doubled angle brackets notation was introduced so that you can invoke Java object methods whose names happen to be reserved in JavaFX Script. For example, the following script uses this feature to invoke the `java.lang.String` class's `replace()` method.

```
var s = "abc def ghi";
s = s.<<replace>> ("def", "DEF");
println (s); // Output: abc DEF ghi
```

Output
abc DEF ghi

The abstract Class

An abstract class is one that is declared with the access modifier **abstract**. Like other classes, this type of class can have data members and member functions; but with a few functions that are not implemented (instead, you just specify the function prototype). These unimplemented functions are described as *abstract functions*. Because a class of this type is incomplete without implementing member functions, you cannot create an object of the class. To access the data members or the member functions of this class, you need to extend this class and implement the incomplete member function—the abstract function. You will learn more about extending classes in Chapter 8. Because this chapter is dedicated to classes, our purpose here is just to introduce you to abstract classes and functions. Listing 6-11 shows an example.

Listing 6-11. *Example of an abstract class*

```
public abstract class    AbstractClassExample {
    var  x: Integer ;

        function  callMe( ) : Void  {      // implemented function
            println("Please call me also. ");
        }
        //unimplemented function
        public abstract function sayHello( ) : String;
    }
```

In this code, **AbstractClassExample** is an abstract class because it contains an abstract member function, **sayHello()**.

■ **Note** It is mandatory to specify the keyword abstract for both the abstract method and the class. Failing to specify either of these will result in a compilation error.

You will learn more about implementing abstract classes, interfaces, and other elements in Chapter 8.

Summary

In this chapter you learned the essentials of working with class definitions and other object-oriented features of JavaFX Script. Following are the main points to keep in mind:

- A well defined class exhibits some or all features of OOP, including at a minimum data abstraction and encapsulation.

- An *object* is an instance of the class. When a program is executed, objects interact with each other by sending messages.

- The variables inside a class are called its *data members* and the functions inside the class are called *member functions*.

- A member function can only access the data members of the class.

- Objects of a class can be created using either JavaFX or Java style. The new operator is used to create an object in Java style.

- The init block is optional and used to initialize the data member of the class. It is called after the objects are created and is the final stage of initializing the object.

- The postinit block is optional and called after the object initialization is completed.

- An abstract class is one that contains abstract functions. Therefore, it is not possible to create instances of an abstract class.

CHAPTER 7

■ ■ ■

Access Specifiers

An important aspect of object-oriented programming is *data encapsulation* (also called *data hiding*), whereby the implementation details of a class are kept hidden from the users of the class. Not only the implementation but also the data can be kept hidden from the user. Or one can choose to provide varying degrees of restricted access to those data members through functions.

In general, this concept can be simply stated as "differentiating things that change from things that do not." This is particularly important when you are writing an API library that the application developer is going to use. Any user of your API library should be able to rely on your API when writing the application and should not be forced to rewrite code when you come up with a newer version of the library. On the other hand, you as a library creator should have the freedom to change the implementation (for the better) without breaking the existing applications written using your API. While you can achieve this by not removing any of the existing methods, there are further problems to handle. Existing applications might have used your data members, and it's hard to for the API author to figure out which of the data members are accessed by the client applications and which are not. So you will finally end up not being able to change anything, fearing incompatibility with existing applications.

So in any object-oriented design, it is important to identify what should be exposed to API users and what should be kept hidden so that the API author can change the hidden things as needed later on. (These revisions are made for many reasons, such as improving functionality, performance, reliability and so on.) In other words, the interface of the class remains the same while the implementation changes. This is where *access specifiers* (also called *access modifiers*) are useful.

The concept of access specifiers—keywords that identify specific levels of access— was developed mainly to control how a class and its members are accessed by the users of the class. With the help of access specifiers, you can clearly define what can and cannot be accessed by users of your library, which gives you the freedom to improve your library at will without breaking any existing applications.

JavaFX Script offers the following access specifiers you may know from Java; you will see each of them in detail in this chapter.

- `public`

- `protected`

- `package`

- Script-private (when nothing is specified explicitly)

While these look similar to the access specifiers that Java offers, there are subtle differences between how Java and JavaFX Script deal with them, as you will learn when we discuss them in detail. They are primary access modifiers that are applicable to all forms of access: creation and reference to classes, defining and calling functions in a class or outside of the class, reading and writing of script or instance variables, and overriding and setting or binding in an object literal of an instance variable.

There are also two access specifiers that are entirely new in JavaFX Script:

- `public-read`

- `public-init`

These are applicable only to variable declarations (`var`) and are additive in nature with respect the primary modifiers specified before. In this chapter, we will refer to these as *secondary specifiers* or *modifiers*.

Now let us see the basic syntax of specifying the primary and secondary access specifiers.

Syntax

```
[<secondary_access_specifier> <primary_access_specifier>] var variable name[: data
type] = <initial value>;
```

or

```
primary access-specifier function function name()[: return data type] { }
```

Any elements appearing between square brackets are optional.

The Script—The .fx File

Before going into the details of the access specifiers, you should understand how JavaFX organizes the code within a JavaFX script. A JavaFX script is the `.fx` file that will have the JavaFX code and can optionally contain zero or more classes. Unlike Java, JavaFX does not require you to write all the code within a class, and an application may or may not have a class. So you don't have to always create a class, and you can write expressions, variable declarations, functions and so on directly within the script. A script is also compiled into a Java class internally, but that's more of an implementation detail. Understanding the script paradigm is important because the concept of script is new in JavaFX and does not exist in Java, and JavaFX offers specific access specifiers at the script level.

The variables and functions created directly within the script are considered to be equivalent of the `Static` modifier in Java. Your script, in addition to expressions, vars, functions, and so on can also have one or more class definitions in itself. You learned about classes in Chapter 6, "Class Definitions," and here you will learn more about how a class member interacts with a script member that resides outside of the class when these members have different access specifiers.

I'll show how to specify access modifiers for the class definitions later in this chapter; first you will see the applicability of access modifiers for the class/script members.

The context in which script variables and functions are defined is called a *static context,* and a class definition is a *nonstatic* context. So accessing a class variable from outside the class would require an instance of the class, because accessing an instance variable of a class is not permitted from a static context. This is true in Java, too, where a nonstatic variable cannot be accessed directly from a static context.

■ **Note** JavaFX Script, unlike Java, allows you to have different names for a script and a class defined within that script. JavaFX Script does not strictly require you to give a script the same name you have given a class within it. Similarly, you can have multiple public classes defined within the same script.

The Script-Private Access Specifier

The default access specifier in JavaFX Script is the script-private. This is the access specifier assigned by the compiler when one is not explicitly specified, as you have seen in all the previous examples.

A script-private member is accessible only within its own script. In other words, within the same .fx file and not outside. The script may or may not have a class definition in it, nevertheless the script-private members will be accessible within the class definition also provided if the class definition resides in the same .fx file.

This access specifier is applicable to variable declarations, functions, class definitions, and so on.

Figure 7-1 illustrates script-only access for members defined within script1 in Package B.

Script-Private Access for the script1 Member

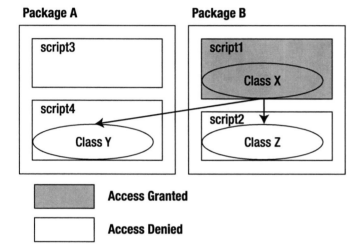

Figure 7-1. *Script-only access*

As you see in the diagram, only script1 has access to the members, and no access is allowed outside of the script. Listing 7-1, a script named Employee.fx, and Listing 7-2, the EmployeeList.fx script, demonstrate this level of access.

Listing 7-1. *Variables with default access: Employee.fx*

```
// Script Private variables
var empId: String;
var firstName: String;
var lastName: String;
var deptId: Number;
var designation: String;

public function populateData(empID: String) {
    empId = empID;
```

```
        // Typically other details are fetched from web-service or database using the
    empid.
        // Hardcoding here
        if (empId == "23456") {
            firstName = "Praveen";
            lastName = "Mohan";
            deptId = 44;
            designation = "Manager";
        } else {
            println("Invalid Employee ID");
        }
    }

    public function printData() {
        println("Details of employee with ID: {empId}");
        println("First Name: {firstName}");
        println("Last Name: {lastName}");
        println("Department ID: {deptId}");
        println("Designation: {designation}");
    }

    public function run() {
        empId = "11111";
        firstName = "Lawrence";
        lastName = "PremKumar";
        deptId = 33;
        designation = "Developer";
        printData();
    }
```

Listing 7-2. *Accessing script-private variables of another script: EmployeeList.fx*

```
    var employee = Employee {};
    var id:String = "23456";
    //employee.empId = id;  - ERROR: Not accessible here
    //employee.firstName = "Praveen"; - ERROR: Not accessible here
    employee.populateData(id);
    employee.printData();
```

First compile and run Employee.fx to see its result.

Output
```
Details of employee with ID: 11111
First Name: Lawrence
Last Name: PremKumar
Department ID: 33.0
Designation: Developer
```

Then compile and run EmployeeList.fx.

Output
```
Details of employee with ID: 23456
First Name: Praveen
Last Name: Mohan
Department ID: 44.0
Designation: Manager
```

In this example, you see many of the variables declared without any access specifier; those variables assume the default access specifier, `script-private`. You see that those variables are accessible directly within the script in the `run()` method. Thus, compiling and executing `Employee.fx` yields the expected result. However, you cannot access those variables from another script directly, and doing so will cause a compilation error—typically demonstrated by the commented lines in `EmployeeList.fx`. So a public function is provided in `Employee.fx` for initializing those variables from a different script. You can uncomment the commented lines in `EmployeeList.fx` and see for yourself what kind of error the compiler throws.

Now let's us see how such variables are accessed from within the class definitions available in the same script. Listing 7-3 is a script named `ScriptPrivateWithClassDef.fx`.

Listing 7-3. *Script-private access from within the class: ScriptPrivateWithClassDef.fx*

```
var PI: Number = 3.14;
var area: Number;
function printArea() {
    println("Area: {area}");
}
class CustomCircle {
    var r: Number;
    init {
        area = calculateArea();
        printArea();
    }
    function calculateArea() {
        PI * r * r;
    }
}
CustomCircle { r: 25 }; //Anonymous Object Literal
```

Output
```
Area: 1962.5
```

As you see, the variables declared outside the class (the *script* variables) can be accessed like static variables from within the class, and there is no need to use an instance or the member operator. However, the reverse situation would require an instance—that is, a script-private variable defined within a class would require an instance of the class to be accessed from a static context. Listing 7-4 redefines the previous example to demonstrate this.

Listing 7-4. Accessing class variables from within the script: ScriptPrivateClassDef2.fx

```
var PI: Number = 3.14;
class CustomCircle {
    var r: Number;
    var area: Number;
    init {
        calculateArea();
    }
    function calculateArea() {
        area = PI * r * r;
    }
    function printArea() {
        println("Area: {area}");
    }
}

var circle = CustomCircle { r: 25 };
circle.printArea();
println(circle.area);
```

Output
```
Area: 1962.5
1962.5
```

In Listing 7-4, notice a change from Listing 7-3: the **area** variable and **printArea** function from the script have been moved into the class definition. Now you need to have an instance of **CustomCircle** in order to access the **area** variable or the **printArea** function and hence we are assigning the **CustomCircle** instance to a variable **circle** (instead of leaving it anonymous, as we did in Listing 7-3) and accessing the class members with the help of this variable.

It is also possible to access the script-private variables defined in one class from another class if both the classes are defined within the same source file. Listing 7-5 demonstrates this approach.

Listing 7-5. Access across multiple classes in the script: ScriptPrivateClassDef3.fx

```
var PI: Number = 3.14;
class CustomCircle {
    var r: Number;
    var area: Number;
    function calculateArea() {
        area = PI * r * r;
    }
    function printArea() {
        calculateArea();
        println("Area: {area}");
    }
}
```

```
class ShapeBuilder {
    var circleRadius:Number = 10;
    var circle: CustomCircle = CustomCircle { r: bind circleRadius }
    init {
        circle.printArea();
        circleRadius = 25;
        circle.printArea();
    }
}
ShapeBuilder{};
```

Output
```
Area: 314.0
Area: 1962.5
```

In Listing 7-5, because the `CustomCircle` and `ShapeBuilder` classes are defined in the same script, the class `ShapeBuilder` can create an instance of the class `CustomCircle` within itself and can access the attributes of class `CustomCircle` using the instance `circle`. Please note that it works only if both the classes are defined in the same script. For instance, if you move `ShapeBuilder` to a different script (a different `.fx` file—ShapeBuilder.fx), you will no longer be able to access `CustomCircle` or its attributes. You would get a compilation error attempting to compile `ShapeBuilder.fx` because the class `CustomCircle` and its attributes are script-private. So when you need separate scripts, you will have to look for other access specifiers that provide broader access than script-private.

Packages

As listed at the beginning of the chapter, the next level of access is `package`. Before going into the `package` access specifier, however, it's a good idea to understand the concept of packages and why they are required. The concept is inherited from Java and its implementation in JavaFX Script is not very different. By definition, a package is a collection of related classes and scripts grouped together under a common package name. Each package is given a name, and the combination of the package and class/script name forms the *fully qualified name* of the class/script, which uniquely identifies it. The package can include Java classes as well. Packages help API developers organize their source files appropriately by combining related classes/scripts into a single collection; This in turn helps the API users (application developers) to use only the collection that the application requires, and not all the classes.

This also helps you avoid naming conflicts in your program. When you use the OOP paradigm to create an application, you typically model the problem domain by creating your own data types and assign each of them an identifiable name. Each type that you create must be unique so that you can identify and use it appropriately in your program. This could get complicated when you start using types from other vendors, especially when writing a larger application. In such a case, you can choose to assign your types their own unique package name that does not conflict with the names that others have chosen. As a result, you don't have to deal with this complexity in your code and can focus on the actual complexity of the application as such. Conflicts can arise not only from external vendor APIs but also with the APIs developed in-house, typically in a multi-developer environment. In such a case, it is very much possible that your co-developer may choose to have the same name as you for one of his/her classes, potentially creating a conflict within the same API library. This is where subpackages become helpful.

You can also organize the packages hierarchically; a package can have subpackages. Anything contained within a package is called a package *member*. These can be classes, scripts, or subpackages.

With the help of access specifiers, you can grant special privileges for the classes/scripts within the same package, and you can share and reuse the code within the same package. The logical grouping of classes and scripts makes it convenient for the users of your API as well to import only the classes that are needed. It improves the readability and maintainability of the whole application over all.

A package can be defined by using the `package` keyword, which should be specified as the first line in each of the source files that you want to organize together.

For example, If you have three source files, `A.fx`, `B.fx`, and `C.fx`, that you want to organize into a single package named `tasks`, add the following line in each of these source files as the first line.

```
package tasks;
```

You should also physically organize the files in the same way, by creating a folder named `\tasks\` and moving these source files into the folder.

A fully qualified name of a class or a script is the class/script name prefixed with appropriate package names, separated by the dot (.) operator.

So for our `tasks` example, the fully qualified names would be

```
tasks.A
tasks.B
tasks.C
```

In order to use these classes in a different package, you have to import these classes specifically. If you want to import all three classes, you can just use a wild-card character, as follows:

```
import tasks.*;
```

Otherwise, you can import only the necessary classes, as in these statements:

```
import tasks.A;
import tasks.C;
```

A typical fully-qualified name of a class looks like the following:

```
com.foo.ui.Bar
```

where `com`, `foo` and `ui` are packages, and `Bar` is the actual JavaFX script (`Bar.fx`) that resides within the `com/foo/ui` package. The `com.foo` portion is typically the reverse domain name of the organization that creates the API library. In this notation `foo` is a subpackage of `com`, and `ui` is a subpackage of `foo`. The Java Virtual Machine does not differentiate between main and subpackages when granting package-specific access, and JVM does not treat these packages in an hierarchical way. As far as JVM is concerned, a sibling package is treated the same way as a subpackage, and whatever rights tare available within a particular package are not granted either to a sibling package or to a subpackage. Thus, subpackages are useful more for the API author/user, because the sources are organized in a much better way and form a hierarchy. They do not make much difference to the JVM.

In all the examples you have seen so far, there is no package name assigned explicitly. In such a case, the compiler uses a default package name implicitly, and all the scripts or classes are considered to be part of this default package automatically.

JavaFX Graphics API has its own set of classes and packages, such as the following:

```
javafx.scene
javafx.scene.shape
javafx.scene.paint
javafx.scene.text
```

and so on. You will see many of them when we introduce you to graphics and animation in later chapters.

Statics in JavaFX Script

Script variables are considered to be equivalent to the `static` modifier in Java and can be imported into another JavaFX Script. A script variable is one declared outside of any class definitions within a script. Such variables can be imported into another JavaFX script—as long as the access specifier for those script variables allows them to be accessed from a different script. In other words, the variables that have script-private default access will not be imported, because their scope is limited to the script where they are created).

Syntax
```
import script name.*;
```

Here, *script name* is the name of the `.fx` file such as `Bar.fx`. Note that we are using the name of the script in the import and not any class or package as such. We will explore the importing of packages and classes in more detail in the next section. In this type of importing, the specified script may or may not contain any class. Listings 7-6 and 7.7 demonstrates static importing.

Listing 7-6. *Defining the statics: AreaUtil.fx*

```
public def PI: Number = 3.14;
public function getAreaOfCircle(radius: Number) {
    PI * radius * radius;
}
protected function getCircumferenceOfCircle(radius: Number) {
    2 * PI * radius;
}
package function getSurfaceAreaOfSphere(radius: Number) {
    4 * PI * radius * radius;
}
```

Listing 7-7. *Importing the statics from AreaUtil: ShapeBuilder.fx*

```
import AreaUtil.*;

class Circle {
    var radius: Number;
    var area = bind getAreaOfCircle(radius);
    var circumference = bind getCircumferenceOfCircle(radius);
}
class Sphere {
    var radius: Number;
```

```
    var surfaceArea: Number = bind getSurfaceAreaOfSphere(radius);
}
var circle = Circle {
    radius: 25
}
var sphere = Sphere {
    radius: 20
}
println("PI value: {PI}");
println("Circle Area: {circle.area}");
println("Circle Circumference: {circle.circumference}");
println("Sphere SurfaceArea: {sphere.surfaceArea}");
```

Run ShapeBuilder.fx to see the following result.

Output
```
PI value: 3.14
Circle Area: 1962.5
Circle Circumference: 157.0
Sphere SurfaceArea: 5024.0
```

In Listings 7-6 and 7-7, all the variables and functions declared in AreaUtil.fx are imported into ShapeBuilder.fx and thus can be accessed within ShapeBuilder.fx as if they were defined there. But the variables declared in this example are either public, protected, or package and not script-private, and hence they are accessible. No script-private variables (var statements with no access specifiers mentioned) would be imported into another script. Likewise, a package-access variable will not be imported when the FX script is imported into a different package. Here no package is specified in either of the scripts, and so both of them belong to the same default package that the compiler assigns. This example is a typical use of statics, in which utility variables and functions that are shared across the whole application are grouped into a single .fx script, which would be imported into other scripts wherever these utilities are needed.

The package Access Specifier

Now that you've seen the concept of packages and the need for them, we can explore the package access specifier. A class or a member of the class or the script having the access specifier defined as package would be accessible anywhere within the same package and not in other packages or subpackages. This is the next wider access level beyond the default script-private access.Listings 7-8 through 7-10 demonstrate package access.

■ **Note** Java's default access is package (or friendly), which is applied when you don't explicitly specify any access specifier. But in JavaFX Script, you explicitly specify package access, and the default specifier is script-private.

Listing 7-8. Implementation that offers package access function: CookDessert.fx

```
package com.foo.dessert;
package var bakeTime: Number;
package var coolingTime: Number;

package function cook(item: String) {
    println("Baking item: {item} for {bakeTime} min");
    println("Cooling item: {item} for {coolingTime} min");
    println("Item {item} is ready!!");
}
```

Listing 7-9. Public interface for accessing package level function in CookDessert: Desserts.fx

```
package com.foo.dessert;
public var item: String;

public function prepare() {
    if (item == "Cake") {
        var cake = CookDessert {};
        cake.bakeTime = 25;
        cake.coolingTime = 10;
        cake.cook ("Cake");
    } else if (item == "Pudding") {
        var pudding = CookDessert {};
        pudding.bakeTime = 10;
        pudding.coolingTime = 5;
        pudding.cook("Pudding");
    } else {
        println("Sorry!! Recipe not available yet!");
    }
}
```

Listing 7-10. Application that accesses the package level functionality in CookDessert through the public interface in Desserts: Dinner.fx

```
package com.foo.meal;
import com.foo.dessert.*;
var dessert = Desserts {};
dessert.item = "Pudding";
dessert.prepare();
```

Compile all the files and run `Dinner.fx` to see the following result.

Output
```
Baking item: Pudding for 10.0 min
Cooling item: Pudding for 5.0 min
Item Pudding is ready!!
```

In Listings-7-8, 7-9, and 7-10, CookDessert.fx and Desserts.fx belong to a package named com.foo.dessert. CookDessert contains the parameters and recipe for cooking desserts that Desserts.fx script makes use of. The members, such as bakeTime and coolingTime, are specific to the com.foo.dessert package and hence have been declared with the package access specifier so that they are accessible only within the package. As a result, the API user cannot access the members of CookDessert.fx from within Dinner.fx, since Dinner.fx belongs to a different package. Hence there is another script—Desserts.fx that offers a public interface to the API user and internally calls the members of CookDessert.fx. Desserts.fx is able to access the members of CookDesserts.fx directly since they belong to the same package, com.foo.dessert.

Note that CookDesserts.fx creates an instance of the Desserts script inside its prepare() function; this can be avoided if you import CookDessert.* into Desserts.fx. We can rewrite Listing 7-9 as follows -

```
package com.foo.dessert;
import CookDessert.*;
public var item: String;
public function prepare() {
    if (item == "Cake") {
        bakeTime = 25;
        coolingTime = 10;
        cook ("Cake");
    } else if (item == "Pudding") {
        ...
    // Same as listing 7.9
```

Here the static variables (script variables) declared in one file are imported into the other so that you don't have to create an instance of CookDessert.fx in Desserts.fx. This will yield the same output as that of Listing 7.8 to 7.10.

■ **Note** Only permitted members of a script are imported into another, and the access specifier of each member of the script is validated at the time of import. For example, if there is a script-private variable declared in CookDessert, it will not be imported into Desserts. And if this import is to a different package (for example, if CookDessert is imported into Dinner.fx), the package access variables will not be imported, and hence the compiler will give an error appropriately when you try to access any of the CookDessert variables from within Dinner.fx.

Fig 7-2 demonstrates package access for members of script1 and summarizes the behavior of the package access specifier that you have seen so far.

Package Access for the script1 Member

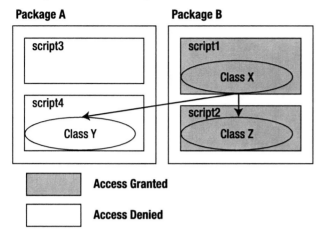

Figure 7-2. *Package Access*

As you see in the diagram, the package members of `script1` can be accessed within `script1` and `script2` since both scripts belong to the same package—Package B. However, no access is granted to package A.

Trying to access the members of `script1` or `script2` from within any of the scripts in package B would cause a compilation error.

Package Access with Class Members

The `package` access specifier behaves the same way when used within the class definitions as with script variables. The access specifiers for the class definitions as such will be discussed later in this chapter; for now, let us assume all the classes are public and hence can be accessed anywhere. Here you will see package access specified for class members such as variable definitions and functions. Listings 7-11 and 7-13 convert the same example you have seen previously to use class definitions.

Listing 7-11. *Class definitions with package level access: CookDessert.fx*

```
    package com.foo.dessert;

package class CookDessert {
    package var bakeTime: Number;
    package var coolingTime: Number;

    package function cook(item: String) {
        println("Baking item: {item} for {bakeTime} min");
        println("Cooling item: {item} for {coolingTime} min");
        println("Item {item} is ready!!");
    }
    }
```

Listing 7-12. Public interface to package-level functionality in CookDessert: Desserts.fx

```
package com.foo.dessert;

public class Desserts {
    public var item: String;
    var cookDessert:CookDessert;

    public function prepare() {
        if (item == "Cake") {
            cookDessert = CookDessert {
                bakeTime: 25
                coolingTime: 10
            };
            cookDessert.cook ("Cake");
        } else if (item == "Pudding") {
            cookDessert = CookDessert {
                bakeTime: 10
                coolingTime: 5
            };
            cookDessert.cook("Pudding");
        } else {
            println("Sorry!! Recipe not available yet!");
        }
    }
}
```

Listing 7-13. Application accessing package-level functionality through a public interface in Dessert.fx: Dinner.fx

```
package com.foo.meal;
import com.foo.dessert.*;
var dessert = Desserts {
    item: "Pudding"
};
dessert.prepare();
//var cookDessert = CookDessert{}; - ERROR: Cannot be accessed
```

Output
```
Baking item: Pudding for 10.0 min
Cooling item: Pudding for 5.0 min
Item Pudding is ready!!
```

The code in this example is self-explanatory. The same code that was previously defined within the script has been moved into a class definition, and the only change you will probably notice is in the way objects are created for the class CookDessert within Desserts; this time, the attributes are initialized directly in the object literal. Apart from that, there is no change with the behavior.

Another change you should note is that the class CookDessert itself has been defined with a package access specifier. This would prevent anyone from creating an instance of the class from a class or script that is outside the package. That's exactly what the commented line in Dinner.fx demonstrates. If the line were uncommented, it would cause the compiler to throw an error, because Dinner.fx belongs to a different package and hence does not have access to the CookDessert class.

Honoring Access Specifiers for Java Classes

Access specifiers specified within the Java classes accessed within a JavaFX script must also be honored in the same way as JavaFX Script or JavaFX classes. Listings 7-14 and 7-15 demonstrate this behavior.

Listing 7-14. A sample Java class: JavaImpl.java

```
package com.foo;
public class JavaImpl {
    int x = 10;
    String technology = "JavaFX";
    public JavaImpl() {
        System.out.println("Constructor called");
    }
}
```

Listing 7-15. JavaFX script accessing the Java class - Main.fx

```
package com.foo;
var jimpl = new JavaImpl();
println("X value: {jimpl.x}");
println("Technology: {jimpl.technology}");
```

    Output
```
Constructor called
X value: 10
Technology: JavaFX
```

As you see in Listing 7-14, the JavaImpl java class members do not specify any access specifiers, and in Java, the default access specifier is package. Hence, these class members must be accessible within the same package—com.foo. An instance of JavaImpl has been created from within the JavaFX script, Main.fx (Listing 7-15), and that script also belongs to the same com.foo package. Hence, the class members of JavaImpl are accessible within Main.fx.

This example indicates that the access specifiers, whether specified in Java or JavaFX Script, are appropriately honored and even the default access specifier type of Java is preserved when accessed from within JavaFX Script, even though the default access type is different than in Java compared to JavaFX.

Similarly, access is also revoked appropriately wherever required. For example, if we change the package in Main.fx from com to jfx, you will see a compilation error.

Now that you have learned how the package access specifier works under different circumstances, we can move on to the protected access specifier, which is closely tied to class definitions and inheritance.

The protected Access Specifier

The next wider access is provided by the `protected` access specifier. Members of the class that are `protected` are accessible within the same package, just like `package`-level members, and also accessible outside the package if it is accessed from within a subclass. The concept of base class (super class) and derived class (sub class) is explained in detail in Chapter 8, "Inheritance," but here is a brief introduction focusing on the use of the `protected` access specifier in the context of inheritance.

Inheritance is about taking an existing class and adding more functionality to it. The existing class is called the *base* class and the new class that `extends` the existing class is called the *derived* class. In addition to adding new functionality, the derived class can also choose to change the behavior of the existing members within its implementation.

Syntax
```
class derived class extends base class {..}
```

Example
```
class Car extends Vehicle {
       }
```

(The rest of this class is pretty much the same as any other class definition.)

Here, when the `Car` and `Vehicle` classes belong to different packages, the only members of `Vehicle` that you will have access to from within the `Car` are the `public` members. But declaring everything as public would leave everything too open to control. There are cases where you would want to expose certain functionality only to those who extend your class and not to all the users of the class. This is where `protected` comes in handy.

Protected members of the class are accessible within the same package, just like `package` members, and they are accessible to classes that reside in other packages provided those classes extend this class.

Figure 7-3 demonstrates the `protected` access specifier.

Protected Access for the script1 Member

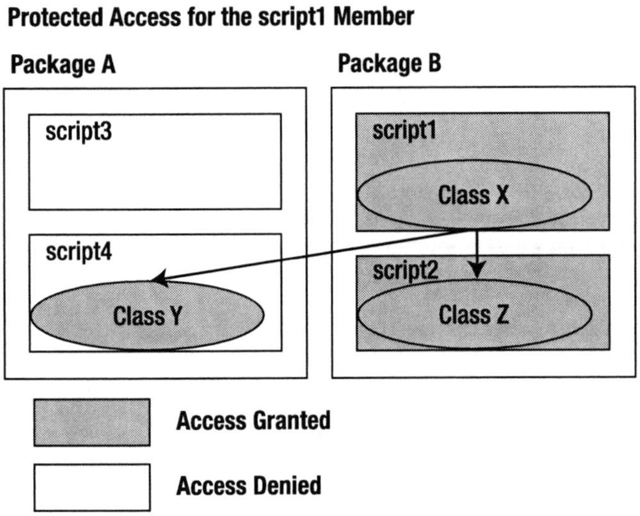

Figure 7-3. Protected access for class X members

As you see in the diagram, class Z and class Y are subclasses of class X, but they are implemented in different packages. When we looked at package access earlier, class Z was granted access but not class Y. With protected access specified for members of class X, all the classes extending class X will also have access to the protected member, regardless of the package where they are implemented. The `protected` level also preserves the package access, so that all the scripts and classes in the same package will have access to the protected member of class X.

The next example clearly shows the difference between `protected` and the other access specifiers you have seen so far. Listing 7-16 shows the `Vehicle.fx` file and Listing 7-17 shows `Car.fx`.

Listing 7-16. *A generic vehicle superclass: Vehicle.fx*

```
package com.automobile;

public class Vehicle {
    package var yearOfManufacture: Integer;
    protected var noOfWheels: Integer;
    protected var noOfDoors: Integer;
    var make: String;
    protected var inspectionDone: Boolean;
    protected function checkQuality(): Boolean { return false; };

    public function getYearOfManufacture() {
        yearOfManufacture;
    }
    init {
        yearOfManufacture = 2009;
        make = "Toyota";
    }
    public function getMake() {
        make;
    }
    public function getNoOfDoors() {
        noOfDoors;
    }
    public function getNoOfWheels() {
        noOfWheels;
    }
}
```

Listing 7-17. *A car implementation that extends Vehicle: Car.fx*

```
package com.automobile.fourwheelers;
import com.automobile.*;

class Car extends Vehicle {
    var noOfSeats: Integer;
    var hatchBack: Boolean;
    protected override function checkQuality(): Boolean {
        // Check engine
        // Check Interiors
```

```
            // Check Painting
            return true;
        }
        init {
            noOfSeats = 4;
            hatchBack = true;
            noOfWheels = 4;
            noOfDoors = 4;
            inspectionDone = true;
            // make = "Honda"; // COMPILER ERROR: Not allowed
            // YearOfManufacture = 2008; // COMPILER ERROR: Not allowed
        }
    }
    var corolla = Car {};
    println("Year Of Manufacture: {corolla.getYearOfManufacture()}");
    println("Make: {corolla.getMake()}");
    println("No Of Wheels: {corolla.getNoOfWheels()}");
    println("No Of Doors: {corolla.getNoOfDoors()}");
```

Compile the two scripts and run `Car.fx` to see the following result.

Output
```
Year Of Manufacture: 2009
Make: Toyota
No Of Wheels: 4
No Of Doors: 4
```

In this example, you can see that the data members of the `Vehicle` class are declared as `protected` and there are equivalent public `get` methods. So the API user will only be able to use the `get` methods, and the attributes cannot be set directly from the customer code. The `Car` class, on the other hand, has access to these `protected` variables and can set the appropriate values, since the `Car` class extends from `Vehicle`. Nevertheless, there are some script-private and package data members, such as `make` and `yearOfManufacture`, that the `Car` class cannot access. Trying to access those variables would cause a compilation error. You can uncomment the commented lines in the `Car` class to see for yourself the compilation error you get.

Also notice that although the `Vehicle` and `Car` classes belong to two different packages, `Car` is able to access the protected members of the `Vehicle` class. This is different from the `package` access specifier, where we were not allowed to access the package data members of a class in one package from another package. Hence, protected members have wider access than package members and can be accessed across packages provided they extend the base class.

The following example, in Listings 7-18 and 7-19, shows a protected member accessed freely within the same package without any inheritance.

Listing 7-18. *Class definition having protected members: Cup.fx*

```
package com.cutlery;

class Cup {
    protected var material: String;
    protected var purpose: String;
}
```

Listing 7-19. *Another class definition in the same package accessing protected members of Cup.fx:*
Saucer.fx

```
package com.cutlery;
class Saucer {
    init {
        var c = Cup{};
        c.material = "porcelain";
        c.purpose = "tea";
        println(c.material);
        println(c.purpose);
    }
}
var s = Saucer {};
```

Compile the two scripts and run **Saucer.fx** to see the following result.

Output
```
porcelain
tea
```

In this example, the protected members of the Cup class can be accessed from within the Saucer
class because both of them belong to the same package. So to summarize, the **protected** access specifier
has all the access that **package** access specifier provides, plus additional access for inherited classes.

The public Access Specifier

The **public** access specifier has the widest access in JavaFX Script. Public members of a class or the script
can be initialized, overridden, read, assigned, or bound from anywhere. Figure 7-4 demonstrates public
access for members of **script1** in Package B.

Public Access for the script1 Member

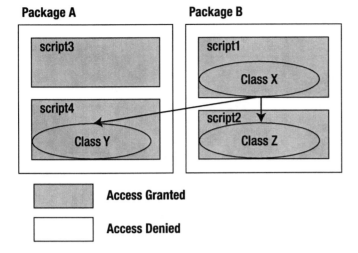

Figure 7-4. Public access for script1 members

As you see in the diagram, the public members of **script1** are accessible everywhere. The example in Listings 7-20 and 7-21 demonstrates public access.

Listing 7-20. A rectangle implementation: Rectangle.fx

```
package com.foo;
public class Rectangle {
    public var x: Number;
    public var y: Number;
    public var width: Number;
    public var height: Number;
    var area: Number;

    public function draw() {
        computeArea();
        drawRectangle();
    }
    function computeArea() {
        area = width * height;
    }
    function drawRectangle() {
        println("Initializing the rect peer");
        println("Creating graphics surface");
        println("Rectangle Drawn");
    }
}
```

Listing 7-22. An application using the Rectangle API: UIBuilder.fx

```
package com.foo.uibuilder;
import com.foo.*;
var borderRect = Rectangle {
    x: 0
    y: 0
    width: 100
    height: 100
}

borderRect.draw();
// borderRect.computeArea(); - ERROR: Will not work
```

Compile the two scripts and run `UIBuilder.fx` to see the following result.

Output
```
Initializing the rect peer
Creating graphics surface
Rectangle Drawn
```

Note that there are two source files here, in two different packages. The public variables declared in `Rectangle.fx` can be accessed in `UIBuilder.fx`. In `UIBuilder`, we are creating an instance of `Rectangle` and accessing `Rectangle`'s public function `draw` using the member operator. However, if you try to access a nonpublic member of `Rectangle` (say `computeArea()`), the compiler will throw an error. Public members of a class or script are accessible everywhere and thus have the widest possible access in JavaFX Script.

■ **Note** Although the `public` access modifier is simple, you should use it with caution, because it limits your ability to make later changes to the API. Such changes will have to be done in a compatible manner so as not to break any existing applications that are using the API, and hence you are limited in what you can change once you get your first version of the API out. So it is wise to keep the access narrower initially wherever possible and expose as public only those APIs that are really needed. You can always widen the access later on without breaking compatibility.

The Enforced run() Function Requirement

When you introduce a `public` member in your Java FX script, or in a class within the script, and the script is going to be the entry point for your application (that is, its name will be the argument to the `javafx` executable), it is mandatory to implement a `run` method for this script where you have declared the public member. The compiler generates this automatically as long as you don't have a public member, but the moment you introduce a public member, the compiler expects you to take care of implementing this. Failing to do this will result in a compilation error. Listing 7-22 is an example that demonstrates the error.

Listing 7-22. *A script with public members but no run() function: ExampleWithoutRun.fx*

```
    // CAUTION: This example will not compile
public var pi : Number = 3.142;
public var radius : Number = 6;
function area_of_circle( ) {
        pi * radius * radius;
}
println("area of circle = {area_of_circle()}");
```

Attempt to compile the script, and you'll see the following output.

Output
```
ExampleWithoutRun.fx:8: Loose expressions are not permitted in scripts with exported ('pu
blic', etc) members.
Any expressions to be run on script invocation should be moved into run().
println("area of circle = {area_of_circle()}");
^
```

Let's correct the previous example so that it works. Listing 7-23 shows the revised code.

Listing 7-23. *A script that tightens loose expressions: ExampleWithRun.fx*

```
public var pi : Number = 3.142;
public var radius : Number = 6;
function area_of_circle( ) {
    pi * radius * radius;
}
function run() {
    println("pi = {pi}   ,   radius = {radius}");
    println("area of circle = {area_of_circle()}");
}
```

Compile and run the script to see its output.

Output
```
pi = 3.142 , radius = 6.0
area of circle = 113.112
```

As you see in Listing 7-23, once you implement the run() method, everything works fine. This run() method must be included directly in the script and not within any class as such. The run() method can also take arguments, typically the arguments that you pass to your application through the command line.

JavaFX Secondary Access Specifiers

As mentioned in the chapter introduction, JavaFX Script offers two more access specifiers, which are applicable only to variables. They are

```
public-init
public-read
```

These access specifiers cannot be used for classes and functions.

Because of the central use of object literals in JavaFX Script, instance variables tend to be externally visible. To provide more control over the **var** declarations, JavaFX Script introduced these access specifiers that offer more-refined access. We will refer to these access specifiers as *secondary* specifiers throughout this chapter. The other access specifiers you have learned so far can be considered *primary* specifiers.

These access specifiers are additive and can be combined with primary access specifiers, such as script-private (no specifier), `public`, `protected`, and `package`.

public-read

As its name suggests, the `public-read` access specifier allows a variable to be read from anywhere. However, the ability to change the variable value depends on other access specifiers mentioned in the **var** declaration.

Syntax
```
public-read [primary access specifier] var var name[:data type] [= value];
```

where not specifying the primary specifier would default to script-private. The *data type* is optional, since the compiler can infer the type automatically from the value assigned.

Example
```
public-read var x = 10.0;
```

Variable x can be read from anywhere—within the script, outside the script, within the package, outside the package, and so on. But let us see who has the privilege to modify this variable.

The primary access specifier is skipped for this variable declaration, which means this variable can be modified only within the script. Hence, within the script where this is declared, one can modify, bind, or assign the value of this variable.

Listings 7-24 and 7-25 present a simple example of a simulated media player.

Listing 7-24. Mock Media Player implementation: MediaPlayer.fx

```
public class MediaPlayer {
        public var url: String;
        public-read var playing: Boolean = false;
        public function play() {
            // play media here
            println("Currently Playing {url}");
```

```
            playing = true;
        }
        public function stop() {
            // stop the playback
            playing = false;
        }
    }
```

Listing 7-25. *A juke box application that uses MediaPlayer: MediaBox.fx*

```
    var player = MediaPlayer {
        url: "http://www.javafx.com/javafx_launch.wmv"
    }
    player.play();
    println("Is Playing? {player.playing}");
    player.stop();
    println("Is Playing? {player.playing}");
```

Compile the two scripts and run MediaBox.fx to see their output.

Output
```
Currently Playing http://www.javafx.com/javafx_launch.wmv
Is Playing? true
Is Playing? false
```

This example demonstrates a simple media player application that defines a URL and play()/stop() functions. The MediaPlayer class also exposes a public-read attribute, playing, that is intended for only the applications to read. The MediaBox application creates an instance of the player and plays the media. Once it starts playing, the application wants to query whether the media is still being played and hence it queries the playing attribute's value. However, no application can set this value except the MediaPlayer class itself, which would typically set this value depending on various conditions such as the user stopping the media, end of media reached, the URL changed while media was played, and so on.

For example if the MediaBox tried to set the value of playing, that would cause the compiler to throw a compilation error since it has been declared as public-read.

Also note that there is no primary access specifier mentioned in the declaration; this means the write-access defaults to script-private. So the value of playing can only be modified within the MediaPlayer.fx script. Another way of allowing write access externally (if needed) is to declare a public function setPlaying(val: Boolean) within the MediaPlayer, and applications that would like to modify the playing value can call this function.

Now let us see some examples that combine primary and secondary access specifiers to offer a varied write-access to the variable.

```
public-read package var x: String = "JavaFX";
```

In this statement, the variable x has its primary access specified as package—it can be assigned, bound or initialized within the same package and the value can be read anywhere.

```
    public-read protected var x: String = "JavaFX";
```

Here , the variable x has its primary access specified as **protected**—it can be assigned, bound, or initialized within the same package or from derived classes in other packages.

```
public-read public var x: String = "JavaFX";
```

The variable x has its primary access specified as **public**. This combination is useless, because the variable is publicly modifiable and hence **public-read** does not make sense anymore. You can remove the **-public-read-** specifier and it will give the same effect. Since this is a potentially useless combination, the compiler will give a warning message if you try to compile this code.

Also note that a **public-read** variable can be unidirectionally bound to another variable from anywhere, but the **public-read** variable must be on the right side of the bind expression. In such a binding, the value of the **public-read** variable is consumed by some other variable without causing any change to the **public-read** variable as such. However, bidirectional binding will cause a compilation error. The example in Listings 7-26 and 7-27 demonstrates this binding.

Listing 7-26. *Script with a single public-read attribute: PublicReadBindExample1.fx*

```
package com.foo;
public-read var x = 100.0;
public function setX(val: Number) {
    x = val;
}
```

Listing 7-27. *Public-read attributes in bind expressions: PublicReadBindExample2.fx*

```
package com.jfx;
import com.foo.*;
var obj = PublicReadBindExample1 {};
var y = bind obj.x;
println("Y Value: {y}");
obj.setX(200);
println("Y Value: {y}");
```

To see the output, compile and run **PublicReadBindExample2.fx**.

Output ()
```
Y Value: 100.0
Y Value: 200.0
```

As you see in the output, changing the x value in this example through the **setX()** method changes the y value as well, since y is bound to x.

With the help of **public-read**, you can expose any variable declaration publicly for read access without worrying about the variable being modified inadvertently by the public code, which still retains the write access as you wish, be it protected, package, or script-only.

public-init

A variable defined with the `public-init` access specifier can be read or initialized anywhere but cannot be bound publicly. Notice that I said "initialized" and not assigned—it can be initialized in an object literal but cannot be changed or assigned or bound from anywhere. Nevertheless, these variables can be modified either within the same script, within the package, or in inherited classes across the package depending on the primary access specified. In other words, once initialization is over, `public-init` would pretty much be treated the same way as `public-read` throughout the life-cycle of that class instance created.

■ **Note** Another important difference between `public-read` and `public-init` is that `public-init` usage is limited to class member variables and is not allowed for script variables. Using it for script variables will throw a compilation error.

Syntax

```
public-init [primary access specifier] var var name[:data type] [= value];
```

Not specifying the primary specifier would default to script-private. Specifying a data type is optional because the compiler can infer the type automatically from the value assigned.

The example in Listings 7-28 and 7-29 demonstrates the usage of `public-init`.

Listing 7-28. *Defining public-int vars: PublicInitExample1.fx*

```
public class PublicInitExample1 {
    public-init var y = 20;
    public-init var x = bind (2 * y);
}
```

Listing 7-29. *Initializing public-init vars: PublicInitMain.fx*

```
var pre1 = PublicInitExample1 {
    y: 100
    x: 20
}
println("X Value: {pre1.x}");
println("Y Value: {pre1.y}");
println("------------");
var pre2 = PublicInitExample1 {
    y: 100
}
println("X Value: {pre2.x}");
println("Y Value: {pre2.y}");
```

Compile the two scripts and run `PublicInitMain.fx` to see the following output.

Output
```
X Value: 20
Y Value: 100
------------
X Value: 200
Y Value: 100
```

In Listing 7-28, there are two `public-init` variables defined within the `PublicInitExample1` class. In a different FX script, you create an instance of the class (`pre1`) and you are initializing x, y within the object literal at the time of creation. According to the definition of `public-init`, this is allowed. Hence, printing those values show the correct values you have assigned (20, 100). Note that the `bind` defined for variable x has been overridden in the object literal and hence will have no effect on the `pre1` instance of the class.

In the second instance of the `PublicInitExample1` class, `pre2`, you are initializing only the y value and not the x value. So the x value will use the original `bind` expression defined within `PublicInitExample1` class for `pre2`, and the last two lines of output indicate that the `bind` defined on variable x has been exercised.

Now with the same example, after the initialization let us try to see if the value of y can be changed outside the object literal block. Listings 7-30 and 7-31 show the code.

Listing 7-30. *A script with public-init vars defined: PublicInitExample1.fx*

```
public class PublicInitExample1 {
    public-init var y = 20;
    public-init var x = bind (2 * y);
}
```

Listing 7-31. *Accessing public init outside the object literal: PublicInitMain.fx*

```
// WARNING: This code will not compile
var pre1 = PublicInitExample1 {
    y: 100
    x: 20
}
println(pre1.x);
println(pre1.y);
pre1.y = pre1.y + 100;
```

Compile and run the scripts to see the following output.

Output
```
PublicInitMain.fx: y has script only (default) write access in PublicInitExample1
pre1.y = pre1.y + 100;
         ^
1 error
```

This example demonstrates the difference between initialization and assignment. Initialization within the object literal is permitted here, but trying to assign or bind to x/y causes a compilation error.

Now let us see some combinations of `public-init` and different primary access modifiers to offer varied access to the variable.

```
public-init var y: String = "JavaFX";
```

Here, the variable y can be read from anywhere, and it can be publicly initialized within an object literal (as seen in the examples given before) from anywhere, but it cannot be assigned or bound publicly. Because the primary access specifier is omitted, it defaults to script-only, allowing y to be modified (assigned or bound) only within the script.

```
public-init package var y: String = "JavaFX";
```

This time the variable y can be read and initialized from anywhere, but it can be assigned and bound only within the same package.

```
public-init protected var y: String = "Cool";
```

Here the variable y can be read and initialized from anywhere, and it can be modified, assigned, or bound anywhere within the same package. It can be modified, assigned, and bound from any class in other packages, provided the class extends from the base class where y is declared.

```
public-init public var y = "JavaFX";
```

This combination would be useless, because you have already made the variable public by defining the primary access specifier as `public`. It is fully open to the public, so it makes no sense to declare it as `public-init`. The compiler in this case would throw a warning to indicate that this is a meaningless combination of access specifiers.

Secondary Specifiers and def

So far, you have seen the usage of secondary access specifiers only with **var** declarations. Technically, it is possible to use **def** in place of **var**. However, the real-world use of such a combination is very limited. A **def** once defined cannot be changed in an object literal, it cannot be overridden by a derived class, nor can it be assigned a different definition or value regardless of what the access permissions are. Hence the usage of access specifiers with **def** is pretty much confined to specifying whether the value of the **def** should be publicly readable or not.

Access Specifiers for Class Definitions

So far, you have only seen access specifiers applied to class members and not to classes themselves. In most of the examples you have seen so far, the widest access, public, has been assigned to the classes. In fact, most of the access specifiers that we have discussed so far are applicable to classes as well as class members. In this section, you will see the applicability of each access specifier with respect to class definitions.

The access specified on the class normally will be wider, with appropriate access restrictions enforced on the class members. Having a too-restrictive access specifier on the class itself can potentially make the class unusable.

Script-private Classes

A class definition that does not have any access specifier mentioned explicitly would default to script-private, meaning that the class can be instantiated and used only within that script. Trying to instantiate or refer to the class in some other script would cause a compilation error. Listing 7-32 shows an example.

Listing 7-32. Script-private class definition: Cup.fx

```
class Cup {
    public var material: String;
}
var c = Cup { material: "ceramic" };
println ("From same script: {c.material}");
```

Output
```
From same script: ceramic
```

In Listing 7-32, the Cup class is script-private, and you don't see any issues using it within the script. However, when you try to use it in some other script, the compiler will throw an error, saying the Cup class has script-only access.

The same error will occur even when the members of the class are public. So normally it does not make sense to have access for the class members that is wider than the class itself.

■ **Note** Having script-only access at the class level is normally too restrictive to be useful, and you should keep the class at a higher access level and restrict the class member's access instead.

Package-accessible Classes

As with class members, you can choose **package** access for the class itself, which will make the class accessible only within the package and not exposed to the public. It is common to apply such access to implementation classes whose interface and implementation are consumed only within the respective package. Listings 7-33 and 7-34 demonstrate this access.

Listing 7-33. A class definition restricted to package-only use: Cup.fx

```
package class Cup {
    package var material: String;
}
```

Listing 7-34. Using a package-only class: Cup1.fx

```
var c1 = Cup { material: "plastic" };
println("From another script {c1.material}");
```

Output
```
From another script plastic
```

In this example, `Cup.fx` and `Cup1.fx` both reside within the same default unnamed package, so the Cup class is accessible from within `Cup1.fx`. However, if you move Cup and `Cup1.fx` into separate packages, there will be a compilation error, because Cup has only `package` access and cannot be accessed from a different package.

Protected Classes

Classes specified as `protected` are different from protected class members. A protected member of a public class (A) can be accessed from within another class that extends A, even if the derived class is in a different package. However, this definition will not work if the class itself is protected, because a protected class cannot be extended by another class in a different package. The compiler will complain that the protected class is being accessed outside of its scope because the usage to extend the class comes directly within the script. Go through the example in Listings 7-35 and 7-36 and you will understand this clearly.

Listing 7-35. A protected class definition: Cup.fx

```
package com.cutlery;
protected class Cup {
    protected var material: String;
}
```

Listing 7-36. Accessing a protected class definition: Cup1.fx

```
//WARNING: This script will not compile
package com.jfxcutlery;
import com.cutlery.*;
class FXCup extends Cup {
    public override var material = "Ceramic";
}
var c2 = FXCup{};
println(c2.material);
```

Compile and run the code to see the following output.

Output
```
Cup1.fx:4: com.cutlery.Cup has protected access in com.cutlery
class FXCup extends Cup {
                    ^
Cup1.fx:8: cannot find symbol
symbol : variable material
location: class com.jfxcutlery.Cup1.fxCup
println(c2.material);
           ^
```

```
Cup1.fx:5: cannot find symbol
symbol : variable material
location: class com.jfxcutlery.Cup1.fxCup
    public override var material = "Ceramic";
                          ^
3 errors
```

As shown in the output, the compiler sees an inappropriate use of the protected class where it has been used within a script directly from a different package. As per the definition, this is wrong because a protected entity is not being used within a derived class. So having a protected class does not bring in any of the advantages of the `protected` access specifier, and the class can be used only within the package. Hence there will be no difference between `protected` and `package` for class definitions.

So in this case, the class has to be defined as public, and if you want to have restrictions in place, keep the class members as protected wherever appropriate.

Public Classes

Public classes do not need much explanation. Just like any other public members of the class or script, they can be accessed from anywhere and can be instantiated or extended from anywhere. You have already seen many such examples in this chapter.

Summary

In this chapter, you have learned about data encapsulation, or data hiding, and the advantages of having appropriate restrictions on data members. In JavaFX Script, data encapsulation can be achieved through *access specifiers* (also called *access modifiers*) such as `public`, `protected`, `package` and the default, in decreasing order of access territory. Public members can be read, written, bound and so on from anywhere. Protected members can be accessed within the same package or from classes in other packages that derive from the class where the protected member is defined. Package members can be accessed from within the same package. If no access specifier is specified, it defaults to script-private, where the member would be accessible only within that script.

JavaFX also offers two new secondary access specifiers, `public-read` and `public-init`. Members having `public-read` access can be read from anywhere. Members having `public-init` can be initialized (within an object literal) or read from anywhere. However, the write access for these members would be decided by the primary modifiers specified along with `public-init/read`. If primary modifiers are omitted, the member will have write access only within the script where it is defined.

In the next chapter, you will learn more about inheritance in object-oriented programming. You'll learn how it can be achieved in JavaFX Script and how its implementation differs from that in Java. You will also learn more about protected access, with real inheritance examples, and you'll learn how to implement Java Interfaces within JavaFX.

CHAPTER 8

■ ■ ■

Inheritance

Inheritance is a form of software reusability in which programmers create classes that "inherit" an existing class's data and behaviors and enhance them with new capabilities. Software reusability saves time during application development. It also encourages the reuse of proven and debugged high-quality software, which increases the likelihood that a system will be implemented effectively. When creating a class, instead of writing completely new data members and member functions, the programmer can designate that the new class should inherit the members of the existing class. The existing class is called the base class, and the new class that is derived from the base class is called the derived class. In Java and the JavaFX scripting language, a base class is called a superclass and the derived class is called a subclass.

Inheritance is an integral part of the JavaFX scripting language. When you inherit, you say "This new class is like that old class with new data members and member functional that adds the additional capabilities." You state this in code by giving the name of the class as usual, but before the opening brace of the class body, put the keyword **extends** followed by the name of the base class or superclass. When you do this, you automatically provide all the fields and methods in the base class to the derived class or subclass, and you can define your own data members and member functions in the derived class.

Listing 8-1 shows a simple example of how we can inherit a class in JavaFX.

Listing 8-1. *A simple inheritance example*

```
class Shape{
    var x : Number=10.0;
    var y : Number=10.0;
    function drawShape(){
        println("Draw the shape");
    }
}
class Circle extends Shape {
    var radius : Number;
    override function drawShape(){
        println("Draw circle at x={x} y={y} with radius={radius}");
    }
}
var circle : Circle = Circle{
    x : 40
    y : 50
    radius : 5
```

```
}
circle.drawShape();
```

Output
```
Draw circle at x=40.0 y=50.0 with radius=5.0
```

In Listing 8-1, the class shape represents any shape to draw on the computer. It's a base class or superclass, which has two data members, x and y, representing X and Y coordinates on the screen, and drawShape(), a method to draw the shape.

Listing 8-1 also shows a class Circle, which is extended from the Shape class. So class Circle is a derived class, since it inherits all the data members and the member functions of the Shape class and also defines its own data as well as member functions, thereby enhancing the functionality of the base class. Since a circle is also a shape, we are overriding member functions of the drawShape( ) method to draw the circle, and the overridden method is marked with the override keyword. (Method overriding is covered in Chapter 5, "Functions.")

Finally, when you create an instance of the class Circle, you have the data members x, y, and radius. When you call the circle.drawShape() method on an instance of the Circle class, the Circle.drawShape() method is invoked. If you need to invoke a member function of the Shape class, then you should invoke drawShape() on a Shape class instance.

The Order of Initialization of Data Members

Since inheritance involves two or more classes, in general there is a relationship established between the base and the derived class. When you create an instance of the derived class, it contains within it a base class member as a subobject. This subobject is the same as if you had created an instance of the base class by itself. It's just that from the outside, the subobject of the base class is wrapped within the derived class object. When we initialize an object of the derived class, first the base class data member is initialized and then the derived class data member. Let us see an example that demonstrates the order in which the data members are initialized across base and the derived classes, through the init block. (Refer to Chapter 6, "Class Definitions," for more information on the init block. Briefly, it is equivalent to the constructor in Java and is called automatically when a class is instantiated. It is used to do any initialization such as grouping different shapes to create a custom UI control.) Listing 8-2 shows the code.

Listing 8-2. Data member initialization order

```
class Base {
    var a : Integer;
    var str:String;
    init{
        println("Base class init block.");
        a = 10;
        str="Base";
    }
}

class Derived extends Base {
    var k:Number;
    init {
```

```
            println("Derived class init block.");
            k=34.34;
        }

        function printValues() : Void {
            println("a = { der.a }  str = {der.str}  k = {der.k}");
          }

    }

    var der:Derived = Derived{}
    der.printValues();      // a = 10  str = Base  k = 34.34
```

Output
```
Base class init block.
Derived class init block.
a = 10  str = Base  k = 34.34
```

Listing 8-2 has two classes, named **Base** and **Derived**. Each class has its own data members and its own **init** blocks to initialize the data members. When we create an object or instance of the class **Derived**, the **Base** class's **init** block is called first and then the **init** block of the **derived** class. Hence the **base** class's data member initialization is done prior to that of the **derived** class. Finally, the **printValues()** method is called to verify the initialized data member values.

Overriding Data Members

Similar to overriding a member function of the base class, you can override the data members or instance variables of the base class as well. Overriding a data member is straightforward and simple. In the derived class, you declare a data member or instance variable with the same name as the superclass data member, but with the **override** keyword as one of its modifiers, and without any type specifier. A data member can be initialized with a different value in the derived class when it is being overridden, and if the variable is left uninitialized in the derived class, the initialization specified in the base class would be considered.

Listing 8-3 shows an example.

Listing 8-3. Overriding data members

```
class Game{
    var player:Integer = 2;
    var item : String="Some Game";
    var location:String="Out Door";

    function printValues() : Void {
        println("player = {player}  item = {item}  location={location}");
    }
}
```

```
class Cricket extends Game{
    override var item="Bat,Ball and stumps";
    override var location;         // data member is not initialized.

    override function printValues() : Void {
        println("player = {player}  item = {item}  location={location}");
    }
}
var game:Game=Game{ }
    game.printValues();
    var cri:Cricket = Cricket{}
    cri.printValues();
```

Output
```
player = 2   item = Some Game   location=Out Door
player = 11   item = Bat,Ball and stumps   location=Out Door
```

In Listing 8-3, we are overriding three data members of the base class Game from within the derived class Cricket, and we are initializing two of the overridden members with new values in the derived class. We are leaving the variable location uninitialized. We are creating an instance of the Game class as well as the Cricket class and printing the values. In the output, notice that the value ofthe location variable in the cri instance is automatically initialized to Out Door, demonstrating that the initialization is inherited from the base class.

■ **Note** Attempting to specify a type specifier in a statement overriding a data member or instance variable will cause a compiler error.

Use of the super Keyword

Like Java, JavaFX Script also supports the super keyword, which can be used to invoke a method available in the base class from within any member function of the derived class. Let us see a simple example of how it can be used in JavaFX, in Listing 8-4.

Listing 8-4. Usage of the super keyword

```
class A{
    function fun1(){
        println("Base class Function-1");
    }
    function fun2(){
        println("Base class Function-2");
    }
}
```

```
class B extends A{
    function bFun1(){
        println("Derived class Function-1");
    }
    override function fun2(){
        super.fun2();
        println("Derived class Function-2");
    }
}
var obj:B=B{}
obj.fun2();
```

Output
```
Base class Function-2
Derived class Function-2
```

The code shown in Listing 8-4 is self-explanatory; we call the base class's `fun2()` function from within the overriding function of the derived class.

It is also possible to call a non-overridden function of the base class using the `super` keyword, but doing that generally does not make sense, since you can already invoke the non-overridden member function directly.

Mixin Classes

JavaFX Script has supported multiple inheritance right from its inception, but the concept of multiple inheritance has been radically changed as of JavaFX 1.2. Prior to 1.2, a normal JavaFX class could directly extend from any number of other classes, but as of version 1.2 this has been streamlined by enforcing certain restrictions on inheriting multiple classes through *mixins*. The `mixin` keyword in JavaFX Script refers to a new form of multiple inheritance with same features as before but with additional benefits such as much simpler and much faster code generation. The concept of a mixin is generic within OOP. Mixins are more or less like interfaces in Java except that they can have variables and implementations that can be inherited by all the classes that extend a mixin class.

The `mixin` keyword is applied to classes, and such a class is described as a mixin class. A mixin class is a like a regular JavaFX class; it contains data members, member functions, an `init` block anda `postinit` block. The difference is that the class cannot be instantiated directly; it is instead designed to be extended and used by subclasses.

Some basic points should be remembered while implementing inheritance in JavaFX:

- JavaFX Script classes are allowed to extend at most one other JavaFX Script class as a superclass. This superclass can be either a Java class or a JavaFX Script class.

- JavaFX Script classes are allowed to extend any number of JavaFX Script mixin classes.

- JavaFX mixin classes are allowed to extend any number of other JavaFX mixin classes and can also extend any number of Java interfaces.

As mentioned earlier, a mixin class can extend one regular (non-mixin) class and any number of `mixin` classes.

Now let us see an example that demonstrates the difference between how Java and JavaFX achieve a similar functionality and how simple JavaFX is compared to Java (Listing 8-5).

Listing 8-5. A comparison of mixins in Java and JavaFX

```
FileName: GreetWorld.java
public interface GreetWorld {
    public void printGreetings();
}
FileName: Greeting1.java
public class Greeting1 implements GreetWorld {
    String courtesy = "Hello";
    String name = "Praveen!";

    public void printGreetings() {
        System.out.println(courtesy + " " + name);
    }
    public static void main (String args[]) {
        Greeting1 g = new Greeting1();
        g.printGreetings();
    }
}
FileName: Greeting2.java
public class Greeting2 implements GreetWorld {
    String courtesy = "Hello";
    String name = "Lawrence!";

    public void printGreetings() {
        System.out.println(courtesy + " " + name);
    }
    public static void main (String args[]) {
        Greeting2 g = new Greeting2();
        g.printGreetings();
    }
}
FileName: Greetings.fx
public mixin class GreetWorld {
    var courtesy: String = "Hello";
    var name: String;

    public function printGreetings(): Void {
        println("{courtesy} {name}");
    }
}

class Greeting1 extends GreetWorld {
    override var name = "Praveen!";
}
```

```
class Greeting2 extends GreetWorld {
    override var name = "Lawrence!";
}

public function run() {
    var g1 = Greeting1 {}
    var g2 = Greeting2 {}
    g1.printGreetings();
    g2.printGreetings();
}
```

Output
```
(Executing Greeting1.java) Hello Praveen!
(Executing Greeting2java) Hello Lawrence!
(Executing Greetings.fx)
Hello Praveen!
Hello Lawrence!
```

As you see in Listing 8-5, the JavaFX code is much simpler than the Java code. You can easily see that there is an implementation for the method printGreetings() in the mixin class, and so the subclasses do not have to implement the method again. The implementations of printGreetings in Greeting1 and Greeting2 are identical, a duplication that is avoided in JavaFX. In addition to this, all the classes are maintained in a single file in JavaFX; in Java you need a separate file for each of the public classes and interfaces.

▓ **Note** A mixin class cannot be instantiated directly and can only be extended. However, you can instantiate a derived class that extends a mixin class, and it is legal to cast a derived class's object to a mixin reference. It is also legal to use a mixin class with the instanceof operator.

Listing 8-6 demonstrates how to create a subclass from a regular class and a mixin class.

Listing 8-6. *Deriving a mixin and a regular class together*

```
class Base {
    var x : Integer;
    function showX() {
        println("x = {x}");
    }
}

mixin class MixBase  {
    var y : Integer;
    function showY( ){
        println("y = {y}");
    }
}
```

```
class SubClass extends MixBase , Base {
    var z : Integer;
    function showZ() {
        println("z = {z}");
    //super.showY(); - ILLEGAL: WILL NOT COMPILE
    //super.showX(); - LEGAL
    }
}

var obj = SubClass{
    x : 10;
    y : 20;
    z : 30;
}

obj.showX();   // x = 10
obj.showY();   // y = 20
obj.showZ();   // z = 30
```

Output
```
x = 10
y = 20
z = 30
```

Listing 8-6 shows how a regular class and a mixin class can be extended by a subclass. Notice that a mixin class can also have data members and functions just like a normal class, and those members can be accessed the same way as we do with a normal class.

Notice also that the contents of the mixin class, such as member functions and data members, are included in the derived class rather than inherited. They become part of the derived class during compilation. Hence, the super keyword can only refer to the extension of a non-mixin class and not a mixin class. That's why super.showY() will not compile if uncommented in this example, whereas super.showX() will compile correctly.

Creating a Subclass from Multiple Mixin Classes

When a class inherits from multiple other classes, the technique is called *multiple inheritance*. Java does not support multiple inheritance through classes, but it can be done using Java interfaces. By contrast, in the JavaFX scripting language, mixin inheritance allows you to extend multiple mixin classes, giving you the benefits of multiple inheritance. Now let us see how we can create a subclass extending from multiple mixin classes (Listing 8-7).

Listing 8-7. Extending multiple mixin classes

```
public mixin class Mixin1 {
    var a : Integer;
    public function getA(){
        return a;
    }
}
```

```
public mixin class Mixin2 {
    var b : Integer;
    public function getB(){
        return b;
    }
}
class Mixee extends Mixin1, Mixin2 {
    var c : Integer;
    public function getC(){
        return c;
    }
}
function run () {
    var obj = Mixee{
        a : 10;b:20;c:30;
    }
    println("a = {obj.getA()}   , b = {obj.getB()}   , c= {obj.getC()}"); // a = 10   , b = 20
, c= 30
}
```

```
output :-
a = 10   , b = 20   , c= 30
```

In Listing 8-7, we have defined two classes, named Mixin1 and Mixin2.Each class contains a single Integer data member and a member function to return its data value. The class Mixee extends both the Mixin1 and Mixin2 classes, inheriting the data members and member functions of both parent mixin classes and thus enabling multiple inheritance. Now with an object of the Mixee class, you can access the data members and member functions of Mixee, Mixin1, or Mixin2.

The Order of Initialization in Multiple Inheritance

Recall from the beginning of this chapter that init blocks are always executed in order from parent class to child class. Now when we have multiple parent classes, the same order of parent-to-child is maintained, and the parents' init blocks would be called before the child's. But the order among multiple parents is chosen by the order in which the parent classes are mentioned after the extends keyword in the derived class. If class A extends from B, C, and D, the order of initialization would be B ▶ C ▶ D ▶ A. Listing 8-8 is an example that demonstrates the order of initialization in a multiple-inheritance scenario.

Listing 8-8. Order of initialization with multiple inheritance

```
public mixin class Mixin1 {
    init{
        println("mixin1 init block");
    }
}

public mixin class Mixin2 {
    init{
        println("mixin2 init block");
```

```
        }
    }

class Mixee extends Mixin1, Mixin2 {
    init{
        println("mixee init block");
    }
  }

function run() {
    Mixee{}
}
```

Output
```
mixin1 init block
mixin2 init block
mixee init block
```

As you see in the output of Listing 8-8, the order is always from parent to child and the order among multiple parents is decided by the order in which the parent classes are extended by the derived class. In this case, Mixee extends Mixin1 first and then Mixin2, and so the init blocks are executed in the order Mixin1 ▶ Mixin2 ▶ Mixee.

Abstract Classes

There are situations in which you would want to define a superclass that declares the structure of a given abstraction without providing a complete implementation of every method. That is, sometimes you will want to create a superclass that only defines a generalized form that will be shared by all of its subclasses, leaving it to each subclass to fill in the details. Such a class determines the nature of the methods that the subclasses must implement. One way this situation can occur is when a superclass is unable to create a meaningful implementation for a method.

In such a scenario, you can create a class and mark certain methods to be overridden by subclasses compulsorily, by specifying the abstract type modifier. The responsibility of implementing these methods is with the subclass, since the parent class will not have any implementation. Thus, a subclass must override them—it cannot simply use the version defined in the superclass.

Any class that contains one or more abstract methods must also be declared abstract. To declare a class abstract, you simply use the abstract keyword in front of the class keyword at the beginning of the class declaration. There can be no objects of an abstract class. That is, an abstract class cannot be directly instantiated, because an abstract class is not fully defined. But you can create a reference of the abstract class.

▪ **Note** A mixin class can have abstract functions if you want to leave the implementation to the derived classes. But the class need not be referred to as abstract, unlike a normal Java or JavaFX Script class.

Using a JavaFX Class to Extend a Java Abstract Class

Because the JavaFX Scripting language is built on top of Java, JavaFX classes can extend Java classes (including abstract classes) and Java interfaces. For example, suppose you have created an application in Java and now want to migrate it to JavaFX. You can just extend those Java classes or implement the Java interfaces in your JavaFX directly to import the same behavior (that is, the interface) that you have already built using Java. Listing 8-9 shows an example; we have a Java abstract class, which is in a separate .java file, and this abstract class is extended and implemented by JavaFX subclasses.

Listing 8-9. *A JavaFX class extending an abstract Java class*

```
Filename : Figure.java
package inheritance;

abstract class Figure {
    public float dim1;
    public float dim2;
    // abstract area class
    abstract float area();
}


FileName : AbstractImplementation.fx
package inheritance;
class Rectangle extends Figure {
    override function area() : Number  {
        println("Overriden area function in Rectangle class");
        return dim1 * dim2;
    }
}

class Triangle extends Figure {
    override function area() : Number {
        println("Overriden area function in Triangle class");
        return dim1 * dim2 / 2.0;
    }
}

function run(){
    var rect = Rectangle{ }
    rect.dim1 = 5.0;
    rect.dim2 = 5.0;
    println(rect.area());

    var triangle  = Triangle{ }
    triangle.dim1 = 10.0;
    triangle.dim2 = 5.0;
    println(triangle.area());
}
```

Output
```
Overriden area function in Rectangle class
25.0
Overriden area function in Triangle class
25.0
```

In Listing 8-9, we have a Java abstract class named `Figure`, which has an abstract method named `area`. This Java abstract class is stored in a file called `Figure.java`. The class is extended by two JavaFX classes, `Rectangle` and `Triangle`, and it overrides the abstract method `area` in a file called `AbstractImplementation.fx`. Both the Java and JavaFX classes are in the package `inheritance`. In the `run()` function, we create instances of the `Rectangle` and `Triangle` classes and assign values to the data members. Finally, we call the `area()` function of the respective implementations.

Anonymous Implementation of Java Interfaces

In Java, we often encounter situations where we need to implement interfaces anonymously, without specifying a class name, and the same thing can be done in JavaFX Script as well. One such example is the implementation of `java.awt.event.ActionListener`, which is demonstrated in Listing 8-10.

Listing 8-10. Implementing Java interfaces anonymously

```
import javax.swing.*;
import java.awt.event.ActionEvent;
import java.awt.event.ActionListener;

var counter: Integer = 0;

var listener = ActionListener {
    public override function actionPerformed(ae: ActionEvent): Void {
        println("Timer Triggered {counter}");
        counter ++;
    }
}

var timer: Timer = new Timer(1000, listener);
timer.start();
```

Output
```
Timer Triggered 0
Timer Triggered 1
Timer Triggered 2
Timer Triggered 3
..
..
```

In Listing 8-10, we are implementing a *swing timer* from Java to do some animation. A swing timer requires an action listener and a time interval at which the action listener's `actionPerformed` must be invoked. Here we are creating an object, named `listener`, of type `ActionListener`, by providing an inline implementation of the interface and using it in the `Timer` constructor. As you see in the output, the swing timer will invoke `listener`'s `actionPerformed()` function every second (1000ms), infinitely. As you see the `ActionListener` implementation, it is the same listener method in Java implemented in JavaFX Script syntax with keywords such as `override` and `function`.

Summary

Inheritance allows a class to be derived from an existing class. The derived class has all the data and functions of the parent class but adds new ones of its own. Inheritance makes possible reusability—the ability to use a class over and over in different programs with enhanced features. JavaFX supports all types of inheritance as Java does, including multiple inheritance, but in a slightly different way, using mixin classes. A mixin class resembles a regular class in that it contains data members and member functions but is prefixed with the `mixin` keyword. A JavaFX Script class can extend at most one Java or one JavaFX Script class, but it can extend multiple JavaFX mixin classes. The class that is extended from the mixin class is called a *mixee* class. JavaFX classes can extend Java abstract classes and implement Java Interfaces. In the next chapter, you will learn more about one of the most important and powerful JavaFX features—data binding.

CHAPTER 9

■■■

Data Binding

Binding is one of the most important, powerful and useful features of JavaFX; it can simplify your code to a great extent. In this chapter, we will start with basic binding concepts and proceed toward more sophisticated binding, with appropriate examples.

What Does Binding Mean?

In general terms, *binding* normally means sticking one object firmly to another, forming a bond, say by tying with a rope. After the objects are bound, anything you do with one of the objects will impact the other. Displacing one of the objects, for example, will displace the other. The definition in JavaFX is on similar lines. It's the ability to create a direct and immediate relationship between two variables, where a change to one variable would change the other.

Binding in JavaFX is achieved through the **bind** keyword, which associates the value of the target variable with the outcome of an expression. The expression could just be anything —another variable, an object, a function call, an expression, a block, and so on. This expression is called a *bound expression* and is illustrated in Figure 9-1. A bound expression can be any expression that does not return **Void**, and so expressions involving increment or decrement operators or loops are not allowed.

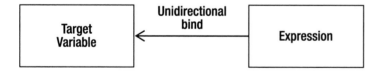

Figure 9-1. *Unidirectional binding*

Listing 9-1 demonstrates a simple bind.

Listing 9-1. *A simple bind*

```
var x = 0;
def y = bind x * x;
x = 10;
println(y); // 10*10 = 100
```

```
x = 5;
println(y); // 5*5 = 25
```

Output
```
100
25
```

In this example, def y is bound to the square of x, which means that whenever the x value changes, the y value will be recalculated but not vice-versa. This is called *unidirectional binding*. The binding happens in one direction—from right to left. In the example, changing the x value changes y, but changing y will not change x. (There is also bidirectional binding, which we will discuss later in this chapter.) Continuing with the example, the expression x*x depends on the value of x, and so x can be considered a dependency. So when the dependency changes, the expression will be re-evaluated.

Also note that y is declared as def, primarily because no value can be assigned directly to y, and y's value can be changed only through x. If you try to change the value of y directly, that would result in a compilation error. You can also define y as a var, but assigning a value to y will still cause a runtime error, since it is not legal to change the value of y when it is unidirectionally bound to an expression already.

Listing 9-2 is an example that is nearly as simple but uses a loop.

Listing 9-2. Changing a bound expression from within a loop

```
var x = 100;
var y = bind x + 100;
for( a in [5..50 step 5]){
    x = a;
    println( "x={x}, y={y}");
}
```

Output
```
x=5,  y=105
x=10, y=110
x=15, y=115
x=20, y=120
x=25, y=125
x=30, y=130
x=35, y=135
x=40, y=140
x=45, y=145
x=50, y=150
```

The code in this example is pretty self-explanatory: whenever the x value changes, y also changes automatically. The only difference from Listing 9-1 is that the value of the expression is changed continuously with a loop, which causes continuous re-evaluation of the expression.

> ■ **Note** It is recommended to use def instead of var for variables whose value depend on a bound expression since it is not legal to assign a value directly to a bound variable, and such errors can be caught at compile time instead of runtime when using def. However, this applies only to unidirectional binds, and it would still make sense to use var in the case of bidirectional binds, as we will see later in this chapter.

Recalculation of Expressions

When the bound expression changes, the outcome is recalculated and assigned to the target variable. However, this recalculation will not be done for all the elements in the expression, as it is optimized to re-evaluate only the changed portion in the expression. Let us see this in detail with the following bound expression:

```
def val = bind expr1 + expr2
```

The value of `val` will be recalculated whenever `expr1` or `expr2` changes. However, only the changed expression will be recalculated and not both if only one of the expressions is changing.

> ■ **Note** There is another important optimization technique, called lazy binding, in which the bound expression will be evaluated only when the result of the expression is being consumed. So it is unsafe to assume that val will be changed immediately when expr1 or expr2 changes when using JavaFX 1.3 or higher, but it is guaranteed to be changed before the first consumption of val's value. For more information, see the last section of this chapter, "Lazy vs. Eager Binding."

Let's prove this with an example; Listing 9-3 shows the code.

Listing 9-3. *Optimized re-evaluation of a bound expression*

```
var x = 10;
var y = 20;
var z = 10;
var sum = bind addConstant() + z;
println(sum);
z = 30;
println(sum);

function addConstant() {
    println("function called");
    30 // This will be considered as the return value.
}
```

Output
```
function called
40
60
```

In Listing 9-3, the bound expression consists of a function call and a variable. When this expression is evaluated the first time, the value of addConstant() is calculated and remembered. It is then added to the z value, and the outcome is assigned to sum. That's why you see the "function called" message in the output.

Now when the z value changes, the outcome of the addConstant() function is not recalculated (since it is not changed), and the same value that was calculated before is fetched and replaced in the expression. However, the new z value is substituted in the expression to give the value of 60 to sum. Since the outcome of addConstant() is not recalculated, the function is not called the second time.

Thus you can see that the recalculation of bound expressions is optimized so as not to evaluate all the elements in the expression but only the changed portions. We will see more about this optimization when we explore how binding works with other forms of expressions later in this chapter.

■ **Note** The value of the function expression is the value of the last line in the expression, which in our example is 30. So there is no need to have an explicit return statement within the function; also note that the return type is not explicitly mentioned, since it is automatically inferred from the last line of the function block.

Binding with Conditional Expressions

Bind can be used along with conditional expressions such as if-else to choose the value of the target variable conditionally.

Syntax
```
def x = bind if (condition) expr1 else expr2;
```

Here, as in any other if-else expression, if *condition* is true, x will have the value of expr1; otherwise, it will equal expr2. If *condition* is true, only *expr1* is recalculated, and *expr2* is ignored even if there is a change in the *expr2*. The inverse of this is also true. Listing 9-4 demonstrates conditional binding.

Listing 9-4. A conditional bind

```
var mark = 50;
var status = bind if (mark >= 50) then "PASS" else "FAIL";
println(status);
mark = 30;
println(status);
```

Output
```
PASS
FAIL
```

When you use bind with if-else, the value of the if expression must always be a valid value and cannot be Void, though a normal unbound if-else expression can have a Void value. In other words, the following requirements must be taken care of when you use bind along with an if expression:

- Having an else clause is mandatory

- if and else expressions (expr1 and expr2 in the syntax shown earlier) must return a valid value and cannot be Void.

Any violation of these requirements would cause a compilation error.

■ **Note** Remember that null is different from Void; null is a valid value and can be used in the bound conditional expressions but Void typically represents "No-value."

Binding with for Expressions

Binding can be used with for expressions as long as those expressions return a valid value and not Void. Listing 9-5 is an example of how the bind keyword can be used with the for expression.

Listing 9-5. A bind with a for expression

```
var min = 0;
var max = 5;
def seq = bind for (x in [min..max]) 2*x;
println(seq);
max = 10;
println(seq);
min = 5;
println(seq);
```

Output
```
[ 0, 2, 4, 6, 8, 10 ]
[ 0, 2, 4, 6, 8, 10, 12, 14, 16, 18, 20 ]
[ 10, 12, 14, 16, 18, 20 ]
```

In Listing 9-5, whenever min/max values change within the for expression, the portion of the sequence that would be impacted by the change would be recalculated and not the entire sequence.

For example, initially the for expression is evaluated fully and the sequence is created when it is defined. Now when the max value is changed to 10, the existing items of the seq (index 0 through 5) will not be recalculated, and only the new items are calculated and added to the sequence.

Now when the min value changes from 0 to 5, the initial five entries in the seq are discarded and the rest of the items are never touched.

There is of course, one exception to this: If an expression uses indexof, then it will be re-evaluated completely, regardless of the min/max values, since it is quite possible that some additions/deletions would obviously change the index of all the items. Listing 9-6 demonstrates how this works.

Listing 9-6. *A bind with a for expression using indexof*

```
var seq = [1..10];
def seq1 = bind for (x in seq) {
    x * (indexof x) + 2;
}
println(seq1);
insert 0 before seq[0];
println(seq1);
```

Output
```
[ 2, 4, 8, 14, 22, 32, 44, 58, 74, 92 ]
[ 2, 3, 6, 11, 18, 27, 38, 51, 66, 83, 102 ]
```

In this example, note that the entire sequence has changed after we insert a value at the beginning of seq; this occurs because seq elements actually depend on the index of the corresponding element in seq. Inserting an item in the beginning alters the index of all the elements in seq, and hence causes the entire seq1 to be recalculated by rerunning the for expression through its entire range.

It is important to re-emphasize here that a bound variable cannot be modified directly, and doing so will result in a runtime error. This is true of a **var**; In the case of a **def**, the variable cannot be modified directly at all, regardless of whether it is bound, and doing so will result in compile-time error.

With **for expressions**, one can have a non-default step value also bound to a variable in addition to the min and max values. Let us see how this works; Listing 9-7 shows the code.

Listing 9-7. *A bind with a for expression using a bound step value*

```
var stepVal = 1;
var max = 20;
var seq = bind for (i in [0..max step stepVal] where i < max/2 )  i;
println(seq);
stepVal = 5;
println(seq);
stepVal = 8;
println(seq);
max = 41;
println(seq);
```

Output
```
[ 0, 1, 2, 3, 4, 5, 6, 7, 8, 9 ]
[ 0, 5 ]
[ 0, 8 ]
[ 0, 8, 16 ]
```

As you see in this example, maximum as well as step values are bound to variables, and any change to either max or the step value would cause the **for** expression to be recalculated. Changing the step value from 5 to 8 would cause the entire sequence to be recalculated; however, changing the max value will just insert additional elements into the sequence and will not recalculate the existing elements.

It is also possible to use functions within a bound **for** expression. Listing 9-8 demonstrates how to do this.

Listing 9-8. *Functions in a bound for expression*

```
var sum = bind for (i in [1..10] where i > 5 )  sumSeq([1..i]);

function sumSeq( seq : Integer[]):Integer {
    var sum = 0;
    for (num in seq) {sum = sum + num;}
    sum
}
println(sum);
```

Output
```
[ 21, 28, 36, 45, 55 ]
```

In this example, the **for** expression actually delegates the sum calculation to a function that is invoked whenever the i value changes. Note that a sequence has been created and passed as an argument to the function.

Binding Block Expressions

A *block* is a set of expressions enclosed within curly braces. The value of the block expression is the value of the last expression in the block. When the block is bound to a target variable, there are certain restrictions as to what can appear within the block. Typically, the following restrictions apply to expressions that are defined before the last statement within a block:

- The last statement in the block must fetch a valid value and cannot be Void. Hence you cannot have statements such as **println()** anywhere within the bound block.

- Only variable declarations (**def/var**) can appear in nonfinal positions.

- Assignment, increment, and decrement operators are prohibited at nonfinal positions. (Assignment is allowed only if it is preceded by a variable declaration.)

- Expressions such as **while** and **insert/delete** (see Chapter 10, "Sequences") are not allowed.

Violating any of these restrictions would result in a compilation error. As far as recalculation of expressions is concerned, any change in the expressions specified within the block would cause the entire block expression to be re-evaluated.

Syntax

```
def xxx = bind {
    def a = expr;
    var b = expr1;
    expr2;
}
```

Listing 9-9 demonstrates an example of a block expression with bind.

Listing 9-9. A bound block expression

```
var x = 10;
var y = 10;
var z = 0;

def sum = bind {
    x + y + z;
}
println(sum);
x = 20;
println(sum);
```

Output

```
20
30
```

In Listing 9-9, changing the x value has caused the block expression to be re-evaluated, and the newly computed value is assigned to the dependent variable sum.

Binding Functions

A function whose outcome is bound to a target variable will be called whenever any argument of the function changes. Let us prove this with a simple example (Listing 9-10).

Listing 9-10. Binding a function

```
var x = 10;
var y = 20;
var z = bind sum (x, y);
println(z);
x = 20;
println(z);
y = 30;
println(z);

function sum(x: Integer, y: Integer) {
    println("added");
    x + y;
}
```

Output
```
added
30
added
40
added
50
```

Here, the sum() function takes two arguments, and its outcome is bound to z. So whenever the arguments of the sum() function change, the sum() function will be invoked to recalculate the value of the function-expression. So initially the sum() function is invoked and its output of 30 is assigned to z. After this, the x value changes. Hence the function is called again to recalculate the value of x+y, and the new value is assigned to z. The same applies to y as well. This is the reason you see three "added" statements in the output, and it proves that the function is invoked whenever the arguments change its values. (Again, remember that the function sum() may not be called immediately when the x/y value is changed but instead is done when the output of z is being consumed within a println after a change to x/y. This is the same lazy binding optimization that you will learn at the end of this chapter.)

The ability to bind a function to a target variable is not limited to JavaFX functions; it is also available to existing functions available in Java classes.

■ **Note** When a bound function is invoked from within a bound context (meaning that it's called automatically because one of its parameters has changed in value), the arguments are passed by reference and so is the return value. Passing by reference means that a pointer to the actual data (the memory address) is sent and not the actual data itself. By contrast, if the same method is called from within a nonbound context (for example, the developer calling it explicitly), the arguments and return value are passed by value and not by reference.

Listing 9-11 is an example of how a Java function can be bound.

Listing 9-11. *Binding a Java function*

```
import java.lang.Math;
var d = 0;
var x2 = bind Math.toRadians(d);

for( r in [0..360 step 60]) {
    d = r.intValue();
    println("d={d}, x2= {x2}");
}
```

Output
```
d=0, x2= 0.0
d=60, x2= 1.0471975511965976
d=120, x2= 2.0943951023931953
d=180, x2= 3.141592653589793
d=240, x2= 4.1887902047863905
```

```
d=300, x2= 5.235987755982989
d=360, x2= 6.283185307179586
```

The code in Listing 9-11 just converts angle to radians using the Java Math API, and you can see that x2 is bound to a Java function—Math.toRadians(). Likewise, you can bind any Java function from within JavaFX, including creating new objects through respective constructors.

Bound Functions

A function that is bound to a target variable using bind as shown in Listings 9-10 and 9-11 is different from a "bound" function, which will have the bound keyword in its definition. In this section you'll see how the behavior of a bound function is different from the normal bind function. First, Listing 9-12 shows an example of an ordinary bind function.

Listing 9-12. A standard bind function

```
var name1 = "JavaFX";
var name2 = "Technology";
var filler = "Cool";

function concat(x: String, y: String) {
    "{x} {filler} {y}";
}

def s = bind concat(name1, name2);
println(s);
name1 = "Java";
println(s);
filler = "mature";
println(s);
```

Output
```
JavaFX Cool Technology
Java Cool Technology
Java Cool Technology
```

In Listing 9-12, you can see that when name1 changes, the function is invoked as we have seen in the previous examples. However, the body of the function is a black-box, and any change in the function's body does not cause the function to be reinvoked even though the function is bound. So with normal functions that are associated with a target variable through bind, recalculation happens only when the argument changes; bind does not really care about the expressions specified in the function body. This is why you don't see filler being changed to mature in the output, because the function is not invoked when filler is changed.

However, there are cases where one would expect bind to evaluate the function even if one of the expressions in the function's body changes. Nevertheless, this is a little expensive and should not be carried out by default unless the developer wants it explicitly. This is where bound functions come into the picture.

A bound function is invoked even when there is a change in one of the expressions specified in the function body and the arguments to the function do not change. Bound functions are explicitly marked with the **bound** keyword. The parameter-passing tips given for the normal **bind** functions apply to bound functions as well—parameters and return values are passed by reference (the memory address of the actual data) when the bound functions are invoked from a bound context and passed by value when they are invoked by the application explicitly.

Now let's change the previous example to use a bound function and see how the behavior changes; Listing 9-13 shows the code.

Listing 9-13. *A bound function*

```
var name1 = "JavaFX";
var name2 = "Technology";
var filler = "Cool";

bound function concat(x: String, y: String) {
    "{x} {filler} {y}";
}

def s = bind concat(name1, name2);
println(s);
name1 = "Java";
println(s);
filler = "mature";
println(s);
```

Output
```
JavaFX Cool Technology
Java Cool Technology
Java mature Technology
```

As you see in Listing 9-13, now the **concat()** function has a **bound** prefix, and **bound** is a keyword. Thus, the last output indeed reflects the new **filler** value and indicates that the function was called when the **filler** value changed.

▓ **Note** Although bound functions look appealing, they come with a cost in performance and therefore should be used with caution. While using bound functions, the developer has to be sure under what circumstances the function will be invoked and when the expressions given within the function body are bound to change.

Binding with Object Literals

As you saw in Chapter 6, "Class Definitions," JavaFX supports class definitions similar to Java, and you can create your own classes. Unlike Java, however, JavaFX does not expect everything to be bundled within a class, and it is possible to have a FX application without any class definitions. Let us see some examples of how binding can be used with these classes.

For example, Listing 9-14 demonstrates how you create a class.

Listing 9-14. *Creating a class*

```
class Employee {
    var name: String;
    var age: Number;
    var department: String;
    var id: Number;
}
```

Now let's see how to create an instance of the class.

```
var emp = Employee {
    name: "Praveen"
    age: 44
    department: "JavaFX"
    id: 334455
};
```

Note that we will have to use the colon character (:)instead of equal to when initializing the object literal. It is legal to omit the initialization of some of the attributes of the class if desired, and those attributes will be assigned with default values.

Now instead of hard-coding the department name for each employee, we could store it in some variable and share it across all employee instances. Let's see how binding helps in this case; Listing 9-15 shows the code.

Listing 9-15. Binding with object literals

```
var deptName = "JavaFX";
var empNames = ["Richard", "Praveen", "Lawrence", "Steve"];
var emp:Employee[] = [];

class Employee {
    var name: String;
    var age: Number;
    var department: String;
    var id: Number;

    function printInfo() {
        println("{name}, {age}, {department}, {id}");
    }
}

emp = for (x in [0..3]) {
    Employee {
        id: x
        name: empNames[x]
        department: bind deptName
        age: 34
    }
```

```
        }

        for (e in emp) e.printInfo();
        deptName = "JavaFX BU";
        println("----------------");
        for (e in emp) e.printInfo();
```

Output
```
Richard, 34.0, JavaFX, 0.0
Praveen, 34.0, JavaFX, 1.0
Lawrence, 34.0, JavaFX, 2.0
Steve, 34.0, JavaFX, 3.0
----------------
Richard, 34.0, JavaFX BU, 0.0
Praveen, 34.0, JavaFX BU, 1.0
Lawrence, 34.0, JavaFX BU, 2.0
Steve, 34.0, JavaFX BU, 3.0
```

In Listing 9-15, we create four instances of the Employee class and bind the department name to the deptName variable. So initially, all four instances are created with JavaFX as the department name. That's what you see in the output. Then we change the deptName value to JavaFX BU, and you see that all four instances are getting updated to the new department name.

This example demonstrates binding at the object level. However, it is also possible to define the binding at the class level so that it applies to all the objects created. Listing 9-16 is an example showing how class-level binding is achieved for members of the class.

Listing 9-16. *Class-level binding*

```
class Cube {
    var x: Number;
    var y: Number;
    var z: Number;
    var area: Number = bind x * y * z;
}

var c1 = Cube {
    x: 10
    y: 10
    z: 10
}
var c2 = Cube {
    x: 2
    y: 2
    z: 2
}
println(c1.area);
println(c2.area);
c1.x = 11;
c2.y = 4;
println(c1.area);
println(c2.area);
```

Output
```
1000.0
8.0
1100.0
16.0
```

As you see in the output of this example, the variable `area` is a multiplication of x, y, and z across all instances of `Cube`, so there is no need to define it once per each instance. Changing the x, y, z values of the cube would automatically recalculate the value of `area` for the respective instance of the class.

What we have seen here is an attribute-level binding within the class or instance. However, this would not be possible in certain cases, such as when the respective attribute is a `public-init` attribute. Such objects are described as *immutable*, and `public-init` attributes can only be initialized once and cannot be bound or assigned. Binding would still be possible in such cases, but in that case the entire object has to be bound . Let's see how this works; Listing 9-17 shows the code.

Listing 9-17. Binding immutable objects

```
class MyCircle {
    public-init var centerX: Number;
    public-init var centerY: Number;
    var radius: Number;

    init {
        println("Init Called");
    }
    override function toString() {
        "centerX: {centerX}, centerY: {centerY}, radius: {radius}";
    }
}

var cx = 100.0;
var cy = 100.0;
var r = 50.0;

var circleObj = bind MyCircle {
    centerX: cx
    centerY: cy
    radius: r
}

println(circleObj);
cx = 200;
println(circleObj);
cy = 200;
println(circleObj);
r = 30;
println(circleObj);
```

Output
```
Init Called
centerX: 100.0, centerY: 100.0, radius: 50.0
Init Called
centerX: 200.0, centerY: 100.0, radius: 50.0
Init Called
centerX: 200.0, centerY: 200.0, radius: 50.0
Init Called
centerX: 200.0, centerY: 200.0, radius: 30.0
```

In this example, we have used the `bind` keyword not for the attribute but for the whole instance. This means that whenever there is a change in the values of `cx`, `cy`, or `r`, the whole object would be recreated and returned, since the individual attribute values cannot be changed. So as you see in the output, the init is called whenever we change the `cx`, `cy`, or `r` values, which indicates that a new object is being created. thus, `init` can be considered an equivalent of a constructor in a Java class that is called for every object creation.

There are many built-in immutable objects like this in the JavaFX APIs, such as `Font`, `RadialGradient`, `LinearGradient`, and so on, and this type of binding will come handy when dealing with those objects.

▓ **Note** Always keep in mind that object creation and disposal are costly operations, especially when there are more members in the class such as attributes and functions. Hence, this kind of binding must be used with caution since the whole object is recreated every time an attribute value changes.

Bidirectional Binding

So far we have only seen unidirectional binding, in which the expression on the right side is bound to the target variable on the left, and any change in the expression causes the target variable to change. This is unidirectional binding and all the examples we have seen so far are of this type. *Bidirectional binding* is a type of binding in which the variables on both the sides listen to each other's changes and change themselves accordingly. This way, the variables on the left and right sides always remain in sync, as shown in Figure 9-2.

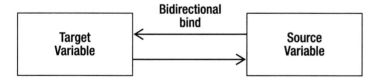

Figure 9-2. Bidirectional binding

The syntax of bidirectional binding is as follows:

```
var x = bind y with inverse
```

When the y value changes, the x value also changes, and vice-versa. Listing 9-18 is an example that demonstrates bidirectional binding.

Listing 9-18. Bidirectional binding

```
var name = "JavaFX";
var name1 = bind name with inverse; // indicates bidirectional binding
println(name1);
name = "Java";
println(name1);
name1 = "C++";
println(name);
println(name1);
```

Output
```
JavaFX
Java
C++
C++
```

In Listing 9-18, please note that the name1 variable is bound to name using with inverse, which means that if name changes, name1 will also change, and if name1 changes, name will likewise change. Also note the line name1 = "C++". The println after this line indicates that both name and name1 have changed to C++. If the binding were unidirectional, name1 = "C++" would have resulted in a runtime error, saying "cannot assign to bound variable."

IMPORTANT POINTS TO REMEMBER

There are three important points to keep in mind about bidirectional binding:

1. Bidirectional binding is implemented using the keywords with inverse.

2. One can assign to a bound variable if it is bound using with inverse. Unidirectional binding would normally throw an exception in this case.

3. When binding bidirectionally, it is better to use var instead of def since def variables cannot be assigned any value directly and might defeat the purpose of bidirectional binding.

Currently bidirectional binding is limited to objects and variables and not expressions. That's because the variables on both the left and the right must be assignable, and you cannot have an expression in place of variables, since no value can be assigned to an expression. This perhaps makes bidirectional binding less interesting for local variables, but it would be very useful in the case of objects.

Listing 9-19 shows an example of how bidirectional binding works with object literals.

Listing 9-19. *Bidirectional binding with objects*

```
class XY {
    var x: Number;
    var y: Number;
    override function toString() { "x: {x}, y: {y}" }
}
def pt1 = XY {
    x: 10
    y: 10
}
def pt2 = XY {
    x: bind pt1.x with inverse
    y: 0
}

println(pt1);
pt1.x = 20;
println(pt2);
pt2.x = 30;
println(pt1);
```

Output
```
x: 10.0, y: 10.0
x: 20.0, y: 0.0
x: 30.0, y: 10.0
```

Listing 9-19 is a classic example of how bidirectional binding works with object literals. As you see in the code, there are two instances of the XY class, and the x attribute of one of them is bound to the other. First pt1.x is changed, and that actually changes pt2.x. After that, pt2.x is changed, which changes pt1.x.

Because bidirectional binding is limited to just variables, it cannot be used with many of the expressions for which unidirectional binding works, such as the following:

- for expressions

- Conditional expressions

- Block expressions

- Arithmetic expressions

- Function expressions

Even though bidirectional binding looks fairly limited, it can still be very useful with objects and primitive types.

With bidirectional binding, you can also create a chain of bound objects up to any level, where one value change will trigger a sequence of changes in the chain of bound variables. Listing 9-20 is an example of bidirectional multi-level binding.

Listing 9-20. Bidirectional multi-level binding

```
var x1 = 10;
var y1 = bind x1 with inverse;
var z1 = bind y1 with inverse;

println("x1: {x1} y1: {y1} z1: {z1}");
x1 = 20;
println("x1: {x1} y1: {y1} z1: {z1}");
y1 = 30;
println("x1: {x1} y1: {y1} z1: {z1}");
z1 = 40;
println("x1: {x1} y1: {y1} z1: {z1}");
```

   Output
```
x1: 10 y1: 10 z1: 10
x1: 20 y1: 20 z1: 20
x1: 30 y1: 30 z1: 30
x1: 40 y1: 40 z1: 40
```

As you can see, x1, y1 and z1 are bound to one another, and any change in any of those values causes all other variable values to change.

Lazy vs. Eager Binding

So far what we have seen is *eager binding*, where regardless of whether the target variable is used or not, the bound expression will be recalculated when there is a change in the bound expression. But there is another type of binding, called *lazy binding*, where the recalculation will occur only when the target variable is accessed. Prior to JavaFX 1.3, it was left to the application developer to decide whether to go with eager or lazy binding, and if the developer chose to go with lazy binding, the expression had to be marked with the lazy keyword.

   Syntax
```
var <varname> = bind lazy <expr>
```

However, in JavaFX 1.3 the compiler has undergone lot of optimization and has the ability to choose eager or lazy binding depending on the expression being bound. Lazy binding offers high performance benefits and hence is made the default in JavaFX 1.3, so you don't have to specify the **lazy** keyword anymore. While it is said to be the default, there are places where lazy binding cannot be employed, especially if the value of a bound expression is consumed immediately within a trigger defined on the bound expression. Triggers are covered later in this book, but essentially, a trigger is a block of code, defined on a variable within the on replace block, that is executed whenever the value of the variable changes.

So when a bound expression changes, the value of the target variable changes and thus its trigger will immediately be called to consume the changed value. In such cases, the JavaFX compiler employs eager binding. So if you really want your binding to be eager for any reason, define a trigger on the target variable.

Let us see the exact difference between eager and lazy binding with a simple example. First, Listing 9-21 demonstrates lazy binding.

Listing 9-21. *Lazy binding*

```
var x = 10;
var val = bind multiplyByTen(x);
for (i in [1..4]) x ++;
println("val: {val}");

function multiplyByTen(y: Integer):Integer {
    println("function called {y}");
    y * 10;
}
```

Output
```
function called 14
val: 140
```

In this example, there is a function that is bound to a target variable, **val**, and takes a single argument, x. So in theory, **multiplyByTen()** is supposed to be called whenever the x value changes. This was the case prior to JavaFX 1.3. But with 1.3, the compiler optimizes this scenario to see if the returned value of the function is actually being consumed anywhere; it performs this check every time the function is invoked. In this case, we are just incrementing the x value five times, but the target value **val** (the consumer of the function's output) is not being used anywhere. So the compiler continues with incrementing x without calling the function. Finally, when we print the value of **val**, at that time the function is called with the last value of x, which is 14, and gets a return value of 140 from the function.

So by default, the bound expression is not evaluated immediately when one of its elements changes. Instead, it is evaluated when the result of the expression is being consumed, and that's what is called lazy binding.

However, if you want to restore the pre-1.3 behavior of eager evaluation, you will have to define a trigger on the target variable. Let us modify the previous example to make the evaluation eager, restoring pre-JavaFX1.3 behavior; Listing 9-22 shows the code.

Listing 9-22. *Eager binding*

```
var x = 10;
var val = bind multiplyByTen(x) on replace {
// Any code that may consume val, validate val
};
for (i in [1..4]) x ++;
println("val: {val}");

function multiplyByTen(y: Integer):Integer {
    println("function called {y}");
    y * 10;
}
```

Output
```
function called 10
function called 11
function called 12
function called 13
function called 14
val: 140
```

In this example, we have used triggers (on replace), a feature that you'll learn about in Chapter 11. For now, just remember that the block after on replace is executed whenever the value of the variable val changes. When you compare Listings 9-21 and 9-22, the only difference is the addition of the on replace clause to the bound expression, and you can see the difference in the output—the function is invoked for every change of x. The trigger indicates that the output of the bound expression is likely to be consumed almost immediately when an element of the expression changes, and so the compiler employs eager binding in this case.

So wherever you need eager binding, define a trigger on the bound expression.

Lazy binding makes execution far more optimized by minimizing the unnecessary evaluation of bound expressions for every bit of change, and in the process offers much better performance for your applications.

Summary

Binding is one of the most powerful features of JavaFX; it has the potential to simplify your code drastically when used wisely. It is commonly used to keep your UI in sync with the back-end model easily, which otherwise would have to be coded explicitly through listeners. You will see more examples of this in Chapter 12, "Introduction to JavaFX Graphics."

The success of binding depends on how judiciously it's been used in the application. Although it is one of the most powerful features in JavaFX, it often comes with a price in terms of performance, and indiscriminate use of bind can significantly bring down the performance of your application. JavaFX 1.3+ has far more performance optimizations, such as lazy evaluation of bound expressions by default, but still striking a good balance between the bind usage and the potential performance trade-offs is critical to the success of your RIA.

Nonetheless, binding when used appropriately will significantly ease development and help you avoid writing a lot of unnecessary code that would otherwise be needed to keep your UI objects in sync with the changing data in the back-end.

CHAPTER 10

■■■

Sequences

A JavaFX Script *sequence* is a special kind of data structure that, like an array in Java, represents an ordered list of items of the same type. But unlike Java arrays, JavaFX Script sequences are not objects. Like arrays, however, they hold elements (individual items in the sequence) of the same type.

Syntax
```
var sequence_name : datatype[];
```
or
```
var sequence_name : datatype[] = [value1, value2 .. value n];
```
or
```
var sequence_name = [value1, value2 .. value n];
```

The examples in Listing 10-1 show several ways to create and initialize a sequence.

Listing 10-1. Different ways of defining a sequence

```
1.    var emptySequence : Integer[];
2.     println(emptySequence);    // []
3.
4.    var intSequence : Integer[] = [2,4,6,8,10];
5.    println(intSequence);         // [ 2, 4, 6, 8, 10 ]
6.
7.    var inferenceSequence = ["Praveen", 'Girish' ,"Cheran" , 'Rabi' , "Lawrence" ];
8.    println(inferenceSequence);    // [ Praveen, Girish, Cheran, Rabi, Lawrence ]
```

In line 1 we create an empty sequence, which is represented as brackets: [ ]. In line 4 we define an Integer sequence named **intSequence** and initialize it. As you can see, a sequence is initialized by specifying its elements within the brackets. In line 7, we define an Inference-type sequence called **inferenceSequence**; this sequence holds String elements.

The sizeof Operator

After creating a sequence, we commonly need to know the number of elements it holds. So JavaFX Script provides a unary operator called sizeof, which returns the number of elements in a sequence.

Syntax
```
sizeof sequence name;
```

The example in Listing 10-2 demonstrates the usage of the sizeof operator.

Listing 10-2. Using the sizeof operator

```
1.    var emptySequence:Integer[];
2.    println("sizeof emptySequence = {sizeof emptySequence }"); // sizeof emptySequence = 0
3.
4.    var inferenceSequence = ["Praveen",'Girish', "Cheran" , 'Rabi' , "Lawrence" ];
5.    println("sizeof inferenceSequence = {sizeof inferenceSequence}"); // sizeof
inferenceSequence = 5
```

Line 2 prints 0 for emptySequence, since it doesn't have any elements, and line 5 prints the size of inferenceSequence as 5, since that variable holds five elements.

Accessing the Elements of a Sequence

Once you create a sequence, you may need to access its elements, either in a specific order, such as from the first element to the last, or randomly. You access an element of a sequence by specifying its index within square brackets ([ ]).

Syntax
```
sequence_name[index] ;
```

The example in Listing 10-3 demonstrates how to access the elements of a sequence.

Listing 10-3. Accessing the elements of a sequence

```
1.    var teamMembers : String[] = [
2.        "Praveen", "Lawrence", "Girish","Rabi","Cheran","Srini","Blessan"
3.    ];
4.    println("My team members");          // My team members
5.    for( i in [0.. sizeof teamMembers - 1] )
6.    println(teamMembers[i]);       //     Praveen
                                            Lawrence
                                            Girish
                                            Rabi
                                            Cheran
                                            Srini
                                            Blessan
```

In Listing 10-3, we declare a String sequence `teamMembers`. Each element of the sequence is accessed using its index, as in line 12. To access the element, we have used a **for** range expression, which starts from zero and ends with `sizeof teamMembers -1`.

Alternatively, you can use the following statements to access the elements of the sequence:
```
for( i in names  )
println(i);
```

Elements of a sequence can also be accessed randomly. For example, if you want to access the third element of the `teamMembers` sequence, you specify it as `teamMembers[2]`, which returns the value `girish`.

▪ **Note** Sequences are "zero based," which means they always starts from zero and end with a value of sizeof the sequence minus 1. For example, if the sequence has 100 elements, the first element is accessed by sequence[0] and the last element by sequence[99].

Nested Sequences

You might come across a situation where you need to combine sequences. When you do this, the JavaFX Script compiler automatically flattens all the sequences to form a single sequence.
The example in listing 10-4 demonstrates the nesting of sequences.

Listing 10-4. Sequence nesting

```
1.    var numSeq1 : Integer[] = [1,2,3];
2.    var numseq2 : Integer[] = [6,7,8,9,10];
3.    var numSeq3 : Integer[] = [ numSeq1 , 4,5, numseq2 ];
4.    println(numSeq1);    // [ 1, 2, 3 ]
5.    println(numSeq2);    // [ 6, 7, 8, 9, 10 ]
6.    println(numSeq3);    // [ 1, 2, 3, 4, 5, 6, 7, 8, 9, 10 ]
```

First we declare three sequences. The last sequence (numSeq3) holds numSeq1 and numSeq2 as individual elements (to form a nested sequence), as well as its own elements. When JavaFX Script executes line 3 it flattens numSeq1 and numSeq2 to form a single sequence, (numSeq3). This can be seen in the line 6 output statement.

Creating a Sequence Using a Range Expression

Range expressions can be used to create either Integer or Number sequences. You have already seen range expression in Chapter 4, "Operators and Expressions." Usually a range expression consists of a starting number, ending number, and optional step value. The step value may be either positive or negative (depending on the requirement); the default step value is 1.

Syntax
```
var sequence_name: datatype[] = [start value ..end value  step value];
```

The example in Listing 10-5 demonstrates how to create sequences using range expressions.

Listing 10-5 . Creating sequences using range expressions

```
1.    var intSeq : Integer[] = [1..10]; // default step positive 1
2.    println(intSeq );     // [ 1, 2, 3, 4, 5, 6, 7, 8, 9, 10 ]
3.    var intSeq1 : Integer[] = [0..100 step 10]; // step  10
4.    println(intSeq1);     // [ 0, 10, 20, 30, 40, 50, 60, 70, 80, 90, 100 ]
5.    var emptySeq : Integer[] = [100..0];  //empty sequence, since step is missing
6.    println(emptySeq);    // [ ]
7.    var intSeq2 : Integer[] = [100..0 step -10 ];
8.    println(intSeq2);     // [ 100, 90, 80, 70, 60, 50, 40, 30, 20, 10, 0 ]
9.    var numSeq : Number [] = [0.5 .. 5.0 step 0.5];  // number sequence
10.    println(numSeq);     // [ 0.5, 1.0, 1.5, 2.0, 2.5, 3.0, 3.5, 4.0, 4.5, 5.0 ]
```

In line 1, we declare an `intSeq` sequence whose value ranges from 1 to 10. Since we have not specified the step value, its default value of 1 is used. In line 3, we declare an `intSeq1` sequence, whose value ranges from 0 to 100 with a step value of 10. Next, in line 5, we declare an `emptySeq` sequence, whose range of values is from 100 to 0. Since the starting number of the range is greater than the end number and we have not specified the step value of this sequence, the result of this range expression is zero; hence, the sequence is empty. To avoid this type of empty sequence creation, it is mandatory to specify the step value of the range expression used to create the sequence. The correct version of the empty sequence is specified in line 7, with the sequence creation `intSeq2`. Finally, line 9 shows a `Number` sequence whose range value is from 0.5 to 5.0 with the step value of 0.5.

When you compile the code in Listing 10-5, you will encounter a warning that the expression will return an empty sequence.

▩ **Note** It's a good practice to specify the step value when creating a sequence using a range expression.

Excluding the End Value in the Sequence

Until now, the sequences that you have created using range expressions included the end value that you specified in the range expression. In some situations, you may need to exclude the end value when creating a sequence using a range expression. To do this, use two dots and a less-than relation operator (..<) in the range expression.

Syntax
```
var sequence_name :  datatype [] = [start value .. end value  step value];
```

The example in Listing 10-6 demonstrates how to create a sequence that excludes the end value of its range expression.

Listing 10-6. *Creating a sequence that excludes the end value of the range expression*

```
1.    var intSeq  : Integer[] = [1..< 10];
2.    println(intSeq ); // output [ 1, 2, 3, 4, 5, 6, 7, 8, 9 ]
3.    var intSeq1 : Integer[] = [0..< 90 step 10];
4.    println(intSeq1); // output [ 0, 10, 20, 30, 40, 50, 60, 70, 80 ]
```

In this example, we declare two sequences and create them using range expressions. In line 1, we have a range expression generating numbers from 1 to 10. While generating the range numbers from 1 to 10 each time, the JavaFX Script compiler checks the condition that generated numbers must be less than 10. Once the generated number reaches 10, then your range expression is stopped, since the condition has failed and the resulting sequence range is from 1 to 9. In line 3, we declare a sequence whose range number is from 0 to 80 with the specified step value of 10. This sequence holds the decade values from 0 to 80, since the condition for this range expression is < 90 and the step value is 10.

Sequence Slicing

Sequence slicing provides access to portions of a sequence. That is, using this technique you create from an existing sequence either a new sequence or an expression that evaluates to a sequence. The newly created sequence elements will be within the range, or equal to the existing elements, of the existing sequence. Usually sequence slicing consists of a sequence name (the existing sequence) or another expression that evaluates to a sequence, followed by a pair of square brackets which has a starting index with an optional ending index separated by two dots (..) or two dots with a less-than relational operator (..<). If the ending index is omitted, JavaFX Script interprets it as accessing all the elements of the sequence started from the specified starting index to the sizeof the sequence minus one.

The example in Listing 10-7 demonstrates sequence slicing.

Listing 10-7. *Sequence slicing*

```
1.    var s1 = [0..8];      // [0,1,2,3,4,5,6,7,8]
2.    var s2 = s1[4..];
3.    println(s2);          // [4,5,6,7,8]
4.    var s3 = s1s2[0..<];
5.    println(s3);          // [0,1,2,3,4,5,6,7 ]
```

In line 1, we declare a sequence s1, which holds the values from 0 to 8. In line 2, we are creating a new sequence (s2) from s1, and we are instructing the JavFX Script compiler to access all the elements of sequence s1 starting from index 4 to the sizeof s1 minus one. In line 4 we are creating a new sequence s3 from s2, in which we access all the elements of s2 starting from index 0 to the last element of s2 sequence; that is, from s2[0] to s2[sizeof s2-1].

Using a Predicate to Create a Subset of a Sequence

A *predicate* is a Boolean expression used to create a new sequence that is a subset of an existing sequence.

Syntax
```
var newSequence = existingSequence[variable | Boolean expression];
```

Here, *existingSequence* is the name of the existing sequence from which you are going to create a new sequence, which will be a subset of *existingSequence*, and assign it to *newSequence*. Notice the pair of square brackets ([ ]) that enclose a predicate in the format of a selection variable. Here, *variable* is just a placeholder within the square brackets that helps the compiler to evaluate *Boolean expression*. The vertical bar | character is used to visually separate the variable from *Boolean expression*. Finally, the *Boolean expression* specifies the criteria to be met before the current item will be copied into the new sequence.

The example in Listing 10-8 demonstrates creating a new sequence from an existing sequence using predicates.

Listing 10-8. Creating a new sequence from an existing one using predicates

```
1.    var integerSequence : Integer[] = [1..10 ];
2.    println(integerSequence);     // [ 1, 2, 3, 4, 5, 6, 7, 8, 9, 10 ]
3.    var subSequence1 = integerSequence[ n | n > 5 ];
4.    println(subSequence1);         // [ 6, 7, 8, 9, 10 ]
5.    var subSequence2 = integerSequence[ n | n < 5 ];
6.    println(subSequence2);         // [ 1, 2, 3, 4 ]
7.    var subSequence3 = integerSequence[ n | indexof n > 4 ];
8.    println(subSequence3);         // [ 6, 7, 8, 9, 10 ]
9.    var subSequence4 = integerSequence[ n | indexof n < 2 or indexof n > 7 ];
10.   println(subSequence4);         // [ 1, 2, 9, 10 ]
11.   var emptySequence = integerSequence[ n | n > 10 ];
12.   println(emptySequence);        // [ ]
```

■ **Note** The difference between sequence slicing and sequence predicates is that in sequence slicing, a range expression is used to create a new sequence, whereas in sequence predicates the vertical bar and a Boolean expression are used to create a new sequence from an existing one.

Working with Sequences

So far, you have created sequences either by explicitly specifying the elements of the sequence or by using range expressions. JavaFX Script also allows you to insert and delete the elements of the sequence dynamically. The following operations can be performed on a sequence:

- Inserting elements into the sequence

- Deleting elements from the sequence

- Reversing a sequence

Inserting an Element into a Sequence

An element can be inserted into a sequence dynamically using the **insert** and **into** keywords.

Syntax
```
insert element into sequence_name;

var  seq : Integer [] ;
insert 120 into seq;
insert 45 into seq;
```

In these statements we first create an empty Integer sequence, **seq**. in the later statements we insert the values 120 and 45 into the **seq** sequence. By default, elements are inserted at the end of a sequence. So when you print the **seq** sequence, you see the following output on the console:

```
[ 120 , 45 ]
```

Suppose you want to insert an element 75 as the first element of the sequence **seq**. To do that, you can use the following syntax:

```
Insert element before sequence_name[ index ] ;

insert 75 before seq[0];
insert 99 before seq[2];
```

In these statements, we are inserting the value 75 as the first element (**seq[0]**) and value 99 as the third element (**seq[2]**). We do this by using the keyword **before** and specifying the index within the sequence where we want to insert. The **before** keyword instructs JavaFX Script that you need to insert the element before the specified index in the sequence. When you print this **seq** sequence, you'll see the following output on the console:

```
[ 75, 120, 99, 45 ]
```

You can insert an element after a specified element in a sequence; this is done using the keyword **after**.

Syntax
```
insert element after sequence_name[index];
```

For example, in the following statements:

```
insert 67 after seq[1];
insert 78 before seq[1];
```

we are inserting 67 as the third element and 78 as the last element of the sequence **seq**. The final output of the **seq** sequence is as follows:

```
[ 75, 120, 67, 99, 45, 78 ]
```

An element or value can also be inserted into a sequence by specifying a negative index.

The examples in Listing 10-9 show how to insert elements into a sequence by specifying the index in different forms.

Listing 10-9. *Different ways of inserting elements into a sequence dynamically*

```
1.    var nums = [0..10];
2.    insert 65 after nums[sizeof nums+1];
3.    insert 23 after nums[sizeof nums];
4.    insert 77 after nums[sizeof nums - 1];
5.    insert 21 before nums[5];
6.    insert 97 after nums[0];
7.    insert 6 before nums[-1];
8.    insert 54 after nums[-2];
9.    println(nums);        // [ 54, 6, 0, 97, 1, 2, 3, 4, 21, 5, 6, 7, 8, 9, 10, 65, 23, 77
      ]
```

We are not restricted to inserting only a single element into a sequence; we can also insert a sequence into an existing sequence. The resulting sequence will be flattened, as you learned in the "Nested Sequences" section of this chapter.

The example in Listing 10-10 demonstrates how to insert a sequence as an element into another sequence.

Listing 10-10. *Inserting a sequence as an element into a sequence*

```
1.    var num : Integer[] = [1..4];
2.    var num1 : Integer[] = [5..10];
3.    insert num1 after num[2];
4.    println(num);        // [ 1, 2, 3, 5, 6, 7, 8, 9, 10, 4 ]
```

In this example, we declare two sequences, num and num1, using range expressions. In line 3 , we are inserting the num1 sequence after num[2].

Deleting an Element from a Sequence

Element of a sequence can be deleted dynamically, using the **delete** keyword. Following are different ways of deleting elements from a sequence:

- Specifying the element of the sequence.

- Specifying the index of the element in the sequence.

- Deleting the whole sequence.

- Deleting the elements using range expression.

Syntax
```
delete element from sequence_name;
delete    sequence_name[index];
```

The examples in Listing 10-11 demonstrate various ways of deleting elements from a sequence.

Listing 10-11. Ways of deleting elements from a sequence

```
1.    var fruits : String [] = ["Applet" , "Mango" , "Orange", "Grapes"];
2.    delete "Mango" from fruits;    // deleting the element by specifying the element
itself.
3.    delete fruits[1]; // deleting the element by specifying the index of the element
4.    println(fruits);       // [ Applet , Grapes ]
```

In line 1, we declare a String sequence named `fruits` with four elements. In line 2, we are deleting an element `Mango` from the sequence `fruits`; here `from` is a keyword that specifies from which sequence you are deleting the element. In line 3 , we are deleting the element by specifying its index within the sequence.

You can delete all of the elements in the sequence by specifying just the **delete** keyword followed by the sequence name, as in this example:

```
var fruits : String [] = ["Applet" , "Mango" , "Orange", "Grapes"];
delete fruits ;
```

Alternatively, you can use the following statement to delete all the elements of the sequence:

```
fruits = [];
```

You have learned how to create an Integer or Number sequence using a range expression. However, there may be situations where you need to delete a portion, or subset, of the sequence. In the previous the example of the `fruits` sequence, if you need to delete all the elements except `Grapes`, you can use the following statements:

```
delete fruits[0..2];
```

▦ **Note** The `delete` command only removes elements from the sequence; it does not delete the sequence from your script. You can still access the sequence and add new items to it as before.

Reversing a Sequence

JavaFX Script provides the **reverse** operator to reverse the order of elements in a sequence. The **reverse** operator produces a new sequence that contains the same elements as the original sequence but in reverse order.

Syntax
```
var sequence = reverse existingSequence;
```

The example in Listing 10-12 demonstrates how to reverse a sequence.

Listing 10-12. Reversing a sequence

```
1.    var namesSeq : String[] = ["Lawrence" , "Yinhe" , "Praveen" , "Vimala Anne"];
2.    var reversedNameSeq = reverse namesSeq; // returns the reversed sequence of namesSeq
3.    println(reversedNameSeq);    // [ Vimala Anne, Praveen, Yinhe, Lawrence ]
```

Here, line 2 returns the reverse of sequence nameSeq to reversedNameSeq. This new sequence has the same elements as namesSeq but in the reverse order.

Sequences as Function Parameters

Unlike Java and its handling of arrays, JavaFX Script allows sequences to be used as function parameters. When a sequence is sent as a parameter to a function, its elements are read-only, like any other parameter to the function. That is, trying to change the elements of the sequence, inserting and deleting them dynamically, will result in a compile-time error. A script-level, package-level sequence can be accessed by any function. Sequences defined within a function, by contrast, cannot be accessed outside the function.

The example in Listing 10-13 demonstrates the implementation of a stack using a sequence; the sequence is passed as a parameter to the function.

Listing 10-13. Implementing a stack using a sequence, by passing the sequence as a parameter to the function

```
1.    var stack: Integer[];
2.    function push(value : Integer){
3.        insert value into stack;
4.    }
5.
6.    function pop( ) {
7.        if(sizeof stack == 0 ){
8.            println("Stack underflow");
9.        }else {
10.            delete stack[sizeof stack -1];
11.        }
12.    }
13.
```

```
14.    function currentStackContent(stk : Integer[] ) {
15.        print(reverse stk);
16.    }
17.
18.    function peak() {
19.        if(sizeof stack == 0 ){
20.            println("Sorry..! there are no elements in the stack.");
21.        }else {
22.            println("\n { stack[sizeof stack -1] } is the topmost element
23.            in the stack.");
24.        }
25.    }
26.
27.    push(5);
28.    push(3);
29.    push(45);
30.    push(25);
31.    push(98);
32.    println("Content of the stack");    // Content of the stack
33.    currentStackContent(stack);         // [ 98, 25, 45, 3, 5 ]
34.    pop();
35.    peak();         //  25 is the topmost element in the stack.
36.    pop();
37.    println("Content of the stack");    // Content of the stack
38.    currentStackContent(stack );        // [ 45, 3, 5 ]
```

In Listing 10-13, the function push inserts an element into the stack; for each call of the push function the element is inserted at the end of the stack Integer sequence. The function pop deletes the last element of the stack using the sizeof operator before deleting the element, because we are checking for the availability of the element in the stack sequence. If the element is available, then the last element of the stack sequence is deleted. The function peep is used to check the last element of the stack sequence. The final and most interesting function is currentStackContent. It is used to display the elements of the stack sequence in reverse order (elements are printed in reverse order to achieve the last-in, first-out concept of stack implementation), where the sequence is sent as the parameter of the function, so that stack sequence is not modified.

Functions can also return a sequence as a return value. Let's modify the curentStackContent function so that it can return the reversed sequence.

```
function currentStackContent(stk : Integer[] ) : Integer[] {
    return reverse stk;
}
```

Function calls to currentStackContent should be modified accordingly.

Binding with Sequences

Unlike binding a variable, it is common to bind a sequence in JavaFX Script. When a variable is bound to an individual element of a sequence, any change either to the value of the element or its position (for example, when an element is inserted or deleted) is reflected in the bound variable.

The example in Listing 10-14 demonstrates how an element of a sequence is bound to a variable.

Listing 10-14. *Binding an element of a sequence to a variable*

```
1.    var seq = [10, 20, 30];
2.    var z = bind seq[1];     // z is bound to seq[1]
3.    println(seq);             // [ 10,20,30 ]
4.    println("z={ z }");       // z=20
5.    insert 55 before seq[1];
6.    println(seq);             // [10,55,20,30 ]
7.    println(" z={ z }");      // z=55
8.    seq[1] = 38;
9.    println(seq);             //[10,38,20,30]
10.   println(" z={ z }");      //z=38
11.   delete seq[1];
12.   println(seq);             // [10,20,30]
13.   println(" z={ z }");      // z=20
```

In line 2, the variable z is bound to the second element of the seq sequence, seq[1]. When a new element is inserted at the second position of seq as in line 5 , the z value changes, reflecting the insertion of a new element at position seq[1]. The z value changes even when the element is updated, as in line 8.

You know that a sequence can be created using a range expression; we can also bind the sequence values to the range expression, Any changes that apply to the range expression directly will reflect the values of the sequence.

Listing 10-15 demonstrates how sequence values are bound to the range expression.

Listing 10-15. *Binding the sequence values to the range expression*

```
1.    var num = 5;
2.    var seq1 : Integer[] = bind [1..num];
3.    println(seq1);     // [ 1,2,3,4,5 ]
4.    num = 10;
5.    println(seq1);     // [ 1,2,3,4,5,6,7,8,9,10 ]
6.    num = 6;
7.    println(seq1);     // [ 1,2,3,4,5,6 ]
```

Here, the seq1 is bound to the range expression, which goes from 1 to the value of num. As the value of num changes, the seq1 sequence values also change, as in lines 1, 4, and 6.

Just as binding can be applied between two variables, it can also be applied between two sequences. Any changes that occur to the source sequence, whether by inserting a new element, deleting an element, or any other change to the existing elements in the sequence, are reflected by changes in the destination sequence. In fact, even bidirectional binding can be applied between sequences, as demonstrated by the example in Listing 10-16.

Listing 10-16. Binding applied between two sequences

```
1.    var seq1  = [1..5];
2.    println(seq1);        // [ 1, 2, 3, 4, 5 ]
3.    var seq2  = bind seq1 with inverse;
4.    println(seq2);         // [ 1, 2, 3, 4, 5 ]
5.    insert 100 before seq1[3];
6.    println(seq1);        // [ 1, 2, 3, 100, 4, 5 ]
7.    println(seq2);        // [ 1, 2, 3, 100, 4, 5 ]
8.    insert 555 into seq2;
9.    println(seq1);        // [ 1, 2, 3, 100, 4, 5, 555 ]
10.    println(seq2);        // [ 1, 2, 3, 100, 4, 5, 555 ]
11.    delete 5 from seq1;
12.    println(seq1);        // [ 1, 2, 3, 100, 4, 555 ]
13.    println(seq2);        // [ 1, 2, 3, 100, 4, 555 ]
```

javafx.util.Sequences Utility Functions

The `javafx.util.Sequences` class in JavaFX Script contains various functions for manipulating sequences. All the functions in this `javafx.util.Sequences` class are *nonmutative;* that is, they do not change the input parameters, but create new instances for output.

Following are the functions of the `Javafx.util.Sequences class; you can see their descriptions in the API documentation:

- sort(*seq*)

- sort(*seq,comparator*)

- binarySearch(*seq, key*);

- binarySearch(*seq,key,comparator*)

- indexByIdentity(*seq,key*)

- indexOf(*seq,key*)

- isEqualByContentIdentity(*seq1, Seq2*)

- max(*seq*)

- max(*seq, comparator*)

- min(*seq*)

- min(*seq,comparator*)

- nextIndexByIdentity(*seq,key,pos*)

- nextIndexOf(*seq,key,pos*)

- reverse(*seq*)

- shuffle(*seq*)

Summary

A sequence is an ordered list of items of the same type. In that respect sequences are like arrays in Java, but with the difference that in Java arrays are objects and in JavaFX Script sequences are not. Elements of a sequence always start from the zeroth index and end at `sizeof` the sequence minus 1. Elements of the sequence can be defined explicitly in the declaration statement by enclosing them within square brackets ([ ]), or they can be inserted into the sequence dynamically using the `insert` keyword with the `before` and `after` keywords to specify a desired position. Likewise, elements of a sequence can be deleted using the `delete` keyword. Range expressions can be used to create a sequence. Sequence slicing provides access to portions (subsets) of a sequence. Predicates are Boolean expressions used to create a new sequence that is a subset of an existing sequence. A sequence can be reversed using the `reverse` keyword. Either a single element of the sequence or the whole sequence can be bound to a variable or to a sequence. Finally, the `Javafx.util.Sequence` class contains various functions for manipulating sequences.

CHAPTER 11

■■■

Triggers

A *trigger* is a block of code that is attached to a variable and executed whenever the value of the variable changes, including the assignment of the initial value. You can also optionally get hold of the old values that were replaced within the trigger. Triggers are very powerful and unique in JavaFX Script, just like bind. Triggers can be attached to normal variables as well as to sequences. First let us see how triggers work for simple variables and then proceed to complicated triggers and sequence triggers.

Defining a Simple Trigger

Here is the typical syntax of a trigger defined on a variable:

Syntax
```
var <var name>[:data type] [= <initial value>] on replace [old value] {
    // block of code to be executed on value change
}
```
or
```
var <var name>[:data type] [= bind expr] on replace [old value] {
    // block of code to be executed on value change
}
```

Up until on replace, both syntax forms are pretty much the same as any variable declaration. The on replace clause indicates that there is a block of code that must be executed whenever the value of *var name* changes. This is what is called a *trigger*.

■ **Note** Please note that "trigger" is just the name of the feature and not a keyword as such. It is typically represented by on replace.

Let us see a simple example of a trigger (Listing 11-1).

Listing 11-1. SimpleTrigger.fx

```
var name="Praveen" on replace {
    println("Name has changed");
    println("New Name: {name}");
}
name = "Lawrence";
```

Output
```
Name has changed
New Name: Praveen
Name has changed
New Name: Lawrence
```

In this example, we are defining a trigger on a variable called name. Typically you would expect this trigger to be invoked when you change the value of name. But as mentioned in the introduction, assigning an initial value is also considered a change. Hence, first the trigger is called when the name variable is assigned the value praveen. That contributes to the first two lines of the output. Right after the declaration, you are changing the value of name to Lawrence. This is another change, so the same trigger gets called again, printing the last two lines of the output.

At this point you may think that the trigger is called the first time because you are specifying an initial value yourself. That is not correct. It gets called even when the compiler assigns a default value.

■ **Note** For any variable, regardless of whether there is an initial value specified by the programmer or not, the trigger gets called during the variable initialization.

So even if you modify Listing-11-1 to the code shown in Listing 11-2, the trigger would still be called twice.

Listing 11-2. SimpleTriggerWithoutInitialization.fx

```
var name on replace {
    println("Name has changed");
    println("New Name: {name}");
}
name = "Lawrence";
```

Output
```
Name has changed
New Name:
Name has changed
New Name: Lawrence
```

As you see in the output of Listing-11-2, the first two lines are printed when the trigger is executed while initializing the object; that's why you see no name printed on the second line of the output. The last two lines are printed because of the application-triggered change.

A Trigger with Access to the Old Value

Now if you want to access the old as well as the new value of the name variable, you can do that by changing the original Listing 11-1 code as shown in Listing 11-3.

Listing 11-3. *TriggerAccessOldVal.fx*

```
var name = "Praveen" on replace oldName {
    println("Name has changed from old: {oldName} to new: {name}");
}
name = "Lawrence";
```

Output
```
Name has changed from old:  to new: Praveen
Name has changed from old: Praveen to new: Lawrence
```

In Listing 11-3, when the name is changed to a new value, the old value is assigned to the oldName variable before the trigger is called and passed to the trigger block. Note that oldName is just a variable name; it can be any name with which you want to access the old data of the variable. The oldName variable need not be declared upfront and can be implicit. However, please note that the scope of this variable is limited to the trigger block, and it cannot be accessed outside the block. Also note that this is like a final variable whose value cannot be modified within the trigger block. The sole purpose of this variable is to read the old value of the actual variable to which the trigger code is attached, and nothing beyond that. Trying to modify oldName within the trigger block would cause a compilation error.

Also note that you may have a variable already defined with the same name (oldName) outside of the trigger definition; that will not conflict with the one used in the trigger definition. These two variables will be treated separately, as you can see in Listing 11-4.

Listing 11-4. *TriggerVarNameSpace.fx*

```
var oldName: String = "JavaFX";

var name = "Praveen" on replace oldName {
    println("Name has changed from old: {oldName} to new: {name}");
}

name = "Lawrence";
println("OLD NAME: {oldName}");
```

Output
```
Name has changed from old:  to new: Praveen
Name has changed from old: Praveen to new: Lawrence
OLD NAME: JavaFX
```

As you see in the output of Listing 11-4, the `oldName` you have defined outside the trigger does not get changed, and what has been defined in the trigger definition is entirely a new variable.

To summarize, the trigger functionality can be pictorially represented as shown in Figure 11-1.

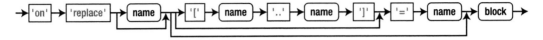

Figure 11-1. *Triggers in JavaFX Script*

This diagram precisely represents the `on replace` clause that constitutes a trigger. As you can see, it is the block between the first `name` clause and the last `block` clause. The use of sequences was explained in Chapter 10, "Sequences." The remaining clauses are pretty much self-explanatory. The first `name` clause is actually the name of the variable that gets the old value of the variable to which the trigger is attached. As you see in Figure 11.1, that `name` clause is optional, so you may choose not to get the old value.

Using Triggers with bind

There is no correlation between a trigger and `bind` as such, apart from the fact that the value of the variable changes through another variable or expression. Listing 11-5 shows a simple example of a trigger with `bind`.

Listing 11-5. *TriggerWithBind.fx*

```
var w = 10;
var h = 10;
var d = 10;
var isCube = true;
var area = bind if (isCube) {w*h*d} else {w*h} on replace  oldVal {
    println("Area Changed from: {oldVal} to {area}");
}
w = 20;
isCube = false;
d = 20;
```

Output
```
Area Changed from: 0 to 1000
Area Changed from: 1000 to 2000
Area Changed from: 2000 to 200
```

In this example, we have a variable `area` that is bound to a conditional expression and has a trigger attached to it. As you learned in the binding chapter, the value of area changes whenever any of the following changes: w, h, d, or isCube. The first line of the output is generated by the variable initialization. The second line is due to the w value changing to 30. After that, we are changing the value of isCube, which again causes a value change in `area` from w * h * d to w * h, yielding 200 (20 x 10). Next we are changing the value of d, which does not cause the trigger to be executed, because the conditional expression is evaluating the expression in the `else` part, which does not include d. So this behavior is correct and expected.

Implementing Binding Using Triggers

While binding can be combined with triggers, it is also possible to implement binding without actually using the bind keyword, using triggers. This kind of implementation is needed when you want the benefit of binding a variable to an expression without losing the flexibility of being able to assign some value directly to the variable. Let us see a simple example (Listing 11-6).

Listing 11-6. BindUsingTriggersError.fx

```
var x = 20;
var y = 30;
var sum = bind x + y on replace {
    println("Sum: {sum}");
}
x = 30;
//sum = 100; // Runtime error
```

Output
```
Sum: 50
Sum: 60
```

In Listing-11-6, we are binding an expression (x + y) to sum, and whenever the x or y value changes, sum will be recalculated. However, if you want the flexibility of overriding the value of sum, it is not possible. The moment you assign some value to sum, the JavaFX Runtime will throw an error, saying you cannot assign to a bound variable. In this case, you cannot do a bidirectional binding, either, since there is an expression on the right side. You may recollect that bidirectional binding is limited to variables.

So in this situation, it would be wise to hand-wire the binding yourself, using triggers. This way, you will have the flexibility to override the value of sum at any time. Let us modify Listing-11-6 to implement hand-wired binding using triggers, as shown in Listing 11-7.

Listing 11-7. BindUsingTriggers.fx

```
var x = 20 on replace {
        sum = x + y;
}
var y = 30 on replace {
    sum = x + y;
}
var sum = x + y on replace {
    println ("Sum: {sum}");
}
x = 30;
overrideSum(100);
function overrideSum(val: Integer) {
    sum = val;
}
```

Output

```
Sum: 20
Sum: 50
Sum: 50
Sum: 60
Sum: 100
```

In Listing 11-7, we have defined a trigger on x as well as y. So whenever the value of x or y changes, we recalculate the sum and assign it to the variable sum. So you pretty much get the same effect as if you'd entered bind x + y. At the same time, you are able to override the value of sum at any time, and here we are assigning a value of 100 through the overrideSum method. Perhaps, in a real-world API library, you could expose this method as public and the library user could actually override the value of sum if needed, from the application code while leveraging on the hand-wired binding.

Similarly, you can implement bidirectional binding as well using triggers. Listing 11-8 shows simple binding code that uses bidirectional binding and demonstrates how you can implement it yourself without using bind.

Listing 11-8. *BidirectionalBind.fx*

```
var name:String;
var name1 = bind name with inverse;
name = "JavaFX";
println ("Name: {name}, Name1: {name1}");
name1 = "Java";
println ("Name: {name}, Name1: {name1}");
```

Output

```
Name: JavaFX, Name1: JavaFX
Name: Java, Name1: Java
```

In this example, you see a simple bidirectional binding that binds two string variables, name and name1. If either of them changes, the other one also changes, as you see in the output.

Now let us implement the same binding using triggers (Listing 11-9).

Listing 11-9. *BidirectionalBindUsingTrigger.fx*

```
var name:String on replace {
    name1 = name;
}
var name1:String on replace {
    name = name1;
}
name = "JavaFX";
println ("Name: {name}, Name1: {name1}");
name1 = "Java";
println ("Name: {name}, Name1: {name1}");
```

Output

```
Name: JavaFX, Name1: JavaFX
Name: Java, Name1: Java
```

The output of Listing-11-9 looks exactly same as that of Listing 11-8, but as you see, Listing-11-9 uses triggers to simulate the effect of bidirectional binding. When looking at the code, you may initially think that this would cause an infinite loop—after all, we are changing one variable from the other trigger, causing the triggers to be called indefinitely. However, that is not what actually happens. Please note that when name is changed to JavaFX, name's trigger is called, and it sets name1 to JavaFX as well. This in turn calls name1's trigger, which tries to set name back to JavaFX. But since name's value is already JavaFX, technically there is *no change* in name's value. Thus name's trigger won't be called in this case.

■ **Note** A trigger is called only when there is a change in the value of the variable. If the variable is assigned the same value that it already holds, the trigger will not be called. In other words, if oldValue and newValue of a variable are the same, the trigger code is not executed.

The implementation of unidirectional and bidirectional binding using triggers provides a lot of flexibility, and you will find it very useful and handy in dealing with situations that demand both the power of binding and the flexibility of overriding the value of the bound variable. This technique also allows bidirectional binding of expressions that cannot be bound with the conventional with inverse clause.

Validation Within the Trigger

Triggers can be used effectively for validating the values of the variables to which they are attached, before the value is used in other bound expressions. When a variable is assigned a value, its trigger gets it first, before it is consumed by other expressions, and hence provides an opportunity to validate the values and eliminate the unwanted ones.

Listing 11-10 demonstrates a simple example of how to avoid a divide-by-zero scenario with triggers.

Listing 11-10. TriggerValidation.fx

```
var x: Number = 10;
var y: Number = 5 on replace oldVal {
    if (y <= 0) {
        y = oldVal;
        println("y value reset");
    }
}

var ratio = bind (x/y);
println(ratio);
y = 0;
println(ratio);
```

Output
```
2.0
y value reset
2.0
```

In this example, the variable `ratio` is bound to an expression (x/y). If the value of y happens to be 0, it would yield an undesirable ratio value of infinity. Hence it is important to validate the y value and reset it appropriately before the ratio is recalculated. The best way to do this is to define a trigger and check the value of y from within that trigger. If the Y value is not appropriate, you can revert back to `oldVal`. This change will cause another trigger call, of course. Triggers can be powerful validators of data values, providing an opportunity for the programmer to veto any value change. This is evident from the output, where y is reset to its old value when it is set to 0, and the value of `ratio` remains unchanged, since the y value has not changed, as needed to force a recalculation of the ratio expression (x/y).

Sequence Triggers

Triggers defined on a sequence are a little more complex than the triggers defined on a normal variable that we have seen so far. Defining a trigger within a sequence has additional clauses that provide you wider access to the data changed in the sequence, from within the trigger. Let us go from a simpler trigger to more complicated examples. You may want to refer back to the diagram given in Figure 11.1 at this point.

The syntax that we have used with normal variables is applicable to sequences as well. Listing 11-11 shows an example of a trigger defined on a sequence.

Listing 11-11. SequenceTrigger.fx

```
var seq = ['A', 'B', 'C', 'D', 'E', 'F'] on replace oldValue {
    println("Seq changed from {oldValue} to {seq}");
}
        1.   insert 'G' into seq;
        2.   delete 'C' from seq;
        3.   insert 'Z' before seq[0];
        4.   seq[1] = 'V';
        5.   seq[3..5] = ['H', 'J'];
        6.   delete seq[1..2];
```

Compile and run the code to see the following result. Note that (here and in the remaining examples) the line numbers are not part of the actual output; they are added for explanation.

Output
```
Seq changed from  to ABCDEF
1.   Seq changed from ABCDEF to ABCDEFG
2.   Seq changed from ABCDEFG to ABDEFG
3.   Seq changed from ABDEFG to ZABDEFG
4.   Seq changed from ZABDEFG to ZVBDEFG
5.   Seq changed from ZVBDEFG to ZVBHJG
6.   Seq changed from ZVBHJG to ZHJG
```

In Listing-11-11, there is a simple trigger defined on the sequence, and the old value of the sequence is obtained through the `oldValue` variable. Now let us analyze the output line by line:

The first line of the output (unnumbered) is due to variable initialization, and the old value is empty. You can relate each line of numbered code to the corresponding line in the output, as explained here.

Code line 1: Tries to insert `G` at the end of the `seq`, and in the output, you see the `seq` value changed from `ABCDEF` to `ABCDEFG`.

Code line 2: Deletes item `C` from the `seq` and you see that the old `seq` `ABCDEFG` changes to `ABDEFG` since `C` is now removed.

Code line 3: Inserts an item `Z` at the beginning of the `seq`, which causes the entire `seq` to change. You see that `Z` gets inserted into the sequence.

Code line 4: Replaces the item at index 1 (`A`), changing it to `V`. Now you see the new value as `ZVBDEFG`.

Code line 5: Replaces items at indices [3..5], which means `seq[3]`. `[4]`, and `[5]` with `['H', 'J']`. Hence `ZVBDEFG` changes to `ZVBHJG`.

Code Line 6: Deletes items at indices 1,2, which changes the sequence content to `ZHJG`.

This output is not complicated, and this is just a simple use of triggers with sequences, where you get the entire unmodified sequence in the `oldValue` variable. Apart from the actual sequence modified and the old sequence, you don't get much information here about which of the indices are updated.

Triggers become more powerful when you start including the additional clauses provided exclusively for triggers. Let us see the syntax of the trigger with new clauses defined:

Syntax

```
var <var name>[: data type[] ] [= value] on  replace [old value [= new element(s)]] { ...
}
```
              or
```
var <var name>[: data type[] ] [= value] on  replace [old value [[ firstIndex .. lastIndex ]
= new element(s)]] { ...
}
```

For both variations the syntax up to `on replace` is pretty much the same as any other example you have seen so far, except that the variable is of type Sequence here. The sequence-specific clauses follow `on replace`; let's examine those in the first syntax in detail:

old value: The implicit variable to which the old sequence value would be assigned. It is similar to the example in the section "A Trigger with Access to the Old Value." The *var* name could be anything.

= new element(s): Another variable, to which the new elements added to the sequence would be assigned. The new elements would be coalesced if there is more than one new element added to the sequence. The new elements can be elements inserted newly into the sequence or can replace a set of existing elements. If you want to have this clause, then *old value* is also required compulsorily.

So the usage of this syntax form would be as follows:

```
    on replace oldValue {}
```

or

```
    on replace oldValue = newElements { }
```

The second syntax format gives additional control over the range of values changed; let us see that clause in detail:

<old value>[startingIndex..endingIndex]: The starting and ending index variables are again just variable names and can be changed to any other variable name. These variables hold the starting and ending index of the sequence where the change has actually happened.

Now let us see an example of each of these syntax formats (Listing 11-12).

Listing 11-12. *SequenceTriggerNewSyntax1.fx*

```
1.   var seq = ['A', 'B', 'C', 'D', 'E', 'F'] on replace oldValue = newElements {
2.       println("Seq changed:  {oldValue} by {newElements} to {seq}");
3.   }
4.   insert 'G' into seq;
5.   delete 'C' from seq;
6.   insert 'Z' before seq[0];
7.   seq[1] = 'V';
8.   seq[3..5] = ['H', 'J'];
9.   delete seq[1..2];
```

Output
```
1.   Seq changed:    by ABCDEF to ABCDEF
2.   Seq changed:  ABCDEF by G to ABCDEFG
3.   Seq changed:  ABCDEFG by  to ABDEFG
4.   Seq changed:  ABDEFG by Z to ZABDEFG
5.   Seq changed:  ZABDEFG by V to ZVBDEFG
6.   Seq changed:  ZVBDEFG by HJ to ZVBHJG
7.   Seq changed:  ZVBHJG by  to ZHJG
```

In Listing 11-12, we have two variables being used after on replace : oldValue is used for getting the old value of the sequence, and newElements is used for getting the changed elements alone. The new sequence is of course, assigned to the seq variable itself.

When you look at the output, the oldValue printed is the value of the sequence before the actual change, and newElements prints out the elements that are added to the sequence—either new or replacing some of the existing elements. Note that newElements does not print anything when an element is deleted from the sequence (line 3 of the output). Another important point to notice is in line 6 of the output, which is triggered by line 8 from the code. This line tries to replace three elements in the sequence with two other elements, H and J. When you look at the output, these two new elements are coalesced to print HJ, and that's what has been assigned to newElements. Again the last line of output (line 7) does not print any newElements value, since it is triggered by a delete statement.

Now let us see the same example with the second syntax (Listing 11-13).

Listing 11-13. *SequenceTriggerNewSyntax2.fx*

```
1.    var seq = ['A', 'B', 'C', 'D', 'E', 'F'] on replace oldValue[fIndex..lIndex] =
newElements {
2.        println ("Seq changed:  {oldValue} [{fIndex}..{lIndex}] by {newElements} to
{seq}");
3.    }
4.    insert 'G' into seq;
5.    delete 'C' from seq;
6.    insert 'Z' before seq[0];
7.    seq[1] = 'V';
8.    seq[3..5] = ['H', 'J'];
9.    delete seq[1..2];
```

Output
```
1.    Seq changed:   [0..-1] by ABCDEF to ABCDEF
2.    Seq changed:   ABCDEF [6..5] by G to ABCDEFG
3.    Seq changed:   ABCDEFG [2..2] by  to ABDEFG
4.    Seq changed:   ABDEFG [0..-1] by Z to ZABDEFG
5.    Seq changed:   ZABDEFG [1..1] by V to ZVBDEFG
6.    Seq changed:   ZVBDEFG [3..5] by HJ to ZVBHJG
7.    Seq changed:   ZVBHJG [1..2] by  to ZHJG
```

In Listing 11-13, the same code shown in Listing-11-12 has been modified to include the range information as well, and with these new clauses, you can precisely identify which part of the sequence is modified. Now let us analyze the output in detail:

Line 1: Triggered by the variable initialization.

Line 2: Triggered by Line 4 from the code, where a new element is inserted into the sequence. The first index changed is actually the new index created by the new element, 6,' and it does not affect any other indices. Hence, the range is shown as [6..5], which denotes the newElements value of G.

Line 3: Caused by deleting the element C at index 2. It is a removal of an element and hence the newElements would not yield a valid value. The impact is just on a single element and hence the range shows [2..2]

Line 4: Caused by inserting Z into the seq at the first index. Pretty much the same behavior as line 2.

Line 5: Caused by replacing A with V at index 1. This is again a change at a single index, and so the range is [1..1]. However, since V is a new element added, newElements returns V.

Line 6: Caused by replacement of three values (index 3, 4, 5) with two values (H, J). The affected indices are 3,4,5, so the range is [3..5]. New elements added to the seq are coalesced and returned as newElements.

Line 7: Two elements have been deleted, so the affected index range shows [1..2]. Since it is a deletion, newElements is empty.

■ **Note** The syntax [firstIndex..lastIndex] denotes a range within which the values/elements are changed within the sequence. This does not represent the index changes as such. For example, deleting an element at index-2 will change the indices of all the subsequent elements. That is not typically captured in the [firstIndex..lastIndex] range, which captures the indices of elements whose values were changed.

Now let us see another example that makes use of `bind` and `for` loops to create a sequence; we will define a trigger on that sequence. Listing 11-14 shows the code.

Listing 11-14. SequenceTriggerWithBind.fx

```
var min = 0;
var max = 5;

def seq = bind for (x in [min..max]) " {x*x}" on replace oldVal[sindx..eindx] =
newElm {
    println("Seq changed from {oldVal} [{sindx}..{eindx}] by {newElm} to {seq}");
}
min = 5;
max = 8;
```

Output
1. Seq changed from [0..-1] by 0 1 4 9 16 25 to 0 1 4 9 16 25
2. Seq changed from 0 1 4 9 16 25 [0..4] by to 25
3. Seq changed from 25 [1..0] by 36 49 64 to 25 36 49 64

In Listing 11-14, we are creating a sequence dynamically through a `for` expression that is bound to the `seq` variable. Note that the `seq` variable is a `def`, meaning that its definition is constant throughout the application life-cycle. Now we have defined a trigger on the sequence with access to the old value, start index, end index, and new element. The `min` and `max` values used in the `for` expression are bound, and so any automatic change to those values would cause the trigger to be executed. Now let us analyze the output in detail.

The initial sequence as shown in line 1 of the output consists of squares of [0, 1, 2, 3, 4, 5]. Now when the `min` value changes to 5, the sequence pretty much reduces to squares of [5..5], which is [25]. That's what has been shown in line 2 of the output. NewElm is empty because it is a removal operation. Now when you look at the difference between lines 1 and 2, the sequence size is reduced from 6 to just 1, and all items except the last one are removed. That's represented by the range [0..4] in line 2. Line 3 of the output represents the range of [5..8] when the `max` value is set to 8. This does not cause any change to the existing value but inserts three more values, which are represented by the `newElm` variable as 36 49 64. The final `seq` shows all the values inserted into the sequence.

Nested Triggers

A trigger can be defined on any variable regardless of where it is declared. It can be defined on a member variable of a class, on a script variable, on a local variable declared within a function, block, and so on. One can also define a trigger within another trigger since a trigger is just another block. Also, it is possible to change the value of a variable from within its own trigger.

Listing 11-15 shows a simple example of how nesting can be implemented.

Listing 11-15. *NestedTriggers.fx*

```
1.    class TriggerSample {
2.        var w = 100 on replace oldVal {
3.            var valid = isValid(w) on replace {
4.                if (not valid) {
5.                    println("Invalid value {w}. Reset to {oldVal}");
6.                    w = oldVal;
7.                } else {
8.                    println("Valid value {w}");
9.                }
10.                println(w);
11.            }
12.        }
13.    }
14.    function isValid(val: Integer) {
15.        val > 0;
16.    }
17.    function run() {
18.        var sample = TriggerSample{};
19.        sample.w = 200;
20.        sample.w = 0;
21.    }
```

Output
```
1.   Valid value 100
2.   100
3.   Valid value 200
4.   200
5.   Invalid value 0. Reset to 200
6.   Valid value 200
7.   200
8 200
```

In Listing 11-15, we are defining a variable w as a member of a class, whose value we are validating within the trigger and resetting it if it is invalid. So there is another trigger defined within the main trigger here, and the nested trigger validates the value of w. As you see in the code, the inner trigger calls a script-level function to validate the value. Now let us analyze the output.

Line 1, 2: Printed when w is initialized.

Line 3: Setting w to 200 in the code calls the trigger, and this value has been validated to true.

Line 4: W is set with the value of 200 after validation.

Line 5: Sets a value of 0 to w. The isValid() function is called and returns false. Since the value is invalid, we are resetting the value to back to 200 (the old value).

Line 6: Note that 200 is not printed yet, which means line 9 from the code is not yet executed. This is because resetting the w value within the validation trigger calls the main trigger again, and this time isValid returns true for the reset value of 200.

Lines 7, 8: 200 is printed twice—once for the reset operation (caused by the inner trigger) and another time for the actual value set by the application (w = 0).

There are a few more things to note in this example: the script-level function isValid() is accessed from within the trigger, a nested trigger is used to validate the value, and the value of the variable is changed from within the same trigger. Also note that the variable w is accessible within the inner trigger of valid, and this is true for any block—it can access the variables of the parent block.

■ **Note** You have to be careful when setting the value of a variable within its own trigger. If the value that is set within the trigger is incremental, that will cause the trigger to be called infinitely. For example, var w on replace { w = w + 1 } will cause the trigger to be called indefinitely and will result in a StackOverflowError.

Summary

In this chapter, you have examined in detail what triggers are. A *trigger* is a block of code that is attached to a variable and is executed when the value of the variable changes. You can access the old value of the variable within the trigger block and you can validate the new value assigned to the variable before it is consumed by other expressions. Triggers on sequences provide more control over the change by exposing the affected range, the old value of the sequence, and the new elements inserted into the sequence. You can define a trigger within another trigger, and the inner trigger can access the variables of the parent trigger. Triggers can be defined on any variable that is part of a class, script, block or function. You can also use triggers to implement your own binding, and you can do both unidirectional and bidirectional binding.

Thus, triggers are one of the most powerful and unique features of JavaFX Script; they can help you create an event-driven logic typically like an EventListener in Java AWT and Swing. Triggers are most widely used in animations in JavaFX, and you will see more of this in Chapter 13, "introduction to Animation."

With this chapter , you have been introduced to all the important features of JavaFX Script, and we have come to the end of our introduction to the language. In the next two chapters, we will dive deep into the JavaFX Graphics and Animation APIs, and you'll see how you can develop a full-fledged rich UI application using JavaFX Script.

CHAPTER 12

■ ■ ■

Introduction to JavaFX UI Elements

As you have learned, JavaFX is a rich client platform for creating and delivering immersive Internet experiences across different screens. So far, you have learned the JavaFX Script language capabilities and features and in this chapter, we will introduce you to various graphics APIs in JavaFX that help you build a rich Internet application. Before going into the actual APIs, you must understand how the APIs are classified in JavaFX. There are two broad categories of the APIs in JavaFX that you will learn in this chapter:

- common profile
- desktop profile

Common profile APIs include classes that work across devices such as desktop, mobile, and TV. So if you are developing an application that is expected to work across multiple screens, you will have to stick only to common profile APIs. But if you are developing a desktop-specific application, you can take advantage of the desktop profile APIs to add specific functionality that enhances your application further for the desktop.

JavaFX common profile graphics offer a richer and wider range of functionality to cater to varied needs of an RIA and the scope of the features extend from drawing basic geometric shapes to virtually any shape, multiple fill and pen styles, enhanced text and imaging capabilities, extensive color definition and composition, multi-stop linear and radial gradience, prefabricated graphical charts, event handling supporting mouse and keyboard interactions across all the UI elements, most standard UI controls of an enterprise UI with multiple layouts, and all kinds of two-dimensional transformations required by the RIA. All these features are built on top of a device-agnostic rendering model, thus making the look and feel uniform across screens.

Here is the broad categorization of the common profile graphical APIs:

- Geometries
- Fill and Stroke Styles
- Colors
- Paints
- Text
- Image
- Charts

- UI Controls

- Input

- Transformations

- Layouts

On the desktop side, JavaFX Graphics provides a way to reuse your existing swing components within your JavaFX application and also offers a richer set of advanced effects such as Lighting, Shadow, Glow, Blur, and so forth that you can apply to any UI element.

The desktop profile graphics APIs can broadly be classified into the following:

- Effects

- Swing Controls

In this chapter, we will go through all the common profile APIs in detail and briefly touch upon some of the desktop-specific APIs as well.

Rendering Model: Immediate Mode vs. Retained Mode Rendering

JavaFX adopts the Retained Mode rendering model where the graphical data is maintained in a data model within the library. Any application-triggered repainting does not directly render the entire UI as is the case with immediate mode rendering, but updates the underlying data model and renders only the required portion of the data model to the display. This is far more optimized than the immediate mode rendering model, where the client code would directly cause the UI elements to be rendered to the display. For example, Java2D Graphics uses immediate mode rendering and the client code has to take care of the rasterization of the UI elements (obtain a graphics context and drawing to it yourself). With retained mode rendering, it is not the actual data that is being transferred to the GPU (Graphical Processing Unit), but only a command that tells which portion of the retained data model has to be updated. At the application level, the rendering process is the same whether the target rendering device is desktop or mobile or TV.

Scene Graph

JavaFX uses the popular *scene graph* data model typically used in 3D graphical systems to implement the retained mode rendering. A scene graph is a device-independent data model that allows the programmers to define what UI elements they need and where they want them to be displayed and the actual rasterization is taken care of internally. In a scene graph, all the UI elements (a.k.a. Nodes) are represented hierarchically in a tree/graph data structure, as seen in Figure 12-1.

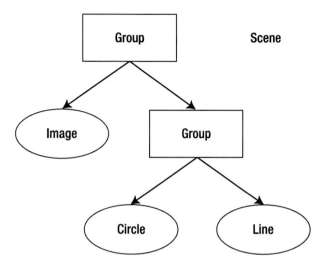

Figure 12-1. *Scene graph containing different nodes*

An example of a scene graph is given in Figure 12-1. A node in the scene graph can have zero or one parent and each node in the scene graph can either be a "leaf" node with no children or a "branch" node with one or more children. A node that does not have a parent is referred to as the "root" node. A scene graph may have multiple trees and only a single node within each scene graph tree can be a root node. For example, the Circle object in Figure 12-1 is a leaf node, the Group object that is a sibling of Image is a branch node, and the other Group object that is the parent of all other nodes is the root node. The root node is added directly to the scene and a scene may have many such root nodes and hence many trees within the scene graph. For example, similar to Figure 12-1, you may have multiple Group nodes added to the scene, in which case each of the Group nodes will be a root of its own tree. What is shown in Figure 12-1 is just a single tree in the scene graph. Any effect such as transformations, clipping, and so forth applied to a parent would implicitly be applied to all its children.

JavaFX scene graph is generic enough to support animations, transformations, clipping, and effects in addition to different node types. The JavaFX SceneGraph implementation has lot more optimizations fine-tuned toward RIAs and hence delivers a superior visual performance than other conventional scene graphs.

A scene graph is exposed to the application through the '**javafx.scene.Scene**' class.

Scene

Scene is the root of the entire scene graph to which you will add your visual elements and it represents the drawing surface. If you are comfortable with Java, you can assume the drawing surface to be something equivalent to '**java.awt.Canvas**' or '**javax.swing.JPanel**'. The **javafx.scene.Scene** class has a **content** attribute that holds all the graphical elements to be displayed. While you assume Scene to be something equivalent to Canvas, in reality you don't have to worry about what it represents internally since JavaFX abstracts those details from the programmer. All you need to do is just to add your visual elements to the scene's content attribute and Scene takes care of drawing them.

Stage

Just having a drawing surface or a scene graph is not sufficient for drawing the visual elements to the display and you still need a top-level container to show it on the screen. You can correlate this back to Java where you would add the 'Canvas'/'JPanel' to a top-level container such as '**java.awt.Window**' or '**javax.swing.JFrame**'. Similarly, Stage (**javafx.stage.Stage**) in JavaFX is an equivalent of the top-level container that holds the drawing surface. What it represents internally is platform-dependent and as a programmer, you don't have to worry about it. Once you have the scene, just associate it to the **scene** attribute of the **Stage** class. A Stage can have only one scene at any point in time but you can change the scene anytime.

■ **Note** Both Scene and Stage offer width/height attributes, but there are subtle differences between the two. A Scene's width/height can only be initialized and cannot be assigned or bound, whereas a Stage's width/height can be bound (must always be bi-directional) and assigned. Another difference is in terms of the actual client area. The width/height set on a Stage does take into consideration the decorations, title bar, and insets and hence the actual area of the drawing surface will be lesser on a desktop and more on platforms where there is no decoration. But in the case of setting Scene's width and height, the drawing surface is guaranteed to have the same size across devices and platforms regardless of whether the Stage is decorated or undecorated. Hence, it is recommended to always specify the required size on the Scene instead of the Stage if you want your application to behave consistently across devices.

Coordinate System

The two-dimensional coordinate system in JavaFX is same as any other graphical system as far as user space is concerned. User space is the coordinate system with which an application developer writes the UI and device space is the coordinate system of the actual device. As an application developer, you need to be bothered only about the user space and the underlying rendering engine will take care of translating the coordinates to the target device space appropriately at the time of rasterization.

In the user space, the coordinate system is right-handed, with its origin (x, y) (0,0) at the top left corner of the display and the orientation semantics being that +y is the local gravitational down and +x is horizontal to the right, as shown in Figure 12-2.

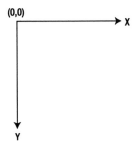

Figure 12-2. *Coordinate system (user space)*

While this looks straight-forward, there is a small caveat here. The SceneGraph supports multiple coordinate systems such as local, parent, and scene, with local being specific to a leaf node, parent coordinate system is that of its parent, and scene is that of the scene to which this node belongs. Nonetheless, all the coordinate systems have the same orientation as shown in Figure-12-2. You will uncover the actual difference later in this chapter, but for now, just remember the orientation given in Figure 12-2.

Since 1.3, JavaFX also offers a basic 3D support with which you can apply three-dimensional transformations on nodes. Additionally, 3D coordinate system will have a Z axis that runs from (0,0) toward you, the reader.

Graphical API Summary

JavaFX offers a wide range of functionality to cater to varied requirements of RIA. In this section, you will see a summary of all the graphics-related packages available in JavaFX with a brief description of what they offer, in Table 12-1. You will find more detailed explanations of the APIs as you read through this chapter further.

Table 12-1. *Graphics API Summary*

Package	Description
javafx.scene	Contains a set of base classes of the scene graph hierarchy such as Node, CustomNode, Parent , and so forth and also the Scene class that represents the scene graph.
javafx.scene.shape	Offers multiple classes for defining geometric primitives such as rectangle, circle, curves, paths, polygons and so forth. The abstract definition of all geometric primitives is provided by the Shape class.
javafx.scene.paint	Offers various color- and paint-related classes that are used to fill and stroke the geometric primitives and text. Includes gradients such as Radial and Linear.
javafx.scene.text	Contains classes that offer text-rendering capabilities and classes that allow to customize the font and text layouts used in text rendering.
javafx.scene.transform	Offers advanced transformation capabilities such as scale, shear, rotate, and translate that you can apply on a node. Transformations can be in two- or three-dimensional space. Most basic transformation needs are addressed with convenience attributes that are part of the Node class, but you can achieve any additional, more customized transformations using this package.
javafx.scene.image	Offers Image loading and rendering capabilities.

Continued

Package	Description
`javafx.scene.control`	Offers a wide range of UI controls such as Button, CheckBox, RadioButton, and so forth, that enterprise RIAs can leverage on.
`javafx.scene.layout`	Offers a wide variety of built-in layouts that take care of organizing the nodes in terms of position and size. Also offers customizable layouts where the application will decide how to organize the nodes.
`javafx.geometry`	Contains classes that represent the node dimensions, bounds, and position in two- or three-dimensional coordinate space.

`javafx.scene.chart`
`javafx.scene.chart.data`
`javafx.scene.chart.part`
	Offers APIs for creating and managing various charts such as BarChart, LineChart, PieChart, and so forth and their customization.

`javafx.scene.effect` `javafx.scene.effect.light`	Offers advanced graphical filter effects that you can apply on one or more nodes to create a rich desktop experience. These APIs are **desktop only**.
`javafx.scene.input`	Offers APIs for supporting keyboard and mouse interactions for any node.
`javafx.ext.swing`	Offers wrapper classes for many swing equivalents. However, many such wrappers are obsolete and replaced by UI control equivalents that are pure JavaFX implementations that offer a uniform user experience across platforms. But these wrappers can be useful if you want to reuse some swing control that is already built and being used in a Java application. All these classes are **desktop only**.

Node – The Base UI Element

Any UI object in JavaFX must extend from a base class–**javafx.scene.Node**–in order to be added to a scene graph and rendered on the screen. The **Node** class abstracts all the common features shared by all the UI elements and all other nodes inherit these attributes and functions from the **Node** class. As you read in the "Scene Graph" section earlier in this chapter, each element added to a scene graph (or Scene from the application standpoint, since scene graph is exposed through the Scene class) must be an object of Node or its subclass. Some examples of Leaf nodes are **javafx.scene.shape.Rectangle,** **javafx.scene.image.ImageView**, and so forth, and these nodes cannot have any children. Branch/Parent nodes are nodes that extend from the **javafx.scene.Parent** class and can contain a set of children and hence form a new branch in the scene graph. Some examples are **javafx.scene.Group**, **javafx.scene.CustomNode**, or sub-classes of these node types. All UI controls extend from the **Parent** class. A node can occur only once within the content of the scene or parent or Group. Trying to add the same node more than once to a same parent or scene will result in a runtime error. Similarly, trying to add a node from one parent to another parent will cause the node to be silently removed from the old parent and added to the new parent. Also, there must not be any cycles in the scene graph where the node is an ancestor of itself in the scene graph. Such cycles will also cause a runtime error. All these restrictions are clearly documented in **javafx.scene.Node**'s class description.

The Node class defines many attributes and functions, some of the important ones of which are shownin Table 12-2. Attributes that require a detailed explanation such as transformations, bounds, events, blocksMouse, and so forth, will be dealt with separately later in this chapter.

Table 12-2. Node Attributes

Attribute	Type	Default Value	Description
id	String	Empty string	A String identifier for a node, just like the "id" element in HTML. This identifier must be unique within the scene graph and it is the responsibility of the application to ensure that. This can be used to lookup for a particular node within a scene graph using the Scene.lookup() method.
visible	Boolean	TRUE	Indicates whether a node is visible or not.
opacity	Number	1	Defines the transparency of the node. A value of "'1.0" indicates the node to be opaque and "0.0" indicates that the node is fully transparent. A transparent node can still receive mouse and keyboard events and can respond to user input.
clip	Node	Null	If specified, this node will be clipped by the geometry of the given node.
disable disabled	Boolean	FALSE	"disable" indicates whether this node is expected to respond to user interactions. If false, the mouse and keyboard events are ignored for this node. It is up to the application to change the visual representation of the node when disabled and for some cases, such as Controls, this is handled implicitly.
			"disabled" is a read-only attribute that is set to true when the node or its parent is disabled. "disable" takes into consideration only the disabled state of this particular node, whereas "disabled" takes into consideration the disabled state of its parent as well. One can track the value of "disabled" to change the visual appearance appropriately.
parent	Node	Null	Gives the parent of this node in the scene graph. If this node is directly added to the Scene or not yet added to the Scene, parent will be null.

Geometries

JavaFX offers several classes that define common geometric objects (shapes), such as lines, curves, ellipses, rectangles, circles, and so forth. All the built-in geometric objects are grouped under the '**javafx.scene.shape**' package. There are many attributes shared by multiple shapes and all such attributes are abstracted in the base class–**javafx.scene.shape.Shape**. Hence, all the geometric shapes extend from the **javafx.scene.shape.Shape** class and this class provides a common protocol for defining and inspecting multiple geometric objects. With the help of multiple shape objects, you can virtually define and use any two-dimensional geometric object. A shape's contour is defined as its path.

The Shape base class primarily defines the stroke-and fill-related attributes that are shared by all the shapes and you need to understand the difference between a stroke and fill.

Stroke vs. Fill

A stroke defines how the contour (or outline) of a shape is drawn and what kind of pen style to be used when drawing the outline. On the other hand, a fill defines the filling pattern, which is basically the pattern with which the geometric area of the shape is filled. An example of a stroke and a fill is given in Figure 12-3.

Both stroke and fill can accept a solid color or a gradience. You can specify a solid color as Color.RED, Color.BLUE, and so forth, whereas a gradience is a fill pattern that is defined in terms of a combination of colors that are distributed across the geometric area of the shape in specific proportions with a smooth transition between the colors. You will learn more about this in the "Paints" section, later in this chapter.

Figure 12-3. Stroke vs. fill

Stroke Attributes

The most important and commonly used stroke attributes are:

- **stroke** – Defines the paint to be used to draw the outline. Can be a solid color or a gradient paint.

- **StrokeWidth** – Defines the width of the stroke; the default value is 1.0. A strokeWidth of 0.0 will still draw a hair-line stroke.

You can also customize the pen style using the following attributes:

- **strokeLineCap** – Defines the end cap style of a stroke segment. This can be SQUARE, ROUND, or BUTT as shown in Figure 12-4.

Figure 12-4. End cap styles (BUTT, ROUND, and SQUARE)

- **StrokeLineJoin** – Defines the pattern when two line segments meet. This can be BEVEL, MITER, or ROUND as shown in Figure 12-5.

Figure 12-5. Line join styles (BEVEL, ROUND, MITER)

- **StrokeDashArray**, **strokeDashOffset** – Defines a dashing pattern for the stroke, where a dash array specifies the length of the dash segment and offset specifies the gap between the dash segments. Figure 12-6 shows the comparison between normal versus dashed stroke patterns.

Figure 12-6. Normal vs. dashed strokes

A shape can choose to have fill alone, stroke alone, both of them, or neither of them. Each shape by design has either a default fill or a stroke defined. Not specifying a fill for a shape will cause the shape to use a default fill if one is defined internally or the default can be null for some shapes. Table 12-3 outlines the default values of fill/strokes for different shapes.

Table 12-3. *Fill/Stroke Defaults*

Shapes	Default Fill	Default Stroke
Line, Polyline, Path	Null	Color.BLACK
All other shapes except Line, Polyline, Path	Color.BLACK	null

Writing your First UI

As you have already learned, JavaFX Script uses a declarative syntax and the usefulness of this syntax will be apparent when you start developing a UI. This syntax will help you code your UI in a structure that will closely resemble how those UI elements are represented visually. Hence, you can actually write the UI in a visual context.

Now let us see how to create a simple UI application using some shapes. You have already read a similar example in Chapter 2, but here you will see more about what is required to create and show a UI using JavaFX. The instructions given in Chapter 2 toward creating a Netbeans JavaFX project and executing it are still applicable for this example as well and hence, let us concentrate more on the UI elements and other requirements.

Let us try to create a UI that is as simple as drawing three circular rings that intersects with each other, as given in Figure-12-7.

Figure 12-7. *Three rings*

For convenience, I have assumed the width of the application to be 240 and the height of the application to be 320. Now let us see how to create the three circular rings first.

Listing 12-1. *Creating Three Rings – Part 1*

```
// WARNING - Not Complete yet !!
import javafx.scene.shape.Circle;
import javafx.scene.paint.Color;
var circle1 = Circle {
        centerX: 100
        centerY: 150
        radius: 40
        fill: null
        stroke: Color.RED
        strokeWidth: 3
}

var circle2 = Circle {
        centerX: 140
        centerY: 150
        radius: 40
        fill: null
        stroke: Color.BLUE
        strokeWidth: 3
}

var circle3 = Circle {
        centerX: 120
        centerY: 170
        radius: 40
        fill: null
        stroke: Color.GREEN
        strokeWidth: 3
}
```

As you see in the code given in Listing 12.1, the first thing you need to do is to import the Circle class from the **javafx.scene.shape** package in your application. Since each circle has to be colored differently, **javafx.scene.paint.Color** must also be imported. Likewise, whatever API you are going to use in your application needs to be imported first. You can import the classes individually or you can use the wildcard import such as '**import javafx.scene.shape.***' if you are planning to use multiple classes from the same package.

Now you have access to the Circle class within your application and hence you can create three circle objects and initialize their attributes appropriately. A circle must have an x, y value representing its center and a radius. We have chosen the x, y, radius values in such a way that the three circles have a reasonable intersection. Here, we have assigned a null value to fill since we don't want the circle to be filled and we have set the stroke attribute to the required color so that only the contour of the circle is drawn with a thickness of 3.0 pixels.

Now you have the circles ready, but you need a drawing surface to draw the circles–the Scene.

Now let us create a scene and add the circles to it.

Listing 12-2. *Creating Three Rings – Part 2*

```
// Continuation of listing 12.1 - part1
var scene: Scene = Scene {
    width: 240
    height: 320
    content: [circle1, circle2, circle3]
}
```

In Listing 12-2, a scene has been created and all the circles are added to it. Please remember to add another import statement to import the **javafx.scene.Scene** class. The scene's width and height have been initialized appropriately to the required size I have assumed earlier on. However, this is optional and not doing so would make the scene fit exactly to the size of its contents by default. Likewise, optionally you can fill the entire scene with a specific color if you want the default white background of the scene to be changed to something of your choice.

There are many other attributes in the Scene class that you can use and please refer to the JavaFX API Documentation for more information on the other attributes.

Please note that certain attributes of scene, such as width, height, are public-init, which means they can only be initialized in an object literal and cannot be assigned or bound. Such attributes will not have a colored marking under the Can Write column in the API documentation.

Listing 12-3. *Create Three Rings – Part 3*

```
// Continuation of listing 12.2 - part2
Stage {
    title: "Three Rings"
    scene: scene
}
```

Now you need the top-level container to hold the scene and render it to the display, hence a stage has been created in Listing 12-3. Please remember to import the Stage class before using it– **javafx.stage.Stage.** In the stage object literal, you are associating its scene attribute to the scene object you have created in your application. Similar to scene, there are many other useful attributes in the Stage class that you can make use of. Please refer to the API documentation.

Now you are ready to build and execute the application; please follow the instructions given in Chapter 2 to execute it, either through Netbeans or from the command line.

Please find the complete code for this example as follows.

Listing 12-4. *Three Rings Application*

```
import javafx.scene.shape.Circle;
import javafx.scene.paint.Color;
import javafx.scene.Scene;
import javafx.stage.Stage;
var circle1 = Circle {
        centerX: 100
        centerY: 150
        radius: 40
        fill: null
        stroke: Color.RED
```

```
                strokeWidth: 3
}
var circle2 = Circle {
        centerX: 140
        centerY: 150
        radius: 40
        fill: null
        stroke: Color.BLUE
        strokeWidth: 3
}
var circle3 = Circle {
        centerX: 120
        centerY: 170
        radius: 40
        fill: null
        stroke: Color.GREEN
        strokeWidth: 3
}

var scene: Scene = Scene {
        width: 240
        height: 320
        content: [circle1, circle2, circle3]
}
Stage {
        title: "Three Rings"
        scene: scene
}
```

The output of this application will look like Figure 12-8 on a desktop and Figure 12-9 on a mobile device.

Figure 12-8. *Output of ThreeRings on desktop*

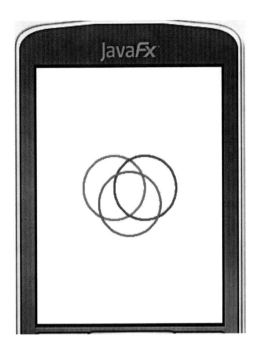

Figure 12-9. *Output of ThreeRings on a mobile emulator*

So when creating a UI, you will have to first import the necessary classes, create the UI elements that you require, and add them to a scene. Then associate the scene with a Stage so that it gets displayed on the screen.

While it is good to create the scene and stage yourself in most cases, it is also possible to not create them explicitly in your application and let the runtime create it for you. However, usefulness of this is very limited and perhaps, limited to just test a standalone UI code before integrating them into an application. When there is no scene/stage in your application, the runtime synthesizes them for you but for this to work, the last statement in your application must be a node construct that can readily be added to a scene. If you have a non-UI element as your last statement in your application, the runtime will not synthesize the scene and stage. An example of this is demonstrated in Listing 12-5 (Figure 12-10 shows the output). The same example also demonstrates the usage of other stroke attributes such as dash array, line cap, and line join.

Listing 12-5. *Dashed Stroke with Auto Synthesis of Scene/Stage*

```
import javafx.scene.*;
import javafx.scene.shape.*;
import javafx.scene.paint.*;
import javafx.stage.*;

var x: Number = 0;
var y: Number = 0;
var width: Number = 200;
```

```
var height: Number = 200;

var colors: Color[] = [Color.BLUE, Color.RED, Color.GREEN, Color.ORANGE,
                                          Color.YELLOW, Color.BLACK, Color.MAGENTA,
Color.GRAY,
                                          Color.CRIMSON, Color.LIME];

var gr: Group = Group {
        content: [
                for (i in [0..100 step 10])
                Rectangle {
                        x: x + i
                        y: y + i
                        width: width - 2 * i
                        height: height - 2 * i
                        arcWidth: if (i mod 20 == 0) then i else 0
                        arcHeight: if (i mod 20 == 0) then i else 0
                        fill: if (i == 90) Color.BLACK else null
                        strokeDashArray: [4.0, 2.0]
                        strokeLineJoin: StrokeLineJoin.ROUND
                        strokeLineCap: StrokeLineCap.BUTT
                        strokeWidth: 5
                        stroke: colors[i/10]
                }
        ]
}
```

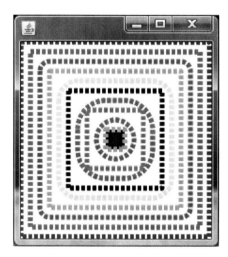

Figure 12-10. Output of the dashed stroke example with auto synthesis of scene/stage

The code given in Listing 12-5 uses a dashing pattern with two elements that give a longer segment to the opaque portion of the dash compared to the transparent portion and hence produces the output shown in Figure 12-10. It also uses a specific Stroke Line Join style and Line Cap style. The arc width/height is set for alternate rectangles and you can visibly see the difference in the output. Also, when width/height become equal or lesser than the arc width/height, the rectangles become circles. Please note that all rectangles except the innermost one are defined only with stroke and not fill. Also note that there is no stage or scene defined in this application and hence runtime synthesizes them and the last statement in the application is a group that gets added to the scene. This is the reason why I have used a group to club all the rectangles together without which only the last created rectangle would have appeared on the scene.

Apart from the built-in standard geometries, you can also create arbitrary shapes using the **javafx.scene.shape.Path** class and using various path elements. One such example is given in Listing 12-6 (with the output shown in Figure 12-11).

Listing 12-6. Creating Custom Shapes

```
import javafx.scene.shape.*;
import javafx.scene.paint.*;

var path:Path = Path {
    id: "Path"
    translateX: -175
    translateY: -150
        fill: Color.GRAY
        stroke: Color.BLACK
    elements: [
            MoveTo {
                x: 200
                y: 150
            },
                LineTo {
                x: 300
                y: 350
            },
                LineTo {
                x: 200
                y: 350
            },
                LineTo {
                x: 300
                y: 150
            },
                LineTo {
                x: 200
                y: 150
            },
                MoveTo {
                x: 250
                y: 250
            },
                CubicCurveTo {
                controlX1: 250
                controlY1: 250
                controlX2: 350
```

```
            controlY2: 150
            x: 300
            y: 350
        },
            MoveTo {
            x: 250
            y: 250
        },
            CubicCurveTo {
            controlX1: 250
            controlY1: 250
            controlX2: 150
            controlY2: 150
            x: 200
            y: 350
        },
            MoveTo {
            x: 250
            y: 250
        },
            ArcTo {
            x: 250
            y: 150
            radiusX: 100
            radiusY: 100
            xAxisRotation: 360
            sweepFlag: true
        },
            ArcTo {
            x: 250
            y: 250
            radiusX: 100
            radiusY: 100
            xAxisRotation: -360
            sweepFlag: true
        },
            MoveTo {
            x: 250
            y: 150
        },
            VLineTo {
            y: 250
        },
            MoveTo {
            x: 235
            y: 200
        },
            HLineTo {
            x: 265
        }
    ]
}
```

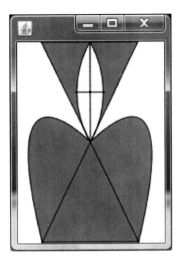

Figure 12-11. *Output of Custom Shape example*

The example given in Listing 12-6 creates an arbitrary shape using the Path API and various path elements and produces the output shown in Figure 12-11. The coordinates of the path elements are hard-coded, but you can make them relative to an x, y variable and hence position the node wherever you want. Also note that this example uses a little bit of transformation–translation to (x, y) -175, -150. This is because the actual node origin is hard-coded to start from 175, 150, and in order to change the origin to 0, 0 (the scene's origin), the node is translated in a negative direction. You will read more about transformations in the "transformation" section of this chapter.

In addition to supporting complex shapes, JavaFX also supports morphing of one shape to another. This is offered by **DelegateShape** class, which inherits its geometry from another shape. **DelegateShape** is initially assigned a shape that later gets morphed into another shape through a timeline (which will be explained in detail in the Animation chapter).

Paints

All the paint-related features are packaged within the **javafx.scene.paint** package. Shape's stroke and fill accepts a **javafx.scene.paint.Paint** object and this class acts as the base class. Paints can be defined in terms of single solid color or a combination of multiple colors following a pattern (gradience). In this section, you are going to see both.

Solid Colors

javafx.scene.paint.Color extends from the Paint class and defines various ways of specifying the colors. A color is a specific combination of red, green, blue, and alpha channel (will be referred as RGB/RGBA henceforth) where alpha defines the transparency of the color–its ability to show through the background. All the colors in JavaFX refer to sRGB color space (Refer to **www.w3.org/pub/WWW/Graphics/Color/sRGB.html** for more information). A color space is basically a system for measuring colors and defines certain rules as to what combination of RGBA transforms to which color. All the colors that you can create using the Color class are classified as "Solid" colors, meaning a single color representation with a specific value of red, green, blue, and alpha.

The Color class offers 100+ built-in named color values that you can use directly and correlate with real-world colors. This would be sufficient for most applications. But for applications for which you would like to use custom colors, the Color class offers multiple ways of constructing colors. You will see some of the common ones in Table 12-4.

Table 12-4. Color Creation

Creation Approach	Description
Using named constants	Use the built-in colors such Color.RED, Color.BLUE, Color.ORANGE, and so forth.
Creating a color instance through object literal: Color { blue: 1.0 green: 0 red: 0 alpha: 1.0 }	Creates equivalent of Color.BLUE. The valid values are 0.0 – 1.0. Optionally, you can omit mentioning other channels and they default to 0.0. Default value of alpha will be 1.0.
Use Color.color() methods to create a color 1. Color.color(1.0, 0, 0) 2. Color.color(1.0, 0, 0, 0.5)	The Color() method accepts values for red, green, blue, alpha channels, in that order. If you don't care about the alpha value, you can use 3 arg method as in (1). 1 – Color.RED, 2 – Color.RED that is 50% transparent.
If you are comfortable defining colors with RGBA values ranging from 0-255, you can use the rgb() method - Color.rgb(0, 0, 255, 1.0) or Color.rgb(0, 0, 255)	Some UI toolkits define colors in terms of 0-255 and JavaFX supports the same through the Color.rgb() method. The example code creates a Color.BLUE equivalent using the rgb() method.
If you are comfortable with HTML/web notation of defining colors, you can use one of the following web notations • Color.web("0x0000FF",1.0) • Color.web("0x0000FF") • Color.web("#0000FF",1.0) • Color.web("#0000FF") • Color.web("0000FF",1.0) • Color.web("0000FF")	• Represents blue as a hex web value, explict alpha • Represents blue as a hex web value, implict alpha • Represents blue as a hex web value, explict alpha • Represents blue as a hex web value, implict alpha • Represents blue as a hex web value, explict alpha • Represents blue as a hex web value, implict alpha

Hence, JavaFX supports all possible notations of defining the color that are common in most UI toolkits. But so far, you have only seen creation of solid colors and it's often necessary to create paints that are combinations of two or more colors so as to make your application look like a real-world RIA. In the next section, you are going to see paints that are composed of multiple colors in a specific proportion.

Gradients

A gradient is a smooth transition of colors. A gradient specifies a range of position-dependent colors whose intensity and magnitude vary based on the current position, providing a smooth transition from one color to the next color. Gradients can be linear or radial in nature and JavaFX supports both.

Linear Gradient

A linear color gradient is specified by two points, and a color at each point. The colors along the line through those points are calculated using linear interpolation, then extended perpendicular to that line. In other words, If `Point P1` (X1, Y1) with `Color` C1 and `Point` P2 (X2, Y2) with `Color` C2 are specified in user space, the `Color` on the P1, P2 connecting line is proportionally changed from C1 to C2. Any point P (X, Y) not on the extended P1, P2 connecting line has the color of the point P that is the perpendicular projection of P on the extended P1, P2 connecting line.

From the application standpoint, you may specify two or more gradient colors, and this Paint will provide an interpolation between each color. The application provides an array of `Stops` specifying how to distribute the colors along the gradient.

The syntax of the Linear Gradient is as follows:

```
LinearGradient {
        startX: Number
        startY: Number
        endX: Number
        endY: Number
        proportional: Boolean
        stops: [
                Stop { offset: Number color: Color (C1)},
                Stop { offset: Number color: Color (C2)}
        ]
}
```

startX, startY – endX, endY defines a straight-line within the geometry of the node on which the color changes from C1 to C2 to C3 etc. The **Stop#offset** variable must be the range 0.0 to 1.0 and act like keyframes along the gradient. They mark where the gradient should be exactly a particular color on the line segment. Proportional indicates whether startX, Y and endX, Y are absolute coordinates or defined in a scale of 0.0-1.0. If proportional is false, the coordinates must be absolute coordinates of the node, and if true (default), the coordinates are defined within a scale of 0 to 1 where 0 represents the origin of the rectangular bounds of the node and 1 represents the right-bottom end point of the rectangular bounds.

For example, in case of a rectangular node having x, y as 10, 10 and width, height as 100, 100, startX, Y will be 10, 10 and endX, Y will be 110, 110 if proportional is false and if proportional is true, startX,Y will be 0 and endX,Y will be 1. Having proportional as true is more convenient since you don't have to calculate the absolute coordinates of the node and you can define the gradient with respect to a virtual space of 0 to 1. So whatever node you apply this gradient to, the runtime will do the appropriate mapping of 0-1 to the actual node geometry. If defined in absolute coordinates, it is tightly coupled with the node's geometry (position and size), whereas if defined in proportional coordinates, it can be applied to any node regardless of its position or size.

Let us see a simple example of filling a rectangle with a LinearGradient of three colors (Listing 12-7, with the output shown in Figure 12-12).

Listing 12-7. *Linear Gradient with Absolute Coordinates*

```
import javafx.scene.shape.Rectangle;
import javafx.scene.paint.*;
import javafx.scene.Scene;
import javafx.stage.Stage;

Stage {
        title: "LinearGradient"
        scene: Scene {
                width: 120
                height: 120
                content: Rectangle {
                        x: 0
                        y: 0
                        width: 100
                        height: 100
                        fill: LinearGradient {
                        startX: 0.0, startY: 0.0, endX: 100.0, endY: 100.0
                        proportional: false
                        stops: [
                                Stop { offset: 0.0 color: Color.BLACK },
                                Stop { offset: 0.5 color: Color.WHITE },
                                Stop { offset: 1.0 color: Color.BLACK }
                                ]
                        }
                }
        }
}
```

Figure 12-12. *Output of Linear Gradient with Absolute Coordinates*

223

In Listing-12-7, the gradient is defined for a rectangle using its absolute coordinates, where startX,Y represents the actual node origin and endX, endY represents (x+width), (y+height). In the stop definition, there are three stops defined–one at origin, one at the mid-point of the rectangle (0.5), and one at the end point of the straight line represented by the startX,Y-endX,Y. So the stop definition says, start filling the rectangle with Color.BLACK at origin, smoothly transition to Color.WHITE at the mid-point, and transition back to Color.BLACK toward the end point. Listing 12-7 will produce the output shown in Figure 12-12.

There are no limitations on the number of stop values that you can define for a gradient and you can define as many stop values as you like. However, the offset values must be unique and each stop must have an offset that is greater than the previous stop's offset. If not, this will result in a runtime error.

Now to differentiate absolute vs. proportional coordinates, let us assume the rectangle's width and height are bound to some variables and gets increased to 200, 200. Gradient attributes cannot be bound, and hence the definition of that would remain the same. In this case, the output of the code in Listing 12-7 will become like what is shown in Figure 12-13.

Figure 12-13. Output of Linear Gradient Absolute for enlarged node geometry

This is certainly not what we would want since we want the gradient to be maintained as-is, regardless of the node dimensions. This is where a proportional attribute comes very handy. Had if we defined the LinearGradient in a proportional way, the same output would have been maintained even when the node size increases. Now let us re-write the example given in Listing-12-7 in a proportional way.

Listing 12-8. Linear Gradient with Proportional Coordinates

```
import javafx.scene.shape.Rectangle;
import javafx.scene.paint.*;
import javafx.scene.Scene;
import javafx.stage.Stage;
```

```
var w: Number = 100;
var h: Number = 100;

Stage {
        title: "LinearGradient"
        scene: Scene {
                content: Rectangle {
                        x: 0
                        y: 0
                        width: bind w
                        height: bind h
                        fill: LinearGradient {
                                startX: 0, startY: 0, endX: 1, endY: 1
                        proportional: true
                        stops: [
                                Stop { offset: 0.0 color: Color.BLACK },
                                Stop { offset: 0.5 color: Color.WHITE },
                                Stop { offset: 1.0 color: Color.BLACK }
                                ]
                        }
                }
        }
}

w = 200;
h = 200;
```

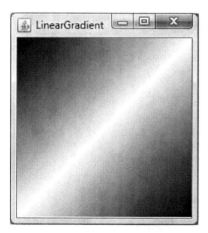

Figure 12-14. *Linear Gradient Proportional*

As you see in Figure 12-14, the gradient definition is maintained even when the node width/height is increased and also the same gradient definition can be applied to a different node that has different dimensions.

But it is not always true that you would want to have endX, endY as 1, 1 always, and sometimes you may define the gradient for a smaller area of the node and you can make the same gradient repeat or reflect for the rest of the area. This is what is defined by '**cycleMethod**'. A cycle method defines how to fill the area beyond the end point endX, endY if the node's geometry extends beyond endX, endY. There are three options for such cases (applicable to both proportional as well as absolute definitions):

- NO_CYCLE–Do not do any cycling and just fill the rest of the area with the color of the last stop. In the rectangle example, such an area would be filled with Color.BLACK.

- REPEAT–Start repeating the same gradient considering the first x, y that lie outside of the gradient definition as startX, startY and proceed until the actual end point of the node's geometry.

- REFLECT–Apply a mirror image of the defined gradient from the x,y that lie outside of the gradient definition, which means the stop values will now be applied in the reverse order.

Now you will see an example of REFLECT and REPEAT –in Listing 12-9.

Listing 12-9. *Linear Gradient REPEAT Cycle*

```
import javafx.scene.shape.Rectangle;
import javafx.scene.paint.*;
import javafx.scene.Scene;
import javafx.stage.Stage;

var w: Number = 100;
var h: Number = 100;

Stage {
        title: "LinearGradient"
        scene: Scene {
                content: Rectangle {
                        x: 0
                        y: 0
                        width: bind w
                        height: bind h
                        fill: LinearGradient {
                                cycleMethod: CycleMethod.REPEAT
                                startX: 0, startY: 0, endX: 0.5, endY: 0.5
                        proportional: true
                        stops: [
                                Stop { offset: 0.0 color: Color.BLACK },
                                Stop { offset: 0.3 color: Color.WHITE },
                                Stop { offset: 0.6 color: Color.RED },
                                Stop { offset: 1.0 color: Color.BLACK }
                                ]
                        }
                }
        }
}
w = 200;
h = 200;
```

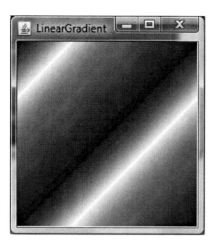

Figure 12-15. *Linear gradient repeat cycle*

Figure 12-15 shows the output of the example given in Listing12-9. In Listing 12-9, you can see a couple of changes. The endX, Y have been reduced to 0.5, 0.5, which means the gradient is defined only for 50% of the node's geometry. Now we have to let the runtime know what it should do with the remaining 50% of the node geometry and hence define a suitable **cycleMethod**. If you don't specify anything, the remaining area will be filled with the last stop color and the output would look similar to Figure-12-13. If you specify the cycleMethod as REPEAT, as given in Listing-12-9, the same gradient that was defined for the first half of the node geometry will be repeated for the rest of the node area as well, as shown in Figure 12-15.

Now when you replace '**cycleMethod.REPEAT**' with '**cycleMethod.REFLECT**' in Listing-12-9, you will get the output shown in Figure 12-16. As you compare Figure 12-15 with Figure 12-16, Figure 12-16 shows a mirror image of the gradient in the lower half of the node, whereas in Figure 12-15, it is more of a repetition of the same gradience.

Figure 12-16. *Linear gradient reflect cycle*

Radial Gradient

A radial gradient is specified as a circle that has one color and a focus (usually at the center of the circle) that has another. Colors are calculated by linear interpolation based on distance from the focus. This class provides a way to fill a shape with a circular radial color gradient pattern. You may specify two or more gradient colors, and this paint will provide an interpolation between each color. You must specify the circle controlling the gradient pattern, which is described by a center point and a radius. You can also specify a separate focus point within that circle, which controls the location of the first color of the gradient. By default, the focus is set to be the center of the circle.

The syntax of radial gradient is as follows:

```
RadialGradient {
        centerX: Number
        centerY: Number
        focusX: Number
        focusY: Number
        radius: Number
        proportional: Boolean
        stops: [
                Stop { offset: Number color: Color (C1)},
                Stop { offset: Number color: Color (C2)}
        ]
}
```

The syntax is pretty much similar to LinearGradient with the only difference that you are defining a circle instead of a straight-line and the circle can optionally define a focus point.

This paint will map the first color of the gradient to the focus point, and the last color to the perimeter of the circle, interpolating smoothly for any in-between colors specified by you. Any line drawn from the focus point to the circumference will thus span all the gradient colors. Specifying a focus point outside of the circle's radius will result in the focus being set to the intersection point of the focus-center line and the perimeter of the circle. All the advantages discussed about the proportional attribute are applicable to **RadialGradient** as well.

Listing 12-10 shows an example of how to use the radial gradient with different focus points.

Listing 12-10. *Radial Gradient with Focus*

```
import javafx.stage.Stage;
import javafx.scene.Scene;
import javafx.scene.shape.*;
import javafx.scene.paint.*;
import javafx.scene.layout.*;

public class RadialGradientSample {
    init {
        var h: Number = 100;
        var w: Number = 100;
        var sceneWidth = 300;
        var sceneHeight = 300;
        var counter = 0;
        var radialGradient: RadialGradient [] = [
            for(y in [10..30 step 10]) {
```

```
                        for(x in [10..30 step 10]) {
                            RadialGradient {
                                cycleMethod: CycleMethod.NO_CYCLE
                                centerX: w / 2,
                                centerY: h / 2,
                                focusX: if (x/10 == 1) (w/2 + 30)
                                            else if (x/10 == 2) (w/2)
                                            else (w/2 - 30)
                                focusY:  if (y/10 == 1) (h/2 + 30)
                                            else if (y/10 == 2) (h/2)
                                            else (h/2 - 30)
                                radius: 50
                                proportional: false
                                stops: [ Stop { offset: 0.0 color: Color.BLACK },
                                            Stop { offset: 1.0 color: Color.RED } ]
                            }
                        }
                    }
        ];

        var tile: Tile = Tile {
                rows: 3
                columns: 3
                content: [
                        for (g in radialGradient)
                        Rectangle {
                            x: 0
                            y: 0
                            width: 100
                            height: 100
                            fill: radialGradient [counter++]
                        }
                        ]
                }
        Stage {
            scene: Scene {
                height: sceneHeight
                width: sceneWidth
                content: [
                    tile
                ]
            }
        }
    }
}

public function run() {
        RadialGradientSample{};
}
```

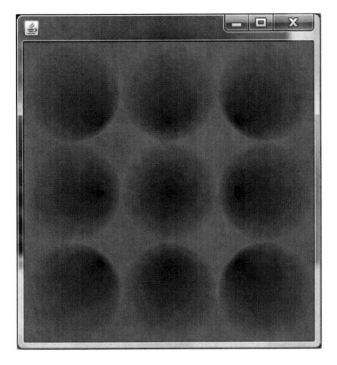

Figure 12-17. *Radial Gradient with focus*

Listing 12-10 demonstrates the usage of **RadialGradient** with different focus points. This sample creates nine Radial Gradient objects, each with a different focus point and each of them is used to fill a rectangle. All the rectangles are added to a Tile (you will learn more about Tile in the "Controls & Layouts" section later in this chapter; just understand that it is a layout for now). The output of this example is shown in Figure-12-17. The default behavior is the circle shown at the middle in Figure 12-17, where the focus and center points are the same.

Radial Gradient also supports the same set of cycle methods that you have already learned for Linear Gradient and it is handled in the same way as Linear Gradient.

Please note that the gradients are common profile APIs and hence supported across multiple platforms/devices, providing a uniform and richer user experience.

Input Handling

Handling user interactions such as keyboard and mouse is critical to any UI application and it has been largely simplified in JavaFX by providing convenient attributes in the Node class itself. When you are defining a node, you will have to define the event-related attributes as well to keep track of the keyboard and mouse interactions from the user.

Keyboard Input

Keyboard operations can be tracked through the following attributes:

- **onKeyPressed: function (ke: KeyEvent) { }**

- **onKeyReleased: function (ke: KeyEvent) { }**

- **onKeyTyped: function (ke: KeyEvent) { }**

All these attributes are of type 'function' and each of them accept a **javafx.scene.input.KeyEvent** object as an argument. This is pretty much similar to the event handling in AWT/Swing toolkits in Java, but here you don't need a separate listener implementation; rather, define the listener code implicitly within the node definition.

For these functions to work properly, a node first should contain the focus so that it can get notified of the key inputs. So first, let us see an introduction on focus.

JavaFX Focus Sub-system

For key events to work, a node should contain the keyboard focus and all the key events should be targeted to the node containing the focus. Focus is a state of the node that indicates whether the respective node is ready to respond to the keyboard inputs from the user. This is visually reflected in some cases, such as controls where an additional border is shown around the control when it has focus. For non-control nodes, it is up to the application to differentiate the node visually based on its focus state.

If a node contains focus, it's 'focused' attribute will be true and it is called the 'focus owner'. If there are multiple stages in the application, you can find out which stage has the focus owner by checking the value of the '**Stage.containsFocus**' attribute. A true value also indicates that the stage is active. A node can be a focus owner but cannot be 'focused' (focused attribute of Node becoming true) until the respective stage in which it resides is active. If not currently active and when subsequently made active, the respective focus owner will become 'focused'.

A node that is not a control has its **focusTraversable** turned off by default, which means it cannot transfer focus automatically to the next node in the focus cycle when pressing TAB. But controls (**javafx.scene.control**) can transfer focus to the next node in the focus cycle. Hence, a non-control node can receive focus from a control through TAB traversal, but then it is up to the application to transfer it to the next node through **requestFocus()**calls.

A call to **requestFocus()**will be entertained only when the node is eligible and eligibility is decided by the following factors:

- Node is added to the scene

- Node and its ancestors are visible

- Node and its ancestors within the scene are not disabled

If any of these conditions are violated, **requestFocus** calls are ignored. If any of these violations occur after the node becomes a focus owner, focus will be moved to the next node in the focus cycle if one is eligible. If no nodes in the scene are eligible, focus owner becomes null. It is up to the traversal engine to pick up the the next eligible node and it may depend on various factors such as proximity of the next eligible node to the current focus owner that is affected, the order in which nodes are added to the scene, and so forth.

Similarly, if the focus owner is moved from one sub-tree to another within the same scene graph, its focus state will be maintained. However, if it is moved to a new scene, its focus state will depend on the new scene's focus state. If the new scene had a focus owner already, that will be preserved and if not, the moved node will gain focus depending on its eligibility. There is one situation where the **requestFocus**() call will be remembered and honored later on and that is when it is called before the nodes are initialized when the scene is shown for the first time. Any call made before the initialization will be remembered and honored when the scene is made visible.

Mouse Input

Mouse operations on a node can be tracked through the following attributes:

- `onMousePressed: function (me: MouseEvent)` – Triggered when mouse is pressed on a node.

- `onMouseReleased: function (me: MouseEvent)` – Triggered when mouse is released on a node.

- `onMouseClicked: function (me: MouseEvent)` - Triggered when mouse is pressed and released on a node.

- `onMouseEntered: function (me: MouseEvent)` – Triggered when the mouse pointer enters a node.

- `onMouseExited: function (me: MouseEvent)` – Triggered when the mouse pointer exits a node.

- `onMouseDragged: function (me: MouseEvent)` – Triggered when the mouse pointer is pressed on a node and dragged. This keeps triggering until the mouse is released, regardless of the mouse position.

- `onMouseMoved: function (me: MouseEvent)` – Triggered when the mouse is hovered on a node.

- `onMouseWheelMoved: function (me: MouseEvent)` – Triggered when the mouse wheel is moved when the mouse pointer is within the node.

All these attributes are of type 'function' and each of them accept a **javafx.scene.input.MouseEvent** object as an argument. This is pretty much similar to the event handling in AWT/Swing toolkits in Java, but here you don't need a separate listener implementation; rather, define the listener code implicitly within the node definition. In other words, you don't have to implement the entire listener interface as in Java; you can implement just the functions that are needed.

While these attributes are self-explanatory, there are a few mouse-related attributes that are worth defining here. They are:

- `Node.pressed: Boolean`

- `Node.hover: Boolean`

- `Node.blocksMouse:Boolean`

`Node.pressed` is set when the mouse is pressed on the node. If you are just interested in the pressed state of the node, you don't have to define the **onMousePressed** and instead you can just use this attribute directly to check if the mouse is pressed. Similarly, **Node.hover** will let you know whether the mouse is moved on a node without you defining the **onMouseMoved** explicitly. These attributes are given for convenience since they are very widely used by most applications.

Please note that mouse-aware area of a node is the geometry of the node for most shapes. However, certain nodes such as Text and controls are exceptions where the mouse-aware area is the bounds of the node and not its geometry. Say if it is based on the geometry, it would be really hard to use some of the controls such as CheckBox, RadioButton, and so forth, and the user has to keep the mouse pointer exactly on the text to produce a selection of the control. This is unintuitive and, perhaps, very difficult. On the other hand, if it is bounds-driven, the user can click anywhere on the area where text is shown and it will change the selection.

While the default behaviors of certain nodes are chosen to be this way, it is valuable to give an option to the developer as to what he would want to choose–geometry-based picking or bounds-based picking. This is achieved through **Node.pickOnBounds**. If this is set to true, it enables bounds-based picking just like the text node. If it is false, the mouse-aware area is defined by the node geometry. This behavior is pictorially represented in Figure 12-18.

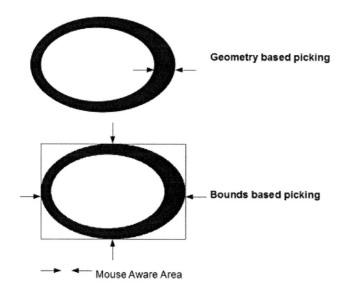

Figure 12-18. *Geometry vs. bounds picking*

BlocksMouse

Node.blocksMouse is an important feature that defines how mouse events are handled for nodes that are overlapping one another. If a node is said to be blocking the mouse events, it means it does not allow the mouse events to pass through to the nodes located beneath or visually obscured by this node (or up the hierarchy in the scene graph). This can be considered equivalent to the event consumption in AWT/Swing toolkits. By default, **blocksMouse** is set to false for all the nodes (except those that descend from the control class) and hence, they allow the mouse events to propagate up the scene graph.

Some interesting facts about **blocksMouse** are that the node acts as if it is isolated from the parent when its **blocksMouse** is set to true. Say you add a rectangle to a group and set **blocksMouse** to true for the rectangle. Now when you enter the mouse into the rectangle from the group, group would trigger onMouseExit and Rectangle will trigger onMouseEnter. Similarly, when moving the mouse out of rectangle and into the group, rectangle will trigger onMouseExit and Group will trigger onMouseEntered. This might look a bit strange at first sight because mouse is actually within the rectangle and hence within the group as well. But this behavior is intentional and as per the design and you can consider the node to be excluded from its parent when its blocksMouse is true.

Another interesting aspect of blocksMouse is with respect to a disabled node. BlocksMouse setting is not honored for a disabled node and hence a disabled node will always allow the events to pass through to the nodes obscured.

Text Rendering

Text rendering in JavaFX is done through the javafx.scene.text.Text class available in the javafx.scene.text package. You can consider a text node as another shape with additional capabilities and Text node indeed extends from the javafx.scene.shape.Shape class. Hence, all the features such as stroke, fill, and so forth that you have learned so far with respect to shapes are applicable for text as well. In this section, you will learn about some of the important aspects of text rendering and the support for different fonts. Before jumping into the API, let us see some basic concepts in text rendering.

A string is commonly thought of in terms of the characters that comprise the string. When a string is drawn, its appearance is determined by the font that is selected. However, the shapes that the font uses to display the string don't always correspond to individual characters. For example, in professional publishing, certain combinations of two or more characters are often replaced by a single shape called a *ligature*. The shapes that a font uses to represent the characters in the string are called *glyphs*. A font might represent a character such as a lowercase *a* in *acute* using multiple glyphs, or represent certain character combinations such as the *fi* in *final* with a single glyph. A glyph is simply a shape that can be manipulated and rendered in the same way as any other shape. An application developer need not worry about glyphs since they are the internal representation of the string to be rendered.

A *font* can be thought of as a collection of glyphs. A single font might have many versions, such as heavy, medium, oblique, gothic, and regular. These different versions are called *faces*. All of the faces in a font have a similar typographic design and can be recognized as members of the same *family*. In other words, a collection of glyphs with a particular style forms a font face, a collection of font faces forms a font family, and a collection of font families forms the set of fonts available on a particular configuration.

Fonts can be manipulated in JavaFX using the javafx.scene.text.Font class. A font can be built by specifying the full font name, which is a combination of font family plus the font style. For example, Arial is a family name and Bold is the style. So you can build a font using the name Arial Bold. Font look-up is done in the following order:

- Embedded fonts

- Fonts shipped with JavaFX

- Fonts available on the system

- Fallback fonts

The runtime looks for the given font in these places and if it cannot find one, it falls back to using the default font available in the runtime. In any case, Font.name is updated to the font being used and you can compare that with what you have specified or some other default font.

Please note that all the attributes in the font class are public-init and hence cannot be bound. If you really want to bind a font, you will have to bind it, as shown in Listing 12-11.

Listing 12-11. *A Text Node with a Bound Font*

```
import javafx.scene.*;
import javafx.scene.text.*;
import javafx.scene.input.*;

var fontNames = ["Arial Bold", "Amble Condensed", "Amble Condensed Italic"];
var index = 0 on replace {
        println("Font Used: {t.font.name}");
}

var t = Text {
        font: bind Font {
                name: fontNames[index]
                size: 25
        }
        content: "JavaFX"
        textOrigin: TextOrigin.TOP

        onMouseClicked: function (me: MouseEvent) {
                if (index < sizeof fontNames) {
                        index ++;
                } else {
                        index = 0;
                }
        }
}
```

Output
Font Used:
Font Used: Amble Condensed
Font Used: Amble Condensed Italic
Font Used: Amble Condensed
Font Used: Arial Bold

In Listing 12-11, the Font object literal as such is bound with the text node's font attribute and no binding is specified at the attribute level within the Font object. So when the user clicks on the text node, the index changes, which causes the entire font object to be re-created and used with the text node and hence, the user will see the font changing visually.

The Font class provides some built-in functions to get all the fonts available on the system (includes JavaFX and embedded fonts as well). It is much safer to use the built-in functions to get the font names instead of specifying a font name yourself, mainly because hard-coding a font name is prone to typographic errors and it will not be very apparent since the runtime will use the default font under the covers if the specified one does not exist.

You can also construct a new font using the built-in functions by specifying your requirements in terms of size, name, weight, size, posture, and so forth and you can do the same through the object literal as well. Font offers lots of additional attributes such as size, embolden, oblique, ligatures, letter spacing, and so forth. Please refer to the API documentation for more information. However, the most predominantly used attributes are font name and font size.

The text node is just another shape, so all the shape attributes are applicable for the text node as well. It supports multi-line rendering in two ways. The developer can break the text into multiple lines by including a '\n' in the string. Another way to do this is to use **wrappingWidth**. Specify **wrappingWidth** in terms of pixels and the given text gets word wrapped when its bounds exceeds the given width. Additionally, you can specify various origins and alignments to form a paragraph of text.

The example given in Listing 12-12 demonstrates various text alignments with respect to multi-line text.

Listing 12-12. *Text Alignments*

```
import javafx.scene.paint.*;
import javafx.stage.*;
import javafx.scene.*;
import javafx.scene.input.*;
import javafx.scene.shape.*;
import javafx.scene.text.*;

public class TextAlignments {

    init {

        var content: String = "The quick brown fox jumps over the lazy dog.\n"
                "Woven silk pyjamas exchanged for blue quartz?\n"
                "Have a pick: twenty six letters - no forcing a jumbled quiz!";
        var alignments: TextAlignment[] = [
                    TextAlignment.LEFT,
                    TextAlignment.CENTER,
                    TextAlignment.RIGHT,
                    TextAlignment.JUSTIFY
        ];

        var alignmentsString: String[] = [
                    "TextAlignment.LEFT",
                    "TextAlignment.CENTER",
                    "TextAlignment.RIGHT",
                    "TextAlignment.JUSTIFY"
        ];

        var counter = 0;
        Stage {
                scene: Scene {
                    height: 160
                    width: 240
                    content: [
                        Text {
                                x: 10
                                y: 10
                                content: bind alignmentsString[counter]
                        },
                        Text {
                            x: 10
                            y: 40
                            font: Font { size: 15 }
```

```
                        content: content
                        fill: Color.BLACK
                        wrappingWidth: 200
                        underline: true
                        textAlignment: bind alignments[counter]
                        focusTraversable: true
                        onKeyPressed: function(e:KeyEvent) {
                            if (e.code == KeyCode.VK_LEFT) {
                                if (counter < alignments.size()-1) {
                                    counter ++;
                                } else {
                                    counter = 0;
                                }
                            }
                        }
                    }
                ]
            }
        }
    }
}

public function run() {
        TextAlignments{};
}
```

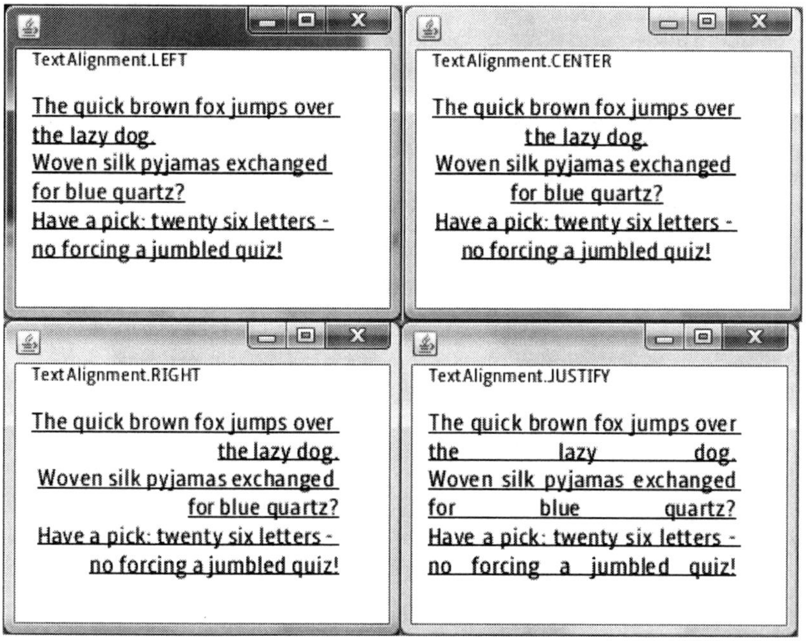

Figure 12-19. Multi-line text with different alignments

Listing 12-12 demonstrates the usage of multi-line text, wrapping width, and text alignments. While running this example, when the stage appears on the screen, press the LEFT arrow key to cycle through various alignments. The given text is wrapped at 200 pixels and various alignments are applied to the text. Figure 12-19 shows the output of Listing 12-12–the various alignments that are possible with JavaFX. A text node is provided with x, y attributes for defining the position within the scene. The font set on the text node does not specify a name and hence, the default FX font (Amble family) would be used. Setting underline to true underlines the content text, as shown in the output.

With the combination of attributes offered by Font and Text classes, you can do any kind of text rendering that is possible with other UI toolkits. The JavaFX controls such as Label, Button, CheckBox, RadioButton, TextBox (multi-line/single-line), and so forth use text nodes extensively to represent textual information (such as label text) and can get as powerful as a multi-line textbox, where you can create and edit multiple lines of text.

Image Rendering

Images are collections of pixels organized spatially. JavaFX offers a comprehensive yet simple API for image rendering through two classes available in the **javafx.scene.image** package. The actual image (bitmap) is represented using the **javafx.scene.image.Image** class and rendering of the image onto a scene is handled by the **javafx.scene.image.ImageView** class. An image has to be first loaded on to the memory before rendered on the scene. The next section shows how to load an image.

Loading an Image

javafx.scene.image.Image is capable of loading an image from a URL that could be a web URL or a local file URL. An image can be loaded in the foreground thread (default) or in a background thread. If the image is of a relatively large size, the developer may not want the application user to wait until the entire image is loaded and hence can choose to load the image in a background thread. Until the entire image is loaded, the Image class allows the developer to show a placeholder image, which is often the thumbnail of the actual image being loaded. This engages the end user appropriately when the image is being loaded in the background. If you are writing a desktop-only application, you can also convert an existing buffered image created in java (**java.awt.image.BufferedImage**) to a JavaFX Image (**javafx.scene.image.Image**) using the following API:

```
javafx.ext.swing.SwingUtils.toFXImage(image: java.awt.image.BufferedImage):
javafx.scene.image.Image
```

Currently (as of 1.3), JavaFX supports loading of the following image formats–GIF, Animated GIF, JPEG, PNG, and BMP. Future version of JavaFX may support additional image formats. However, if you are developing a common profile application, you may have to restrict the image type to PNG and GIF since mobile implementation currently only supports these formats.

▨ **Note** The image format support for desktop applications comes from the underlying ImageIO implementation from Java (javax.imageio.*) that JavaFX leverages on. Hence, if you have an imageio plug-in to recognize a new image format, just add the plug-in to your classpath and JavaFX will automatically be able to support the new format without any code change.

As mentioned already, images can be loaded from the local file system or from the Web. The Image class also allows the developer to specify a preferred width and height for the image optionally, and the image loaded gets scaled to the specified width/height. You can choose the appropriate scaling algorithm to control the rendering quality, by giving priority either to the performance or smoothness of the image.

Listing 12-13 shows a simple example of loading an image.

Listing 12-13. Simple Image Loading

```
import javafx.scene.image.*;

var img = Image {
        url: "{__DIR__}duke.gif"
}

ImageView {
        image: img
}
```

Figure 12-20. Default image loading from local file system

In Listing 12-13, the code tries to load an image–*duke.gif*– from the directory where classes are available (represented by __DIR__) and uses the default width and height of the original image. The

ImageView is used to render the image on to the scene and you will see that in a while. The output of this example is shown in Figure 12-20.

Now let us customize the image width and height for an image loaded from the Web (Listing 12-14).

Listing 12-14. *Image Loading–Custom Size*

```
import javafx.scene.image.*;

var img = Image {
        url: "http://www.apress.com/img/masthead_logo.gif"
        width: 200
        height: 200
}

ImageView {
        image: img
}
```

Figure 12-21. *Image loading from the Web with a custom size*

Listing 12-14 is loading an image from the Web (the Apress logo from **www.apress.com**) and changing its default size to 200, 200. Please note that the actual size of this image is 422x80, and hence changing it to 200, 200 alters the aspect ratio between the width and height. It's pretty apparent from the output shown in Figure-12-21 that the ratio has gone for a toss. If you want to preserve the aspect ratio while resizing the image (either width alone, or height alone, or both), you can set **preserveRatio** to true and you will get an output as shown in Figure 12-22.

Figure 12-22. *Image loading from the Web with custom size–aspect ratio preserved*

■ **Note** It is always better to specify the appropriate width and height when loading the image, depending on your requirements, since it optimizes the image that resides in the memory. While it is also possible to do the scaling at rendering time using ImageView, it is better doing it at loading time since it helps you manage the memory appropriately by keeping a smaller-size image in memory if your usage is likely to scale down the image from it's original size.

Now let's see another example where we load the image in the background while keeping the user engaged through a placeholder (Listing 12-15).

Listing 12-15. *Background Loading of Images*

```
    import javafx.scene.image.*;
import javafx.scene.Scene;
import javafx.stage.Stage;

var width = 800;
var height = 600;

var img = Image {
        url: "http://c0278592.cdn.cloudfiles.rackspacecloud.com/original/191195.jpg"
        backgroundLoading: true
        placeholder: Image {
                url: "{__DIR__}191195.png"
        }
}

Stage {
        scene: Scene {
                width: width
                height: height
                content: ImageView {
                        image: img
                        x: bind (width/2 - img.width/2)
                        y: bind (height/2 - img.height/2)
                }
        }
}
```

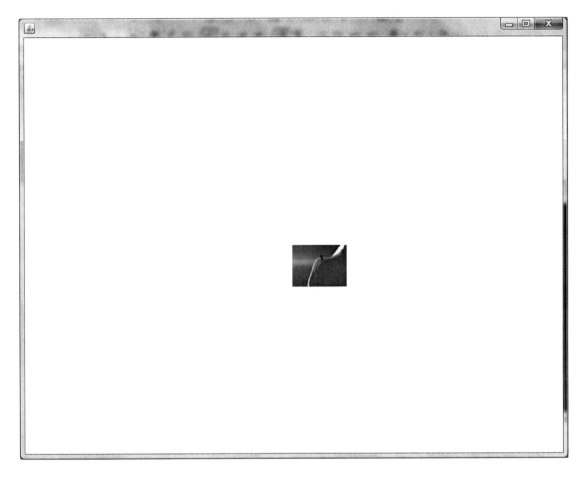

Figure 12-23. *Placeholder image shown while the actual image being loaded*

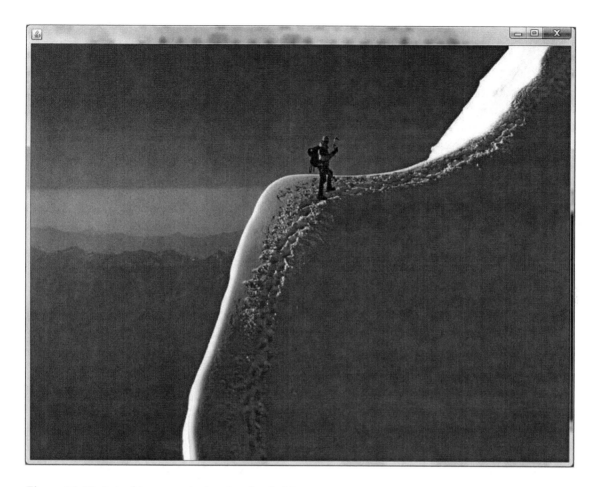

Figure 12-24. Actual image replacing the placeholder

Listing 12-15 loads a larger image in the background thread and while the image is being loaded, a placeholder image (thumbnail version of the image being loaded) is shown to the user, as shown in Figure 12-23. When the actual image completes loading, the placeholder image is replaced with the actual image, as shown in Figure 12-24. Another use of this placeholder image is that when there is an issue with loading the actual image, the placeholder will be retained forever, thus avoiding a blank screen for the end user. In such cases, the placeholder could be an image that indicates an error in image loading such as the ones we typically see on web pages with a red colored X on one of the corners.

■ **Note** Loading an image in the background is optional and often decided by the size of the image and probability of an error when loading it. But please note that the runtime should not have any issues in loading the placeholder image, if you have specified one. An invalid placeholder image will prevent proper loading of the actual image and will not load the actual image even if the actual image is correct. So please take extra care when specifying the placeholder to ensure the placeholder is correct. However, this is not an issue if the placeholder is skipped altogether.

Rendering an image

Images are rendered on to the scene through the **javafx.scene.image.ImageView** class. So far, you have seen a basic use of the image view class, but **ImageView** has lot more features to offer. It is possible to alter the width and height of the image view using the **fitWidth** and **fitHeight** attributes, and it is also possible to preserve the aspect ratio just like you did with Image.

■ **Note** The width and height attributes of the Image class are public-init and hence cannot be bound, whereas fitWidth and fitHeight of image view are normal public attributes and hence can be bound. So if there is a need to alter the width and height of the image in response to another variable, it is better to do it with fitWidth/fitHeight where you can just bind them. On the other hand, specifying it at Image level will offer better optimization in terms of the size of the image kept in the memory.

Additionally, you can specify an 'x' and 'y' location for the image view if you want the image view to be placed at a specific point. This has already been demonstrated in Listing 12-15, where the image is placed at the center of the scene through the use of 'X'/'Y' attributes of **ImageView**.

When scaling the image up or down, you can control the rendering quality by choosing the appropriate algorithm by toggling the '**smooth**' attribute. If smooth is true, runtime chooses an algorithm that offers better smoothness compromising on the performance, and if you set it to false, focus will be on the performance compromising on the smoothness of the image.

ImageView also offers a way to specify a view port into the original image. Viewport is a rectangle within the image which indicates that only those pixels that fall within the viewport must be shown and not others. Viewport rectangle is independent of image view's transformations or scaling. If viewport is not specified, the entire image is shown.

Listing 12-16 shows a simple example of the viewport usage.

Listing 12-16. ImageView Viewport

```
    import javafx.scene.image.*;
import javafx.scene.Scene;
import javafx.stage.Stage;
import javafx.geometry.*;

var width = 200;
var height = 200;

var img = Image {
        url: "http://noelschweig.com/photos/gallery/nature/nature4.jpg"
        width: 200
        height: 200
}

Stage {
        x: 0
        y: 0
        scene: Scene {
                width: width
                height: height
                content: ImageView {
                        image: img
                }
        }
}

Stage {
        x: 200
        y: 0
        scene: Scene {
                width: width
                height: height
                content: ImageView {
                        image: img
                        viewport: Rectangle2D {
                                minX: 0
                                minY: 0
                                width: 100
                                height: 100
                        }
                }
        }
}
```

Figure 12-25. *ImageView with and without viewport*

Listing 12-16 demonstrates the use of viewport where it creates an image object and displays it using two image view objects, one with view port and another one without it. If there is no viewport, the entire image is shown as given in the left half of Figure-12.25. The code specifies a viewport of 0, 0, 100, 100 within the image, which is of size 0, 0, 200, 200, and that's what is shown in the right half of Figure 12-25. If the viewport is smaller than the actual image, only the pixels that fall within the viewport area are shown. If the viewport is bigger than the actual size of the image, the entire image is shown.

Also note that the same image instance can be used by multiple image view objects and can be displayed differently on the scene.

Transformations

Any **Node** can have transformations applied to it. These include translation, rotation, scaling, or shearing transformations. Transformations can be two-dimensional or three dimensional (available since 1.3). Let's see each of the 2-D transformations in detail.

Translation

A translation is applied to a node by repositioning it along a straight-line path from one coordinate location to another. The node is translated by adding translation distances tx and ty to the original coordinate position (x,y) of the origin of the node. For example, if you create a rectangle that is drawn at the origin (x=0, y=0) and has a width of 100 and a height of 50, and then apply a translation with a shift of 10 along the x axis (x=10), then the rectangle will appear drawn at (x=10, y=0) and remain 100 points wide and 50 points tall. Note that the origin was shifted, not the x variable of the rectangle.

In JavaFX, you can translate a node in two ways. One way is to use the convenience attributes available in the Node class–translateX, translateY. The other way is to use the '**Node.transforms**' attribute. For most basic transformations, it is sufficient to use translateX, translate, but if you want to combine multiple transformations to create a composite transformation, it is better to go for '**transforms**' attribute, which accepts an array of transformations and the order of transformations will also be preserved.

▓ **Note** It is not advisable and potentially dangerous to use both convenience variables and the '**transforms**' attribute together for a node and the behavior would be unpredictable since you do not know the order in which transformations will be evaluated. Hence, if you decide to use either of the ways to apply transformations, better stick to the same for that node and do not mix up both.

Listing 12-17 shows a simple example of a translate transformation applied on a rectangle through translateX, translateY attributes.

Listing 12-17. Translate Transformation Using translateX, Y

```
    import javafx.scene.*;
import javafx.scene.shape.*;
import javafx.scene.paint.*;
import javafx.scene.input.*;
import javafx.stage.Stage;

var tx: Number = 0;
var ty: Number = 0;

var rect: Rectangle = Rectangle {
        x: 0
        y: 0
        width: 100
        height: 100
        fill: Color.GRAY
        translateX: bind tx
        translateY: bind ty

        onKeyPressed: function (ke: KeyEvent) {
                if (ke.code == KeyCode.VK_RIGHT) {
                        tx = tx + 10;
                } else if (ke.code == KeyCode.VK_LEFT) {
                        tx = tx - 10;
                } else if (ke.code == KeyCode.VK_UP) {
                        ty = ty - 10;
                } else if (ke.code == KeyCode.VK_DOWN) {
                        ty = ty + 10;
                }
        }
}

Stage {
        scene: Scene {
```

```
                width: 400
                height: 400
                content: [rect]
        }
}

rect.requestFocus();
```

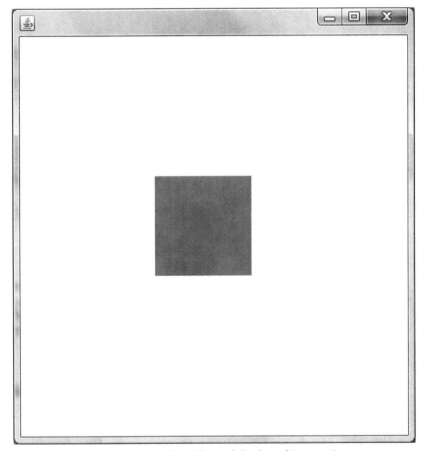

Figure 12-26. *Rectangle translated through keyboard interactions*

In Listing 12-17, a rectangle is drawn at 0, 0 with a width/height of 100, 100 and its translateX, translateY are bound to two variables tx, ty. A key listener is added to the node that changes the tx, ty values based on what key is pressed. UP/DOWN arrow keys move the node along the y-axis and LEFT/RIGHT arrow keys move the node along the x-axis. Please note that the x, y values of the rectangle are unchanged and translation is applied to the rectangle's origin and not to the x, y value of the rectangle. The output of Listing 12-17 is shown in Figure 12-26.

Now let's re-write example 12-17 to use the **transforms** attribute instead of translateX,Y.

```
var rect: Rectangle = Rectangle {
        x: 0
        y: 0
        width: 100
        height: 100
        fill: Color.GRAY
        transforms: bind Transform.translate(tx, ty)
        . . . .
        . . . .
}
```

As you can see in the re-factored code, there is not much difference between translateX, Y and the **transforms** attribute with respect to translate transformation. However, you will see a significant difference for transformations that depend on a pivot point such as scale, rotate, and shear, and you will learn it while learning those transformations.

Rotation

A rotation is applied to a node by repositioning it along a circular path in the xy plane. A rotation transformation needs a rotation angle and the pivot point (x, y) about which the node is to be rotated. For example, if you create a rectangle that is drawn at the origin (x=0, y=0) and has a width of 100 and height of 30 and you apply a 90-degree rotation (angle=90) and a pivot at the origin (pivotX=0, pivotY=0), then the rectangle will be drawn as if its x and y were 0 but its height was 100 and its width -30. That is, it is as if a pin is being stuck at the top left corner and the rectangle is rotating 90 degrees clockwise around that pin. If the pivot point is instead placed in the center of the rectangle (at point x=50, y=15) then the rectangle will instead appear to rotate about its center. Note that as with all transformations, the x, y, width, and height variables of the rectangle (which remain relative to the local coordinate space) have not changed, but rather the transformation alters the entire coordinate space of the rectangle.

Similar to translate, you can apply rotate either using the '**Node.rotate**' attribute or the '**Node.transforms**' attribute of the Node class. The '**rotate**' attribute, by default, assumes the center of the node as the pivot point, whereas in the case of transforms, you need to explicitly specify the pivot point.

Listing 12-18 shows a simple example of a rotate transformation applied on a node using **rotate**, with the output being shown in Figure 12-27.

Listing 12-18. Rotate Transformation Using Rotate on a Custom Node

```
    import javafx.scene.*;
import javafx.scene.shape.*;
import javafx.scene.paint.*;
import javafx.scene.input.*;
import javafx.stage.Stage;
import javafx.scene.transform.*;

var rotate: Number = 0;

var svgNode: SVGNode = SVGNode {
        rotate: bind rotate
```

```
        onKeyPressed: function (ke: KeyEvent) {
                if (ke.code == KeyCode.VK_RIGHT) {
                        rotate++;
                        if (rotate > 360) rotate = 360;
                } else if (ke.code == KeyCode.VK_LEFT) {
                        rotate --;
                        if (rotate < 0) rotate = 0;
                }
        }
}

Stage {
        scene: Scene {
                width: 150
                height: 150
                content: [svgNode]
        }
}

svgNode.requestFocus();

class SVGNode extends CustomNode {

        public override function create(): Node {
                var gr: Group = Group {
                        content: [
                                SVGPath {
                                content: "M70 20 L30 100 L110 100 Z"
                        },
                        Rectangle {
                                x: 30
                                y: 20
                                width: 80
                                height: 80
                                fill: null
                                stroke: Color.RED
                        }
                ]
        }
    }
}
```

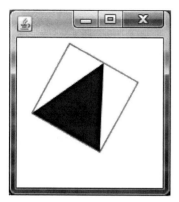

Figure 12-27. *Rotating a custom node with the rotate attribute*

In Listing 12-18, there is a new concept being introduced–**CustomNode**.

Custom Node

A Custom Node is the base class for defining new node types that are not available as part of built-in nodes in the API. This is perhaps one of the most-used classes in JavaFX since every application will have the need to define its own nodes. As you see in the Listing 12-18, you can create a custom node by extending the javafx.scene.CustomNode class and overriding its create method. You can return any node or a composite node such as a group from the create method and the object of this class will be treated as a node by itself. Whatever you do with your custom node, such as transformations, clipping, and so forth will be applied to all its children (the nodes returned by the create method). Instead of overriding the create method, alternatively you can also override the 'children' attribute of the custom node and assign your own node to it.

Now, coming back to the rotation aspect of it, Listing 12-18 creates an instance of the custom node and binds its rotate attribute to a rotate variable. The value of the rotate variable changes based on the keyboard input. When the rotate value increments or decrements, the custom node rotates in the clockwise or counter-clockwise direction visually. Please note that the pivot point is assumed to be the center of the custom node and hence the node rotates with respect to its center, as shown in Figure 12-27.

However, if you want to have more control over the pivot point, you can use the '**transforms**' attribute of the node to rotate the node instead of the '**rotate**' attribute and, for example, you can re-factor the code to use '**transforms**' to use a pivot point of the origin 0,0 instead of the center, as follows:

```
...
...
...
var svgNode: SVGNode = SVGNode {
    transforms: bind Transform.rotate(rotate, 0, 0)
    ...
    ...
}
```

The re-factored code uses a pivot point of 0, 0 instead of the default center of the node and you can see the difference yourself when you run the application.

■ **Note** The rotation example clearly differentiates the difference between the convenience attributes and the `'transforms'` attribute, where `transforms` offers you more control over the transformation than the convenience attributes. On the other hand, people who just use simple basic transformations will definitely find convenience attributes to be handier than the `transforms` attribute. Nevertheless, use the approach that is appropriate for you and do not mix up both.

Scaling & Shear

A **scaling** transformation alters the size of the node, causing a node to either appear larger or smaller depending on the scaling factor. Scaling alters the coordinate space of the node such that each unit of distance along the axis in local coordinates is multiplied by the scale factor. As with rotation transformations, scaling transformations are applied about a "pivot" point. You can think of this as the point in the Node around which you "zoom." For example, if you create a rectangle with a `strokeWidth` of 5, and a width and height of 50, and you apply a scale transformation with scale factors (x=2.0, y=2.0) and a pivot at the origin (pivotX=0, pivotY=0), the entire rectangle (including the stroke) will double in size, growing to the right and downward from the origin.

A **shearing** transformation, sometimes called a skew, effectively rotates one axis so that the x and y axes are no longer perpendicular.

■ **Note** A shear transformation does not have the convenience attribute and hence has to be specified only through the `'transforms'` attribute of the node, whereas the scale transformation has scaleX, scaleY in the node class.

Listing 12-19 shows how you can apply scaling and shear transformation for the custom node you saw in the previous example, with the output shown in Figure 12-28.

Listing 12-19. Scale and Shear Transformations

```
    import javafx.scene.*;
import javafx.scene.shape.*;
import javafx.scene.paint.*;
import javafx.scene.input.*;
import javafx.stage.Stage;
import javafx.scene.transform.*;

var scaleX: Number = 1;
var scaleY: Number = 1;
```

```
var shearX: Number = 0.0;
var shearY: Number = 0.0;

var svgNode: SVGNode = SVGNode {
        transforms: bind [
                Transform.scale(scaleX, scaleY, svgNode.layoutBounds.maxX/2,
svgNode.layoutBounds.maxY/2),
                Transform.shear(shearX, shearY)
        ]

        onKeyPressed: function (ke: KeyEvent) {
                if (ke.code == KeyCode.VK_UP) {
                        scaleX += 0.2;
                        scaleY += 0.2;
                        if (scaleX > 3.0) {
                                scaleX = -3.0;
                                scaleY = -3.0;
                        }
                } else if (ke.code == KeyCode.VK_DOWN) {
                        scaleX -= 0.2;
                        scaleY -= 0.2;
                        if (scaleX < -3.0) {
                                scaleX = 3.0;
                                scaleY = 3.0;
                        }
                } else if (ke.code == KeyCode.VK_LEFT) {
                        shearX += 0.2;
                        shearY += 0.2;
                        if (shearX > 1.0) {
                                shearX = -1.0;
                                shearY = -1.0;
                        }
                } else if (ke.code == KeyCode.VK_RIGHT) {
                        shearX -= 0.2;
                        shearY -= 0.2;
                        if (shearX < -1.0) {
                                shearX = 1.0;
                                shearY = 1.0;
                        }
                }
        }
}

Stage {
        scene: Scene {
                width: 150
                height: 150
                content: [svgNode]
        }
}

svgNode.requestFocus();
```

```
class SVGNode extends CustomNode {

        public override var children: Node[] = [
                SVGPath {
                        content: "M70 20 L30 100 L110 100 Z"
                },
                Rectangle {
                        x: 30
                        y: 20
                        width: 80
                        height: 80
                        fill: null
                        stroke: Color.RED
                }
        ];
}
```

Figure 12-28. Scaling and shearing a custom node

In Listing 12-19, the custom node you saw in Listing 12-18 has been applied with a scale and a shear transformation. Please note that both the transformations are applied using the '**transforms**' attribute of the node and scale also requires a pivot point (x, y) about which the node is to be scaled. In this case, the center of the node has been specified. **Node.layoutBounds** returns the rectangular bounds of the node, excluding any transformations or clipping, but inclusive of its stroke width. The code is calculating the center point of the node, which is used as the pivot so that it appears as if the node zooms about its center. The default pivot points when using '**Transforms.scale (x, y)**' will be 0, 0, which is the origin of the node. Pressing UP/DOWN arrow keys will scale the node up and down appropriately, and pressing LEFT/RIGHT arrow keys will shear the node up and down. Scaling using a negative value will invert the node to look as if it is a mirror image of the original node and it is often used to create reflection-like effects.

Also note one other difference in the implementation of the custom node in Listing 12-19. The example does not override the '**create**' method of the **CustomNode** class, but instead overrides the '**children**' attribute of the **CustomNode**. This is the preferred approach over overriding the create **method** and the advantage of this approach is that you do not have to create an intermediate group to represent multiple nodes within a custom node as we had done in Listing-12-18. The **children** attribute is a node array as opposed to a single Node return value of **CustomNode.create**.

You may apply multiple transformations to a node by specifying an ordered chain of transforms. The order in which the transforms are applied is defined by the sequence specified in the **transforms** variable.

Controls & Layouts

JavaFX offers a wide set of controls and layouts that are useful for creating front-ends for enterprise applications. All these controls are pure JavaFX implementations and hence provide a uniform look and feel across all devices. Controls provide additional variables and behaviors beyond those of Node to support common user interactions in a manner that is consistent and predictable for the user. However, controls are no different from normal nodes as far as developers are concerned and you can add a control wherever you can add a node. All controls extend from the **javafx.scene.Control** class, which in tern extend from **javafx.scene.CustomNode**. Each control comes with its own skin that you can customize to suit your application requirements. By default, all controls except Label blocks mouse events and hence the nodes obscured by controls will not get the mouse events when interacting with the control unless you turn off **blocksMouse** explicitly.

All controls except for a few, such as ProgressBar, Label, are focus-traversable by default. So you don't have to explicitly make them focus-traversable and they all support keyboard focus traversal in the forward and reverse directions by default, unlike nodes. A control can transfer focus to a focus-traversable node available in the focus-traversal cycle when pressing TAB but after that, it is the responsibility of that node to transfer the focus to the next node in the focus cycle. Whereas, controls do this by default for you.

JavaFX as of 1.3 offers the set of controls shown in Figure 12-29.

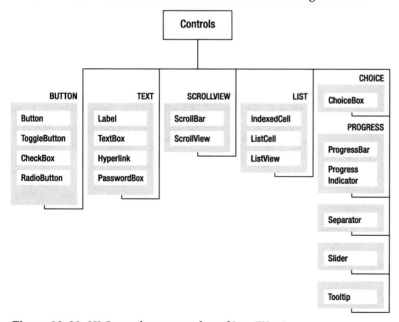

Figure 12-29. *UI Controls supported as of JavaFX 1.3*

In addition to what is shown in the diagram, there is also a set of preview controls that are available purely on an experimental basis in the **com.javafx.preview.control** package and you can try them out. Some of those controls are:

- CheckMenuItem
- CustomMenuItem
- Menu
- MenuBar
- MenuButton
- MenuItem
- MenuItemBase
- PopupMenu
- RadioMenuItem
- SplitMenuButton
- ToolBar
- TreeCell
- TreeItem
- TreeItemBase
- TreeView

However, these controls are not for production use and may change in the next release. You can just play with them and provide your feedback.

Similarly, there are many layout managers available under **javafx.scene.layout** and these layouts can accept controls as well as nodes. Lot of improvements have gone into layouts and controls in JavaFX 1.3. Listing 12-20 shows one of the most typical usecases of controls and layouts—a simple login form created using the Panel layout and a set of controls (see Figure 12-30).

Listing 12-20. *Login Form Using Controls*

```
package layout;

import javafx.stage.Stage;
import javafx.scene.Scene;
import javafx.scene.CustomNode;
import javafx.scene.Node;
import javafx.scene.layout.Panel;
import javafx.scene.control.Label;
import javafx.scene.control.TextBox;
import javafx.scene.control.PasswordBox;
import javafx.scene.control.Button;
import javafx.scene.paint.Color;
```

```
import javafx.scene.paint.LinearGradient;
import javafx.scene.paint.Stop;
import javafx.scene.shape.Rectangle;
import javafx.stage.StageStyle;

public class LoginForm extends CustomNode{

    def width = bind scene.width on replace {
        panel.requestLayout();
    }
    def height = bind scene.height on replace {
        panel.requestLayout();
    }
    var panel : Panel;

    var paddingTop = 20.0;
    var paddingLeft = 20.0;
    var paddingBottom = 20.0;
    var paddingRight = 20.0;

    var saveButton:Button = Button {
        text: "Save"
        action: function() {
                saveButton.scene.stage.close();
        }
    }
    var cancelButton:Button = Button {
        text: "Cancel"
        action: function() {
                cancelButton.scene.stage.close();
        }
    }

    var idLabel = Label { text: "Login Name" };
    var idText = TextBox { columns : 20};
    var passwordLabel = Label { text: "Password" };
    var passwordTxtBox = PasswordBox { columns : 20};

    override function create() : Node {
        panel = Panel{
            content: [
                idLabel, idText,
                passwordLabel, passwordTxtBox,
               saveButton, cancelButton
            ]
            onLayout: onLayout
        }
    }

    function onLayout() : Void {
```

```
            var hSpacing = 10.0;
            var vSpacing = 5.0;
            var gridW = 50.0;
            var gridH = 25.0;

            idLabel.height = gridH;
            var w = panel.getNodePrefWidth(idLabel);
            var x = (paddingLeft + gridW) - w;
            var y = paddingTop;
            var h = gridH;
            panel.layoutNode(idLabel, x, y, w, h);

            x = paddingLeft + gridW + hSpacing;
            w = panel.getNodePrefWidth(idText);
            panel.layoutNode(idText, x, y, w, h);

            w = panel.getNodePrefWidth(passwordLabel);
            x = (paddingLeft + gridW) - w;
            y = idLabel.layoutY + gridH + vSpacing;
            panel.layoutNode(passwordLabel, x, y, w, h);

            x = paddingLeft + gridW + hSpacing;
            w = panel.getNodePrefWidth(passwordTxtBox);
            panel.layoutNode(passwordTxtBox, x, y, w, h);

            w = panel.getNodePrefWidth(cancelButton);
            var buttonPanelWidth = (w * 2) + hSpacing;
            x = (scene.width - buttonPanelWidth)/2.0;
            y = passwordTxtBox.layoutY + (gridH * 2);
            panel.layoutNode(saveButton, x, y, w, h);

            x = saveButton.layoutX + hSpacing + w;
            panel.layoutNode(cancelButton, x, y, w, h);
    }
}

function run(){
    Stage {
        title: "Login Form"
        style : StageStyle.UNDECORATED
        scene: Scene {
            width: 280
            height: 140
            content: [
                Rectangle {
                    width: 280
                    height: 140
                    stroke: Color.BLACK
                    strokeWidth: 2
                    fill: LinearGradient {
                        startX: 0.491
                        startY: -0.009
```

```
                    endX: 0.509
                    endY: 1.009
                    proportional: true
                    stops: [Stop {
                            offset: 0
                            color: Color.color(0.639, 0.639, 0.639, 0.239)
                        }, Stop {
                            offset: 1
                            color: Color.color(0.078, 0.078, 0.078, 0.988)
                        }]
                }
                arcHeight: 20
                arcWidth: 20
            },
            LoginForm{}
        ]
    }
}
}
```

Figure 12-30. *UI controls & layouts–login form*

Listing 12-20 demonstrates a common usecase of designing a login form using the Panel layout and a set of UI controls. Panel is the layout that offers maximum flexibility to you and you can customize the way controls/nodes must be displayed within the panel by defining your own coordinates. As you can see in Listing 12-20, there is an '**onLayout**' function that is defined within the Panel object literal and this method takes care of positioning the controls appropriately within the panel. Also, this method is invoked indirectly by '**Container.requestLayout**' whenever the scene width/height changes. The actual positioning code is self-explanatory.

Covering controls and layouts further in this chapter will really be overwhelming since they are huge topics by themselves. There is pretty good online documentation available for controls and layouts at **www.javafx.com** and please refer the same for more information, in addition to the API documentation shipped with the SDK. For example, the following document is worth referring to for controls: **www.javafx.com/docs/articles/UIControls/overview.jsp**

StyleSheets

JavaFX 1.3 offers a powerful and comprehensive CSS engine that allows you to customize the built-in look of the nodes and controls. Using CSS in JavaFX is similar to using it with HTML since CSS implementation is fully adherent to the CSS specification specified at **www.w3.org/Style/CSS/**. You can define the styles at the application level through a .css file that you can embed into the scene using the **javafx.scene.Scene.stylesheets** attribute that accepts an array of string URLs to multiple style sheets. Alternatively, you can also customize the style on a per-node basis using the **'id'** and **'styleClass'** attributes available in the node class. Please refer to the online documentation at **www.javafx.com/docs/articles/UIControls/theming.jsp** for more information on how to use CSS with JavaFX. Also note that this is available on desktop as well as mobile devices, as of JavaFX 1.3.

Charts

Charts allow the user of the chart to visualize and interpret a large volume of data in an easy way and derive appropriate business conclusions from it. JavaFX offers a wide range of APIs to create and manipulate charts and graphs and it supports creation of the following charts that are most commonly used in a RIA (also demonstrated in Figure 12-31):

- **Area Chart:** Displays quantitative data like a line chart but with the area between the line and the horizontal axis shaded. Good for comparing the magnitude of two or more series of data.

- **Bar Chart:** A good way to show data in a way that makes it easy to see how the data changes over time or under a set of different conditions.

- **Bubble Chart:** Plot data points on a two-dimensional grid and have the extra ability to display the relative magnitudes of the data by controlling the diameter of the point (or bubble) displayed at each XY coordinate.

- **Line Chart:** A simple way to display two-dimensional data points where each point is connected to the next point in the data series by a line.

- **Pie Chart:** Typically used to display the relative percentages of a series of values on a circle. The value of each piece of data, as a percentage of the total, dictates how much of the circle's area it takes up. In other words, the chart shows how big a slice of the pie each value represents.

- **Scatter Chart:** Used to plot the points of one or more series of data. These charts are typically used to show the correlation (or not) of the data by comparing how the data points are clustered (or not).

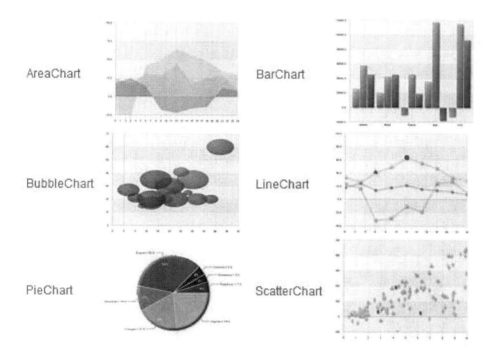

AreaChart

BarChart

BubbleChart

LineChart

PieChart

ScatterChart

Figure 12-31. *JavaFX Charts*

Listing 12-21 shows a simple example of how to create a pie-chart using JavaFX Chart APIs, with the output shown in Figure 12-32.

Listing 12-21. *A Pie Chart*

```
    import javafx.stage.Stage;
import javafx.scene.Scene;
import javafx.scene.chart.*;

def pieChart = PieChart {
    title: "Health Pie"
    data: [
        PieChart.Data { label: "Carrot" value: 22  }
        PieChart.Data { label: "Eggplant" value: 27 }
        PieChart.Data { label: "Potato" value: 16 }
        PieChart.Data { label: "Tomato" value: 50 }
        PieChart.Data { label: "Cauliflower" value: 6 }
        PieChart.Data { label: "Mushroom" value: 7 }
    ]
}

Stage {
```

```
    title: "Pie Chart"
    scene: Scene{
            width: 540
            height: 410
            content: pieChart
    } //Scene
}//Stage
```

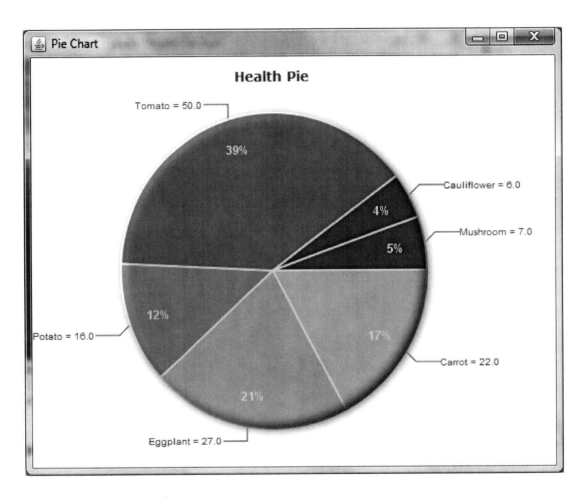

Figure 12-32. *JavaFX pie chart*

In Listing 12-21, a pie chart has been defined with a title and a set of data, where each data is provided with a label and a value of this pie. As you see in Figure 12-32, all the labels and the pie value are displayed in the output. Additionally, you can use other attributes **PieChart.Data** to customize the chart or make it interactive by responding to user input.

For some of the other charts, such as BarChart, you will have to define the X and Y axis of the chart where you can have the category on one axis and a set of numeric values on the other and define a lower and upper bound for the numeric values with appropriate tick values. There is a detailed article on charts at http://java.sun.com that will help you build more complex charts using JavaFX. Please refer to the following article for more information:
`http://java.sun.com/developer/technicalArticles/javafx/v1_2_charts/`.

Effects

An effect is a graphical algorithm that produces an image, typically as a modification of a source image. Effects primarily add richness to your UI by manipulating the default look of your node in various ways, such as adding a glow effect, a shadow within the node, a drop-shadow outside of your node, blurring certain pixels of your node, and so forth. You can associate an effect with a scene graph Node by setting the **Node.effect** attribute. Some effects change the color properties of the source pixels (such as **ColorAdjust**), others combine multiple images together (such as **Blend**), while still others warp or move the pixels of the source image around (such as **DisplacementMap** or **PerspectiveTransform**). All effects have at least one input defined and the input can be set to another effect to chain the effects together and combine their results, or it can be left unspecified, in which case the effect will operate on a graphical rendering of the node it is attached to. All effects available in **javafx.scene.effect** descend from the **javafx.scene.effect.Effect** class. Effects are **desktop-only** APIs and not available on other devices.

■ **Note** Advanced effects are visually intensive and often require a good video card (with OpenGL or Direct3D support) so that the operations can be hardware-accelerated for better performance. Without a good video card, these operations will use the software pipeline and may cause sluggishness or a drop in visual performance in some cases.

Bounds

The visuals displayed within a JavaFX scene are fully represented by a 2D scene graph, where each visual element (line, path, image, and so forth) is represented by a distinct node with variables that can be easily manipulated dynamically. The node's size and position (otherwise known as its *bounds*) become complicated when considering these many variables that contribute to its bounds, such as shape geometry (for example, startX/startY, width, and radius), transformations (for example, scale and rotate), effects (for example, shadows and glow), and clipping. Understanding how each of these variables affects the bounds calculations of a node is crucial to getting the scene layout you want.

Bounds Class

A node's rectangular bounds are represented by the **javafx.geometry.Bounds** class, which provides init-only **minX**, **minY**, **maxX**, **maxY**, **width**, **height** variables. Keep in mind that since the bounding box can be anywhere in the 2D coordinate space, *the X/Y values may often be negative*.

■ **Note** The Bounds class was introduced in JavaFX1.2 in anticipation of adding Z in the future. BoundingBox (concrete 2D implementation of Bounds) has replaced Rectangle2D for bounds values, however Rectangle2D still exists as a general-purpose geom class for other uses.

Node Bounds Variables

A **Bounds** object is always relative to a particular coordinate system, and for each node it is useful to look at bounds in both the node's local (untransformed) coordinate space, as well as in its parent's coordinate space once all transforms have been applied. The **Node** API provides three variables for these bounds values and are listed in Table 12-5.

Table 12-5. bounds related attributes in Node class

Attribute	Access	Description
boundsInLocal	(public-read)	physical bounds in the node's local, untransformed coordinate space, including **shape geometry**, space required for a non-zero **strokeWidth** that may fall outside the shape's position/size geometry, the **effect** and the **clip**.
boundsInParent	(public-read)	physical bounds of the node after ALL transforms have been applied to the node's coordinate space, including **transforms[]**, **scaleX/scaleY**, **rotate**, **translateX/translateY**, and **layoutX/layoutY**.
layoutBounds	(public-read protected)	*logical* bounds used as basis for layout calculations; by default only includes a node's **shape geometry**, however its definition may be overridden in subclasses. It does not necessarily correspond to the node's physical bounds.

It's worth pointing out that a node's visibility has no affect on its bounds; these bounds can be queried whether its visible or not.

It might be easier to visualize in Figure 12-33, which shows the sequence in which the bounds-affecting variables are applied; variables are applied left-to-right, where each is applied to the result of the one preceding it (geometry first, layoutX/Y last).

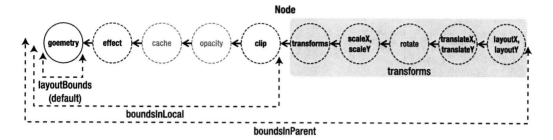

Figure 12-33. *Semantics of various bounds variables in the Node class*

The reason we need a more malleable definition for layout bounds (versus just using **boundsInParent**) is because a dynamic, animating interface often needs to control which aspects of a node should be factored into layout versus not.

Figure 12-34 shows a simple example of how bounds computation is done for a simple rounded rectangle with no effects, transforms, or clipping.

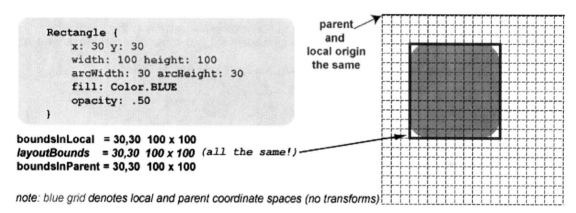

Figure 12-34. *Demonstration of bounds on a rounded rectangle with no transformations*

In Figure 12-34, note that x and y are variables specific to rectangle and that they position the rectangle within its *own* coordinate space rather than moving the entire coordinate space of the node. On the other hand, transformations change the coordinate space of the node instead of the actual geometry. All of the **javafx.scene.shape** classes have variables for specifying appropriate shape geometry within their local coordinate space (for example, Rectangle has x, y, width, height; Circle has centerX, centerY, radius; and so forth) and such position variables should not be confused with a translation on the coordinate space.

Figure 12-35 shows how a simple translation works for this case.

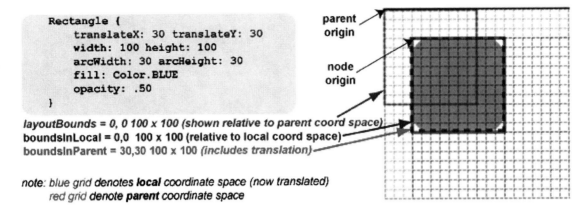

```
Rectangle {
    translateX: 30 translateY: 30
    width: 100 height: 100
    arcWidth: 30 arcHeight: 30
    fill: Color.BLUE
    opacity: .50
}
```

layoutBounds = 0, 0 100 x 100 (shown relative to parent coord space)
boundsInLocal = 0,0 100 x 100 (relative to local coord space)
boundsInParent = 30,30 100 x 100 *(includes translation)*

*note: blue grid denotes **local** coordinate space (now translated)*
  *red grid denote **parent** coordinate space*

Figure 12-35. *Rounded rectangle with a translation*

Now in Figure 12-35, **boundsInParent** has changed to reflect the translated rectangle; however, **boundsInLocal** and **layoutBounds** remain unchanged because they are relative to the rectangle's coordinate space, which was what was shifted. Although **layoutBounds** is relative to the node's local coordinate space, I'm showing it in the parent's to emphasize how a parent container interprets its value when laying out the node.

Figure 12-36 demonstrates the bounds of a rectangle when it is rotated and scaled.

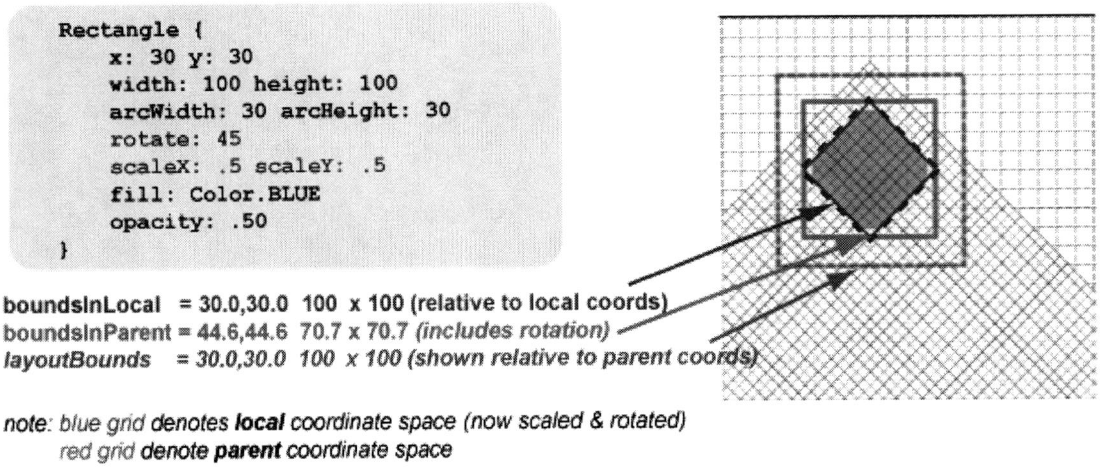

```
Rectangle {
    x: 30 y: 30
    width: 100 height: 100
    arcWidth: 30 arcHeight: 30
    rotate: 45
    scaleX: .5 scaleY: .5
    fill: Color.BLUE
    opacity: .50
}
```

boundsInLocal = 30.0,30.0 100 x 100 (relative to local coords)
boundsInParent = 44.6,44.6 70.7 x 70.7 *(includes rotation)*
layoutBounds   = 30.0,30.0 100 x 100 *(shown relative to parent coords)*

*note: blue grid denotes **local** coordinate space (now scaled & rotated)*
  *red grid denote **parent** coordinate space*

Figure 12-36. *Rounded rectangle with rotation and scale*

Please note that **layoutBounds** remains unchanged (from the perspective of the parent), even as the node's local coordinate system is scaled and rotated.

The bounds of a Group node have a slight twist: **layoutBounds** is calculated by taking the union of the **boundsInParent** on all *visible* children (invisible children are not factored into its bounds). **boundsInLocal** will take the **layoutBounds** and add any effect or clip set on the group. Finally, the group's

boundsInParent is calculated by taking **boundsInLocal** and applying any transforms set on the group. This is demonstrated in Figure 12-37.

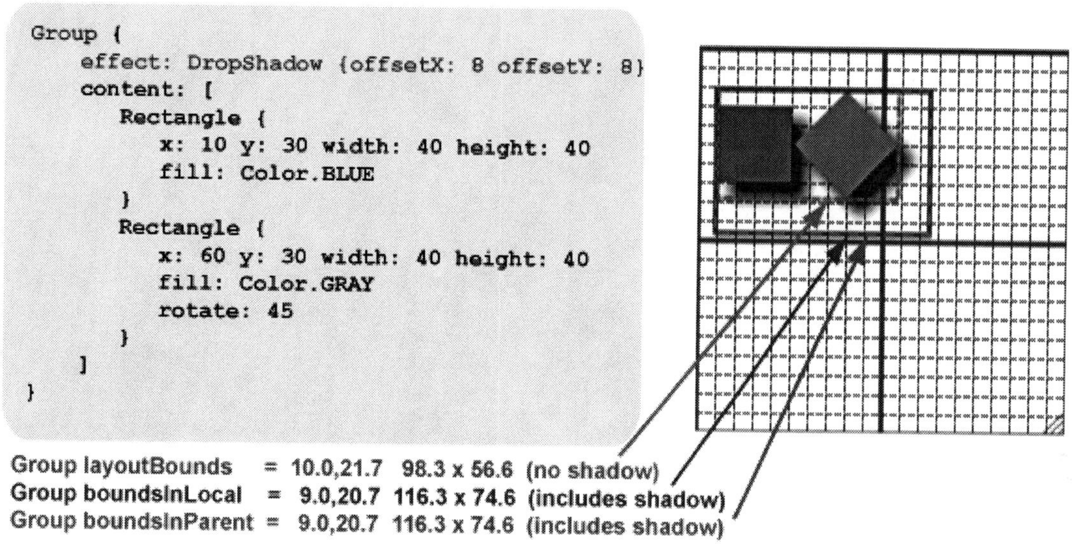

```
Group {
    effect: DropShadow {offsetX: 8 offsetY: 8}
    content: [
        Rectangle {
            x: 10 y: 30 width: 40 height: 40
            fill: Color.BLUE
        }
        Rectangle {
            x: 60 y: 30 width: 40 height: 40
            fill: Color.GRAY
            rotate: 45
        }
    ]
}
```

Group layoutBounds   = 10.0,21.7 98.3 x 56.6 (no shadow)
Group boundsInLocal = 9.0,20.7 116.3 x 74.6 (includes shadow)
Group boundsInParent = 9.0,20.7 116.3 x 74.6 (includes shadow)

Figure 12-37. Group bounds

The group's **layoutBounds** are tightly wrapped around the union of its children **boundsInParent** and do not include the drop shadow.

Summary

In this chapter, you have learned about all the graphical features available in JavaFX right from the fundamentals such as the rendering model, scene graph, scene and stage, and various graphics APIs that JavaFX offer such as shapes, strokes, fills, font, text, images, colors, gradience, bounds, transformations, controls, layouts, and so forth. You have also learned about how to make your applications interactive by handling the keyboard and mouse events appropriately. Already you have learned about the JavaFX Script language extensively in the previous chapters, and now you have gained all that is required to build a wonderful RIA.

The next and final chapter will help you learn more about how to add dynamic contents to your application through various animations and will give you a good introduction on the animation framework that is built-in to the JavaFX Script language.

CHAPTER 13

■ ■ ■

Introduction to Animation

Animation is one of the basic building blocks of any RIA, and any RIA technology need to have good animation support in order to deliver an immersive Internet experience to the end user. Animation adds liveliness to the content you are presenting and makes it far more expressive and interactive to the end user than static content.

What is Animation?

Before going into the animation support JavaFX provides, let us first see what animation is. Animation is a process of creating and displaying a sequence of frames (or simply pictures) within a given time period to create an illusion of movement. The retina of the human eye (some psychologists argue that it's the human brain) can persist, or hold, the picture that is exposed to it for a certain time period even after the exposure to the picture has ceased. For example, you can easily recall seeing a glowing light float in your eye for some time after you look into a light source and then switch off the light. This is due to the *persistence of vision*, in which the retina persists the image that has been exposed to it for approximately one twenty-fifth of a second. So you can create an optical illusion of motion by presenting 24 or more frames per second (FPS) for the human eye to recognize smooth animation.

Animation in JavaFX

In JavaFX, animation can be achieved simply by changing the value of any variable over a specific time period. Note that this is not directly related to the UI but rather is built into the language syntax. The visual behavior of the animation is brought in through the usage of the variable whose value is changed over a timeline. If, for instance, you are changing the value of a variable x from 0 to 360 within 5 seconds, this is just a language feature and there is no UI involved until you bind this variable to, for example, a node's `rotate` attribute. Once it is bound, this ordinary value change transforms into a visual animation of rotating the specified node from 0 to 360 within a span of 5 seconds. If you bind the same variable to `scaleX`/`scaleY` of the node, it would be a zoom transformation instead of rotation. Technically, you can also refer to this as a state transition of your scene or node, where animation is basically a sequence of transitions of a node's state over a timeline.

Thus animation in JavaFX is independent of the UI and is a feature of the language through which you can change the value of any attribute over a timeline. Application developers have the freedom to map such value changes into a visual animation appropriately, as illustrated in our example of binding a rotate variable to the `rotate` attribute of a node.

JavaFX offer various animation capabilities through the APIs, available in the following packages:

- `javafx.animation`

- `javafx.animation.transition`

Animation also uses some special operators, such as `=>` and `tween`, that are built into the language. You will learn about them as you read further.

JavaFX animation can be described as *keyframe* animation, which is the traditional animation technique used in visual design tools. It is also considered the one of the most effective techniques for defining animation programmatically. In a keyframe animation, you constitute a series of state transitions where you define the starting and ending snapshots of your scene's state at specific points in time and leave it to the interpolation mechanism to generate the intermediate states. Interpolation is a mechanism by which the intermediate states of an animation with starting and ending states defined are calculated automatically using either a predefined algorithm or a custom algorithm that is specified explicitly. These intermediate states ensure there is a smooth transition from the beginning state to the end state, which is critical for the visual illusion of motion.

So a timeline (`javafx.animation.Timeline`) is defined by one or more keyframes (`javafx.animation.KeyFrame`), and each keyframe has a specific time and a set of values. This timeline processes the keyframes sequentially in the order specified by `KeyFrame.time`. The values defined by `KeyFrame` are interpolated to or from the targeted key values depending on the direction of the animation at the given time.

Now let us see a simple example of how to create a timeline to cause a circle to zoom in and zoom out. Listing 13-1 shows the code, and Figure 13-1 shows the output.

Listing 13-1. Zooming in and out of a circle

```
import javafx.stage.Stage;
import javafx.scene.Scene;
import javafx.scene.shape.Circle;
import javafx.scene.paint.Color;
import javafx.animation.Timeline;
import javafx.animation.KeyFrame;
import javafx.animation.Interpolator;

var rad : Number = 10.0;
var circle : Circle =  Circle {
    centerX: 100, centerY: 100
        radius : bind rad
    fill: Color.RED
}

Timeline {
    repeatCount: Timeline.INDEFINITE
    keyFrames : [
        KeyFrame {
                time : 0s
                values : [rad => 80 tween Interpolator.LINEAR]
            },
        KeyFrame {
                time : 2s
                values : [rad => 0 tween Interpolator.LINEAR]
```

```
                }
        ]
    }.playFromStart();

    Stage {
        title: "Animation Example-1"
        scene: Scene {
            width: 200
            height: 200
            content: [   circle   ]
        }
    }
```

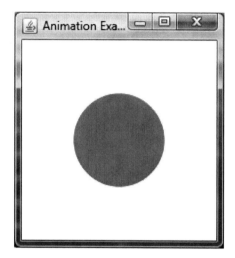

Figure 13-1. *Output of zooming of a circle*

In Listing 13-1, there is a timeline defined with two keyframes. The first keyframe is a starting snapshot state, which initializes the `time` variable to 0 seconds and the `radius` of the circle to 80. The second keyframe is the ending snapshot of the state transition, where `time` is defined as 4 seconds and the `radius` value is 0. Basically, this timeline instructs JavaFX to initialize the `radius` of the circle to 80 at 0 seconds and, within a time period of 4 seconds, reduce the `radius` of the circle from 80 to 0. Then repeat this animation indefinitely. The interpolation to be used for calculating the value of `radius` between 0 and 4 seconds is `LINEAR` interpolation, which means that calculation of radius will happen at a steady rate from beginning to end.

Let us analyze the code in more detail, since there are some new operators and data types.

KeyFrame.time

This accepts a data type called `Duration` (`javafx.lang.Duration`). The `Duration` class accepts values in terms of time. Duration can be specified in terms of milliseconds, seconds, minutes, and so on. For example, you can express a 2½ minute value in the following ways:

```
Duration t = 2m + 30s;
Duration t = 2.5m;
Duration t = 2500ms;
```

In addition to this, there are multiple utility methods available in the `Duration` class to manipulate time values, convert from one type to another, add/divide/subtract one time value to/from another, and compare two duration objects. Animation uses this data type extensively since it is a time-bound feature.

```
=>
```

The `=>` operator is a literal constructor (a shortened form) that specifies the target value for a given attribute.

tween

The `tween` operator denotes the type of tweening (also called inbetweening) to be used. Tweening is the process of generating intermediate frames between two given frames to give the appearance that the first frame evolves smoothly into the second one, using the appropriate interpolation mechanism. In short, `tween` specifies the interpolation technique to be used in the state transition, in this example `Interpolator.LINEAR`.

Timeline.keyFrames

As you see, `Timeline.keyFrames` is a sequence of keyframes, which means you are not just restricted to specifying the first and last keyframes; you define as many intermediate keyframes as you wish at each time period. Even in this example, you can specify individual keyframes for `1s`, `2s`, `3s`, and so on —each specifying a target value for the radius.

KeyFrame.values

`KeyFrame.values` is also a sequence, which means you are not limited to just changing a single attribute; you can change as many attributes as you like. In this example, you could also change the `centerX, centerY` of the circle when changing the radius. The code for doing that would be similar to the following:

```
KeyFrame {
    time: 0s
    values: [rad => 80 tween LINEAR, circle.centerX => 400 tween LINEAR, circle.centerY =>
200 tween LINEAR]
}
```

This would initialize the `centerX, centerY` of the circle to different values when the animation starts.

Timeline.repeatCount

This specifies the number of times you want the animation to repeat. The default value is 1, which means it will just be executed once. To change that, you can either give a specific value or say `INDEFINITE`, as in this example, if you want the timeline to run indefinitely. An important point to note here is that the animation repeats again from 0 seconds after reaching 4 seconds. In this example, it would mean that the value of `radius` changes in the following order:

10 (initial value) ▸

First cycle: 80 (0 sec) ▸ (radius value decrements in linear fashion as time increases)...▸ 0 (4 sec)

Second cycle: 80 (5 sec) ▸ (radius value decrements in linear fashion as time increases)...▸ 0 (8 sec)

Third cycle: 80 (9 sec) ▸ (radius value decrements in linear fashion as time increases)...▸ 0 (12 sec)

and so on.

Note that radius suddenly changes from 0 to 80 at the beginning of every animation cycle and gradually reduces to 0 from 0 to 4 seconds.

Now let us revisit the Listing 13-1 code in detail to summarize our understanding.

The first KeyFrame defines the initial state of the circle when the animation is about to start. So at 0 seconds, radius will be initialized to 80 and circle will be resized to the new radius.

The second KeyFrame defines the final state of the animation, which concludes at 4 seconds. At this time, the radius of the circle should have become 0.

The interpolation is LINEAR, which means radius should change at a constant rate when time increments from 0 to 4th second.

Timeline should be repeated indefinitely as explained in the Timeline.repeatCount section.

The rad value is bound to circle.radius, which will refresh the circle visually when the rad value changes.

But all these are just definitions, and the timeline is not actually running. A timeline is like a movie in the sense that you will have to play it, and so we are calling the Timeline.playFromStart() function, which will play the animation from 0 seconds. There are methods available in the Timeline class to play, stop and pause the animation, which you will learn in the next section.

You will see the output as shown in Figure-13-1 and the circle will zoom out from 80 to 0 gradually in 4 seconds, after which it will suddenly zoom to the size of 80 again.

Currently the animation effect appears little jerky, because the radius resets to 80 from 0 every time a new cycle starts. Instead of this, wouldn't it be nice to zoom in the circle gradually back to 80 from 0 instead of a sudden switch? You don't need to define another keyframe to do this, and there is a built-in attribute in Timeline which does it for you:

Timeline.autoReverse

This is a Boolean value that when True indicates that the timeline should reverse its direction for every alternate cycle. It is set to False by default. Now let us assume that we have revised Listing 13-1 to set this to True, and see how the values change (following the flow given under Timeline.repeatCount):

10 (initial value) ▸

First cycle: 80 (0 sec) ▸ (radius value decrements in linear fashion as time increases)...▸ 0 (4 sec)

Second cycle: 0 (5 sec) ▸ radius value increments in linear fashion as time increases)...▸ 80 (8 sec)

Third cycle: 80 (9 sec) ▸ (radius value decrements in linear fashion as time increases)...▸ 0 (12 sec)

As you see, the timeline has reversed its direction for the second cycle, and radius will now gradually increase from 0 to 80, giving a smooth zooming experience. Add this attribute to Listing 13-1 and try it out yourself.

Play, Pause, or Stop a Timeline

A timeline is like a movie that you can play, pause and stop, just as you do with your DVD player. Following is a brief overview of the attributes for starting and stopping a timeline:

play : Plays the timeline from the current position. This is typically used after a pause, where it resumes play from the time where it was paused before.

playFromStart: Plays the timeline from the beginning; that is, from 0 seconds. This must be used when you are starting the timeline for the first time and not after a pause, since typically you would want a paused timeline to resume from where it was paused

pause: Pauses the animation temporarily. Can be resumed subsequently through play

stop: Stops the animation permanently and resets the current time position to 0.

Now let us see a simple example which demonstrates each of the playing options as applied to an animating circle. Listing 13-2 shows the code and Figure 13-2 shows the output.

Listing 13-2. Play/pause/stop demonstration

```
import javafx.stage.Stage;
import javafx.scene.Scene;
import javafx.scene.shape.Circle;
import javafx.scene.paint.Color;
import javafx.animation.Interpolator;
import javafx.animation.KeyFrame;
import javafx.animation.Timeline;
import javafx.scene.control.ToggleGroup;
import javafx.scene.control.RadioButton;
import javafx.scene.layout.HBox;

var xAxis : Number = 0.0;
def toggleGroup = ToggleGroup {};
var timeline : Timeline;

var playRB : RadioButton = RadioButton {
    text: "Play"
    toggleGroup: toggleGroup
}

var playFromStartRB : RadioButton = RadioButton {
    text: "PlayFromStart"
    toggleGroup: toggleGroup
}

var stopRB : RadioButton = RadioButton {
    text: "Stop"
    toggleGroup: toggleGroup
}

var pauseRB : RadioButton = RadioButton {
```

```
            text: "Pause"
        toggleGroup: toggleGroup
    }

    var selectedButton = bind toggleGroup.selectedToggle on replace {
            if (selectedButton == pauseRB) {
                timeline.pause();
            } else if (selectedButton == stopRB) {
                timeline.stop();
            } else if (selectedButton == playRB) {
                timeline.play();
            } else if (selectedButton == playFromStartRB) {
                timeline.playFromStart();
        }
    }

    var layout : HBox  = HBox{
        translateX : 10
        translateY : 20
        spacing : 10
        content: [playFromStartRB, stopRB, playRB, pauseRB]
    }

    var circle : Circle = Circle {
        centerX: 20.0
        centerY: 100.0
        radius: 40.0
        fill: Color.BLACK
        translateX: bind xAxis
    }

    timeline = Timeline {
        keyFrames : [
            KeyFrame {
                time : 2s
                values : xAxis => 400 tween Interpolator.EASEBOTH
            }
        ]
        autoReverse: true
        repeatCount:  Timeline.INDEFINITE
    }
    timeline.play();

    Stage {
        title: "play/pause/stop demo"
        scene: Scene {
            width: 450
            height: 200
            content: [ layout, circle ]
        }
    }
```

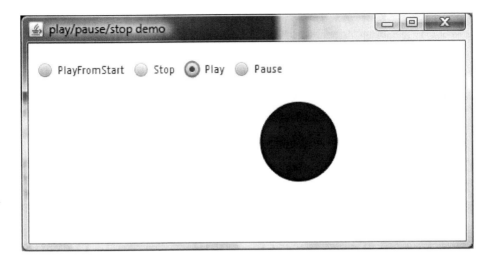

Figure 13-2. *Output from the Play/Pause/Stop demo*

In Listing 13-2, we are animating a circle by translating it on the x-axis back and forth, as illustrated in Figure 13-2. The timeline is set with autoReverse true, and so the animation changes its direction for alternate cycles and continues indefinitely. You will notice the following behaviors with this application:

- Select the Pause radio button, and animation will stop at the current position. Selecting Play subsequently will play the animation from the same position where it was stopped. On the other hand, if you select PlayFromStart after a pause, it will start from the starting position (which might be either the leftmost or the rightmost end, depending on the direction of the animation cycle at the time of the pause).

- Select the Stop radio button, and animation will stop at the current position. Please note that Stop resets the current position to its initial position, so selecting Play or PlayFromStart will only start the animation from the starting position.

There are read-only variables in the Timeline class that give the current status of animation such as running or paused, and that are set when the animation is played/paused or stopped.

Another important aspect that you should notice here is that we have defined only a single keyframe, whose time value is specified as 2s (2 seconds). This is actually the end point of the timeline; the timeline will automatically synthesize a starting keyframe, whose time value will be 0 seconds if none is specified explicitly. So for keyframe 0, the value of the xAxis variable would be its initial value, which is 0 in this case. So the timeline aims to translate the circle from 0 to 400 within a span of 2 seconds.

KeyFrame Attributes

As you have learned, a keyframe defines a snapshot of the animation at a given point in time by specifying the time and respective values of the animation at the given time. There are also additional attributes that can be defined as part of the keyframe, such as action and canSkip. This section looks at each of them in detail.

KeyFrame.action

The action function of the KeyFrame class is called when the elapsed time of the animation cycle passes the specified time of the keyframe. The function is called when the elapsed time passes the specified time even if it never equaled the indicated value exactly. This function is handy when you want to execute something at the end of each keyframe.

KeyFrame.canSkip

This attribute indicates whether the timeline can skip calling the action function of the keyframe if the master timer gets behind and more than one timeline cycle is skipped between time pulses. If it is set to True, only one call to the action function will occur for each time pulse regardless of how many cycles have occurred since the last execution of the action.

Listing 13-3 and Figure 13-3 illustrate how to use the action attribute of the keyframe.

Listing 13-3. KeyFrame action

```
import javafx.stage.*;
import javafx.scene.shape.*;
import javafx.scene.paint.*;
import javafx.animation.*;
import javafx.scene.*;


var scaleX: Number = 1.0;
var scaleY: Number = 1.0;
var rotate: Number = 0;
var timeline : Timeline;
var scene:Scene;
var sceneWidth = bind scene.width;
var sceneHeight = bind scene.height;
var colors = [Color.RED, Color.BLUE, Color.GREEN, Color.LIME, Color.BROWN,
Color.GOLD, Color.PINK];
var colorIndex = 0 on replace {
    if (colorIndex >= sizeof colors - 1) {
        colorIndex = 0;
    }
}
var fillColor = bind colors[colorIndex];
var rect: Rectangle = Rectangle {
    x: bind sceneWidth/2 - 50
    y: bind sceneHeight/2 - 50
    width: 100
    height: 100
    fill: bind fillColor
    stroke: Color.YELLOW
    strokeWidth: 2.0
    scaleX: bind scaleX
    scaleY: bind scaleY
    rotate: bind rotate
```

```
}

var counter = 0;

timeline = Timeline {
    keyFrames : [
        KeyFrame {
            time : 0s
            values : [scaleX => 0 tween Interpolator.LINEAR,
                      scaleY => 0 tween Interpolator.LINEAR,
                      rotate => 0 tween Interpolator.LINEAR]
            action: function() {
                print("0 ");
                colorIndex ++;
            }
        },
        KeyFrame {
            time : 3s
            values : [scaleX => 1.5 tween Interpolator.LINEAR,
                      scaleY => 1.5 tween Interpolator.LINEAR,
                      rotate => 120 tween Interpolator.LINEAR]
            action: function() {
                print("3 ");
                colorIndex ++;
            }
        },
        KeyFrame {
            time : 5s
            values : [scaleX => 4.0 tween Interpolator.LINEAR,
                      scaleY => 4.0 tween Interpolator.LINEAR,
                      rotate => 360 tween Interpolator.LINEAR]
            action: function() {
                print("5 ");
                colorIndex ++;
            }
        }
    ]
    autoReverse: true
    repeatCount:  Timeline.INDEFINITE
}
timeline.play();

scene = Scene {
    width: 400
    height: 400
    content: [rect]
}

Stage {
    title: "KeyFrame Action demo"
    scene: scene
}
```

Output
0 3 5 3 0 3 5 3 0 3 5 3 0 3 5 ...

Figure 13-3. KeyFrame action

Listing 13-3 is a simple application that defines three keyframes, each of which defines a snapshot of animation with respect to the scaleX, scaleY, and rotate attributes of a rectangle. Notice that the range of value change for first two keyframes is much less than from the second to the third keyframe, and so it appears as if the animation accelerates after 3 seconds when you execute this application.

Each keyframe is defined with an action that changes the fill color of the rectangle from a set of pr-defined values and also prints out a message to indicate that the action is called. When you look at the output message printed, the timeline starts from 0s => 3s => 5s during the first cycle and then the direction of the animation reverses because autoReverse is True. So the next cycle of animation proceeds as follows: 5s => 3s => 0s. Once again the direction will be reversed at this point and will proceed in the forward direction. This continues indefinitely because `repeatCount` is set to `Timeline.INDEFINITE`. You can also visually verify the change of the rectangle's fill at every time point defined by the keyframes.

Now we can explore how `canSkip` fits into this paradigm. First let us see how the default behavior of `canSkip` works; Listing 13-4 is a version of the code from Listing 13-3, slightly modified to create a problem we might want the code to skip.

Listing 13-4. KeyFrame action program modified to introduce a delay

```
//Preceding code is the same as Listing 13-3
....
....

timeline = Timeline {
    keyFrames : [
        KeyFrame {
            time : 0s
            values : [scaleX => 0 tween Interpolator.LINEAR,
                      scaleY => 0 tween Interpolator.LINEAR,
                      rotate => 0 tween Interpolator.LINEAR]
            action: function() {
                print("0s ");
                colorIndex ++;
            }
        },
            KeyFrame {
            time : 3s
            values : [scaleX => 1.5 tween Interpolator.LINEAR,
                      scaleY => 1.5 tween Interpolator.LINEAR,
                      rotate => 120 tween Interpolator.LINEAR]
            action: function() {
                print("3s ");
                for (x in [1..1000]) {
                    java.lang.Thread.sleep(7);
                }
                colorIndex ++;
            }
        },
        KeyFrame {
            time : 5s
            values : [scaleX => 4.0 tween Interpolator.LINEAR,
                      scaleY => 4.0 tween Interpolator.LINEAR,
                      rotate => 360 tween Interpolator.LINEAR]
            action: function() {
                print("5s ");
                colorIndex ++;
            }
        }
    ]
    autoReverse: true
    repeatCount:  Timeline.INDEFINITE
}
```

```
timeline.play();

// Same as listing 13-3
....
....
```

Output
0s 3s 5s 3s 0s 3s 5s 3s 0s 3s 5s 3s

Listing 13-4 is the same animation code you saw in Listing 13-3 but with a slight change in one of the action functions. A delay of 7000 ms is introduced in the action function of the second keyframe. The execution of the timeline begins normally with the first keyframe, but when the control completes the second keyframe and executes its action, there is an unexpected delay of 7 seconds, when the timeline is supposed to be executing the third keyframe. So the timeline is behind its own schedule because of the delay we have introduced. When the timeline comes out of the second action function and is about to continue with other keyframes, it realizes that it has to miss the next two keyframes because it is already lagging behind the actual schedule. At this time, it just skips the next two keyframes. However, if canSkip is set to False (the default value), then it cannot skip the action function of the next two keyframes. Thus it is compelled to call the next two actions, though in quick succession.

So if you are doing something important within the action of the keyframe that you don't want the timeline to skip at any cost, leave the default canSkip behavior as is and your action will not be skipped, though the keyframe may be skipped due to the time lag.

However, there could be cases where your action is pretty much tied to the modifications you are doing within your keyframe and has to be executed only when the keyframe is executed successfully and not otherwise. In such cases, you will have to set canSkip to True. Then the timeline will have the freedom to skip the action when it skips the respective keyframe because of unforeseen delays that your app may have introduced in the previous actions. Timeline delays may be introduced not just by the previous actions in all cases; sometimes they are introduced by the complex operations defined within the keyframe values as well.

Now let's see how canSkip works with a True value, by modifying Listing 13-4 to create Listing 13-5, and see how the output differs.

Listing 13-5. Execution with canSkip set to True

```
// Preceding code is the same as Listing 13-4
...
...

timeline = Timeline {
    keyFrames : [
        KeyFrame {
            time : 0s
            canSkip: true
            //Same as Listing 13-4
            ....
        },
            KeyFrame {
            time : 3s
            canSkip: true
            // Same as listing 13-4
```

```
    .....
    },
    KeyFrame {
        time : 5s
        canSkip: true
        //Following code is the same as Listing 13-4
        .....
    ]
    autoReverse: true
    repeatCount:  Timeline.INDEFINITE
}
timeline.play();

// Following code is the same as listing 13-4
```

Output
0s 3s 3s 0s 3s 5s 3s 3s 0s 3s 5s 3s

In Listing 13-5, `canSkip` is set to true for all the keyframes, and so the timeline can choose to skip the subsequent keyframes and associated actions if there is a time lag. This is what is reflected in the output, where you see that the palindrome model shown in the output of Listing 13-4 is broken, and some of the keyframes are indeed skipped.

Simplified Syntax

Although keyframe animations are typical JavaFX objects, a special syntax is provided to make it easier to express animation than is possible with the standard object-literal syntax. The **trigger** clause enables you to associate an arbitrary callback with the keyframe.

Listing 13-6 illustrates how we can rewrite the code from Listing 13-1 in a simplified manner.

Listing 13-6. Simplifying the syntax of the Circle Zoom program

```
import javafx.stage.Stage;
import javafx.scene.Scene;
import javafx.scene.shape.Circle;
import javafx.scene.paint.Color;
import javafx.animation.Timeline;
import javafx.animation.KeyFrame;
import javafx.animation.Interpolator;

var rad : Number = 10.0;
var circle : Circle =  Circle {
    centerX: 100
    centerY: 100
    radius : bind rad
        fill: Color.RED
}

Timeline {
    repeatCount: Timeline.INDEFINITE
```

```
            autoReverse: true
            keyFrames : [
                at (0s) { rad => 80 tween Interpolator.LINEAR },
                at (4s) { rad => 0 tween Interpolator.LINEAR }
            ]
        }.play();

        Stage {
            title: "Animation Example-1"
            scene: Scene {
                width: 200
                height: 200
                content: [    circle    ]
            }
        }
```

The output is the same as for Listing 13-1.

In Listing 13-6, you are seeing the same application as in Listing 13-1, but the syntax for defining the keyframes is much simpler here. The time defined within the at clause is the value of the KeyFrame.time attribute that you defined in Listing 13-1, and the curly braces include the values of the keyframe.

Simplified syntax has its own limitations. If you have multiple values for the keyframe, you cannot include them within the curly braces, and you will have to define two at clauses with the same time value. Similarly, action and canSkip attributes cannot be specified when using at syntax.

So the following code snippet will not compile:

```
at (4s) { rotate => 400, scaleX => 5.0 }   //WRONG
```

Instead, you will have to write it as follows:

```
at (4s) { rotate => 400 }
at (4s) { scaleX => 5.0 }
```

This is not very convenient when you have multiple values to be changed in a keyframe, so it's important to choose the right syntax appropriate for your requirement.

The keyframe 0 can also be skipped with this syntax if you don't have a need to assign a different starting value for the keyframe than what is initialized.

Transitions

Transitions are a set of animation classes created to lighten the burden on the developers who create animated transitional effects. These classes offer a set of predefined transitions that can be utilized by merely setting a few variables, instead of going through the creation of a series of keyframes. These classes are available in the javafx.animation.transition package and include the following set of transitions:

PathTransition

ScaleTransition

FadeTransition

TranslateTransition

RotateTransition

As you'll see, multiple transitions can be combined using parallel and sequential transitions to create complex animations. Table 13-1 lists the attributes of the `Transition` class you will typically have focus on to create a meaningful animation.

Table 13-1. Transition Attributes

Attribute	Description	Default Value
Duration	Length of the animation in time. Accepts a value in `javax.scene.Duration`.	400 ms
Node	Target node to which the transition has to be applied.	Null
Interpolator	The type of interpolation to be applied.	`Interpolator.EASEBOTH`
AutoReverse	Direction of the alternate animation cycles. Same as `Timeline.autoReverse`.	FALSE
RepeatCount	The number of cycles for which this animation has to be repeated.	1
Rate	The speed at which the animation is played.	1

As you see in Table 13-1, many of the timeline attributes are applicable here, and all the transitions can be controlled just as in a keyframe animation using play/pause/playFromStart/stop methods. Transition classes can be considered a set of utility classes that offer convenience in creating transitional effects on the nodes without going through the creation of each and every keyframe.

Path Transitions

The *path transition* allows you to create a translation animation of a node along the given path. The translation is achieved by altering the `translateX`, `translateY` variables, but the object is moved along the geometric contour of the given path defined by the `path` attribute. Listing 13-7 shows an example, and Figure 13-4 illustrates its output.

Listing 13-7. A path transition

```
import javafx.stage.Stage;
import javafx.scene.*;
import javafx.scene.paint.*;
import javafx.animation.transition.*;
import javafx.scene.shape.*;
import javafx.scene.text.*;
import javafx.animation.*;
```

```
var rad : Number = 10.0;
var path:Path = Path {
    id: "Path"
    translateX: -150
    translateY: -130
    fill: Color.GRAY
    stroke: Color.BLACK
    elements: [
        MoveTo {
            x: 200
            y: 150
        },
            LineTo {
            x: 300
            y: 350
        },
            LineTo {
            x: 200
            y: 350
        },
            LineTo {
            x: 300
            y: 150
        },
            LineTo {
            x: 200
            y: 150
        },
            MoveTo {
            x: 250
            y: 250
        },
            CubicCurveTo {
            controlX1: 250
            controlY1: 250
            controlX2: 350
            controlY2: 150
            x: 300
            y: 350
        },
            MoveTo {
            x: 250
            y: 250
        },
            CubicCurveTo {
            controlX1: 250
            controlY1: 250
            controlX2: 150
            controlY2: 150
            x: 200
            y: 350
        },
```

```
                MoveTo {
                x: 250
                y: 250
            },
                ArcTo {
                x: 250
                y: 150
                radiusX: 100
                radiusY: 100
                xAxisRotation: 360
                sweepFlag: true
            },
                ArcTo {
                x: 250
                y: 250
                radiusX: 100
                radiusY: 100
                xAxisRotation: -360
                sweepFlag: true
            },
                MoveTo {
                x: 250
                y: 150
            },
                VLineTo {
                y: 250
            },
                MoveTo {
                x: 235
                y: 200
            },
                HLineTo {
                x: 265
            }
        ]
    }

    var node = Text {
        content: "JavaFX"
        fill: null
        stroke: Color.RED
        font: Font { size: 15 }
    }

    var pathTransition = PathTransition {
        duration: 10s
        path: AnimationPath.createFromPath(path)
        repeatCount: Timeline.INDEFINITE
        autoReverse: true
        node: node
    }
```

```
pathTransition.play();


Stage {
    title: "Path Transition"
    scene: Scene {
        width: 300
        height: 300
        content: [path, node]
    }
}
```

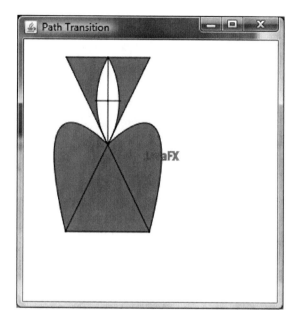

Figure 13-4. *Output from the path transition program*

In Listing 13-7, the code demonstrates the animation of a text node along the geometric contour of a path object, which you saw in Chapter 12. A path is constructed and given to the `PathTransition.path` attribute through `AnimationPath.createFromPath()`, which creates an animation path from the specified path object. The node to the path transition has to be applied is specified in the `node` attribute of the path transition. Finally, both paths have been added to the scene. The animation is set with other standard animation attributes, such as `duration`, `repeatCount`, and `autoReverse`, which you have already seen in the previous examples. Note that the `duration` attribute denotes the duration of one animation cycle, not the duration of a single snapshot of the animation as defined by `KeyFrame.time` attribute previously.

When you run this example, the output will resemble the screen capture shown in Figure 13-4; the text will animate along the path of the given sample path. One important thing to note in this example is that orientation is set on the `PathTransition`, which means the orientation is defaulted to `OrientationType.NONE`. Thus the targeted node's rotation matrix remains unchanged along the geometric path, and so the text always stays horizontal with no rotation.

There is also a way you can apply a rotation matrix to the target node so that the node changes its orientation when it is animated along the given path, keeping the node's rotation matrix perpendicular to the path's tangent. You will see the difference if you run the next example, Listing 13-8. Your output should resemble Figure 13-5.

Listing 13-8. *Applying a rotation matrix to a targeted node*

```
// Preceding code is the same as Listing 13-7
...
...

var pathTransition = PathTransition {
    duration: 10s
    path: AnimationPath.createFromPath(path)
    repeatCount: Timeline.INDEFINITE
    autoReverse: true
    orientation: OrientationType.ORTHOGONAL_TO_TANGENT
    node: node
}

pathTransition.play();
// Following code is the same as listing 13-7
...
...
```

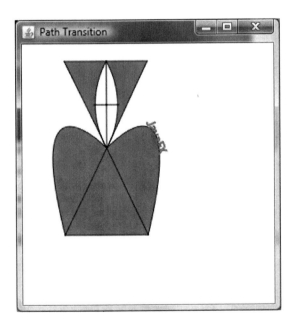

Figure 13-5. *PathTransition with orientation output*

In Listing 13-8, the only extra code added from Listing 13-7 is `PathTransition.orientation`, which is set to `ORTHOGONAL_TO_TANGENT` instead of implicitly to `NONE` (the default) as in the previous version. Compare the output shown in Figure 13-5 with Figure 13-4. You will notice that the text is now rotated in such a way that it stays perpendicular to the path's tangent.

■ **Note** A path can be a `javafx.scene.shape.Path` object or an SVGPath defined by `javafx.scene.shape.SVGPath`, where the coordinates of the path are defined in SVG notation.

Path transition is a very powerful animation technique, as it allows you to animate a node along the contour of an arbitrary path constructed by the `Path` object and can be used to construct very powerful animations in JavaFX.

Scale Transitions

A *scale transition* allows you to zoom into or out of a node by altering its `scaleX`, `scaleY` attributes over a timeline. This approach is slightly different from the one presented in Listing 13-1, where we altered the node geometry directly by changing the radius of the circle. In a scale transition, the node geometry stays the same but a scaling transformation is applied on the node to zoom into or out of the node.

■ **Note** A scale transformation does not alter the node geometry, and so the bounds of the node in local coordinates (`boundsInLocal`) remain unchanged. Only `boundsInParent` is altered (by the scale factor), whereas changing the radius of the node changes the node geometry and thus the `boundsInLocal` value as well.

A scale transformation can be done using absolute or incremental values, and absolute values always take precedence over incremental ones.

Now let us see how we can rewrite Listing 13-1 to use `ScaleTransition` to achieve the same effect; Listing 13-9 shows the code, and Figure 13-6 shows the output.

Listing 13-9. Applying a scale transition

```
import javafx.stage.Stage;
import javafx.scene.Scene;
import javafx.scene.shape.Circle;
import javafx.scene.paint.Color;
import javafx.animation.*;
import javafx.animation.transition.*;
import javafx.animation.Interpolator;

var rad : Number = 10.0;
var circle : Circle =  Circle {
```

```
            centerX: 100, centerY: 100
                radius : bind rad
            fill: Color.RED
    }

    var scaleTransition = ScaleTransition {
        fromX: 0.0
        fromY: 0.0
        toX: 8.0
        toY: 8.0
        node: circle
        duration: 4s
        repeatCount: Timeline.INDEFINITE
        autoReverse: true
    }

    scaleTransition.play();

    Stage {
        title: "Scale Transition"
        scene: Scene {
            width: 200
            height: 200
            content: [circle]
        }
    }
```

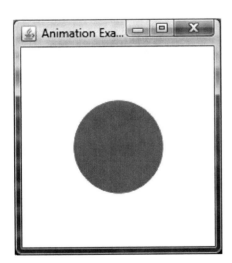

Figure 13-6. *Output of the scale transition program*

In Listing 13-9, we have rewritten our original code to create the same zoom effect. As in Listing 13-1, the radius of the node is increased from 0 to 80, which is equivalent to scaling the node by a factor of 8. Hence we have specified the starting `scaleX,Y` values as 0, 0 and the final `scaleX, Y` values as 8.0, 8.0 and the duration is the same 4 seconds. The transformation is applied on the node; `circle` and rest of the animation attributes are pretty much the same. When you run this example, you will get the same behavior as that of Listing 13-1 although the approach is different here. The `scaleX, Y` values of the given node change from `fromX/Y` to `toX/toY` over a time period of 4 seconds, and you don't have to explicitly bind anything to make the node scale appropriately.

■ **Note** `ScaleTransition` always scales the node with respect to its center, which means that any scale animation targeted with respect to an arbitrary point on the scene has to be done through the keyframes demonstrated previously and cannot be done by the `transition` class.

Rotate Transitions

A *rotate transition* is similar to a scale transition but rotates the node instead of scaling, using the `node.rotate` attribute. The rotation is specified in degrees and starts from `fromAngle` and ends with `toAngle`. Alternatively, you can make the transition incremental by specifying the `byAngle` attribute of the `RotateTransition` class.

Translate Transitions

A *translate transition* applies a translate transformation on the node through `Node.translateX, Y` attributes and thus translates the given node along the X,Y axis by the specified offset. You can specify either absolute values, using `toX/Y`, or incremental values, using `byX/Y`. The node will be translated along the X or Y axis appropriately.

Fade Transitions

A *fade transition* allows you to creating a fading effect by making the node disappear and reappear through the `node.opacity` attribute, whose value is altered from 0 to 1 or vice-versa. You can specify absolute values using `fromValue` and `toValue` or incremental values through `byValue` attributes available in the `FadeTransition` class.

    Now let us see an example that combines various transitions to create a nice animating application. Listing 13-10 shows the code, and Figure 13-7 illustrates the output.

Listing 13-10. Combining multiple transitions

```
import javafx.animation.*;
import javafx.animation.transition.*;
import javafx.scene.Group;
import javafx.scene.image.Image;
import javafx.scene.image.ImageView;
import javafx.scene.input.MouseEvent;
import javafx.scene.paint.Color;
```

```
import javafx.scene.paint.CycleMethod;
import javafx.scene.paint.RadialGradient;
import javafx.scene.paint.Stop;
import javafx.scene.Scene;
import javafx.scene.shape.ArcTo;
import javafx.scene.shape.Circle;
import javafx.scene.shape.MoveTo;
import javafx.scene.shape.Path;
import javafx.stage.Stage;

var x: Number;
var y: Number;
var stgX: Number = 0;
var stgY: Number = 0;
var scene: Scene;
var stgWidth: Number = bind scene.width;
var stgHeight: Number = bind scene.height;

var rgp: RadialGradient = RadialGradient {
    centerX: 0.5
    centerY: 0.5
    radius: 1.0
    proportional: true
    cycleMethod: CycleMethod.REFLECT

    stops: [
        Stop {
            offset: 0.0
            color: Color.RED
        },
        Stop {
            offset: 0.4
            color: Color.BLACK
        },
        Stop {
            offset: 0.7
            color: Color.GRAY
        }
    ]
}


var path: Path = Path {
    fill: rgp
    stroke: Color.LIGHTBLUE
    strokeWidth: 2
    elements: [
        MoveTo {
            x: 15
            y: 15
        },
        ArcTo {
```

```
                    x: 50
                    y: 10
                    radiusX: 20
                    radiusY: 20
                    sweepFlag: true
                },
                ArcTo {
                    x: 70
                    y: 20
                    radiusX: 20
                    radiusY: 20
                    sweepFlag: true
                },
                ArcTo {
                    x: 50
                    y: 60
                    radiusX: 20
                    radiusY: 20
                    sweepFlag: true
                },
                ArcTo {
                    x: 20
                    y: 50
                    radiusX: 10
                    radiusY: 5
                    sweepFlag: true
                },
                ArcTo {
                    x: 15
                    y: 15
                    radiusX: 10
                    radiusY: 10
                    sweepFlag: true
                },
        ]
};

var blueCircle: Circle = Circle {
    centerX: 15
    centerY: 15
    radius: 4
    fill: Color.BLUE
}

var redCircle: Circle = Circle {
    centerX: 70
    centerY: 20
    radius: 4
    fill: Color.RED
}

var greenCircle: Circle = Circle {
```

```
            centerX: 20
            centerY: 50
            radius: 4
            fill: Color.GREEN
    }

    var gr: Group = Group {
            translateX: bind x
            translateY: bind y
            content: [path, blueCircle, redCircle, greenCircle]
    }

    var pathTransition = PathTransition {
            duration: 5s
            node: blueCircle
            path: AnimationPath.createFromPath(path)
            orientation: OrientationType.ORTHOGONAL_TO_TANGENT
            repeatCount: Timeline.INDEFINITE
            rate: 0.5
    }
    pathTransition.play();

    var pathTransition1 = PathTransition {
            duration: 5s
            node: redCircle
            path: AnimationPath.createFromPath(path)
            orientation: OrientationType.ORTHOGONAL_TO_TANGENT
            repeatCount: Timeline.INDEFINITE
            rate: 1.0
    }
    pathTransition1.play();

    var pathTransition2 = PathTransition {
            duration: 5s
            node: greenCircle
            path: AnimationPath.createFromPath(path)
            orientation: OrientationType.ORTHOGONAL_TO_TANGENT
            repeatCount: Timeline.INDEFINITE
            rate: 2.0
    }
    pathTransition2.play();

    var xTimeline: Timeline = Timeline {
            repeatCount: Timeline.INDEFINITE
            autoReverse: true
            keyFrames: [
            at (0s) {x => scene.x},
            at (7s) {x =>
                stgWidth - 90 tween Interpolator.LINEAR},
            ]
    };
```

```
var yTimeline: Timeline = Timeline {
    repeatCount: Timeline.INDEFINITE
    autoReverse: true
    keyFrames: [
    at (0s) {y => scene.y},
    at (4s) {y => stgHeight - 75 tween Interpolator.LINEAR},
    ]
};

var fadeTransition = FadeTransition {
    duration: 10s
    node: bind path
    fromValue: 1.0
    toValue: 0.2
    repeatCount: Timeline.INDEFINITE
    autoReverse: true
    interpolate: true
}
fadeTransition.playFromStart();

var rotTransition = RotateTransition {
    duration: 4s
    node: bind gr
    fromAngle: 0
    toAngle: 360
    repeatCount: Timeline.INDEFINITE
    autoReverse: true
}
rotTransition.playFromStart();

scene = Scene{
    fill: Color.WHITE
    width: 240
    height: 320
    content: [ gr ]
}

Stage{
    title: "Cloud"
    visible: true

    scene: scene
    onClose: function() {
        java.lang.System.exit(0);
    }
}
xTimeline.play();
yTimeline.play();
```

Figure 13-7. Output of the cloud animation program

In Listing 13-10, you see an application that combines various transitions to animate an object. This example basically creates an arbitrary path that looks like a cloud and applies two transitions on the object, RotateTransition and FadeTransition. As the names suggest, RotateTransition keeps rotating the cloud object, and FadeTransition alters its opacity to create a fading effect. Apart from this, there are two other timelines that keep changing the node's translateX and translateY to keep the node moving.

In addition, there are three path animations defined along the path of the cloud object, in which three circles animate along the path. The animation rates of these three circles are set with different values so that the blue circle animates slowly, the red circle animates at medium speed, and the green circle animates quickly. When you run this application, you will notice that the red and green circles often overtake the blue circle thanks to their higher animation rates.

This application demonstrates various transitions and how to use them in conjunction with other timelines.

Parallel and Sequential Transitions

So far, you have seen various transitions available in JavaFX, and even begun to combine them, but now let us see how to combine these transitions in a more focused way to create advanced animation effects. In Listing 13-10, we indeed used multiple transitions together, but there is no order or dependency between the various transitions, and so they are executed in arbitrary order with no relation to one another. If we try to group the transitions in more meaningful ways, however, we soon see that there are two basic ways to do so. We can create a chain of transitional effects where one transition starts when another one completes; this is sequential in nature. On the other hand, we can also create transitions that are guaranteed to run in parallel irrespective of when the previous transition completes.

Parallel and *sequential transitions* are the JavaFX tools that implement this distinction. Containers themselves, they can hold other transitions and execute them in parallel or sequential order.

Our next two examples demonstrate these transition types. We'll begin with a simple example of parallel transitions: creating and animating star-shaped paths within the scene, triggered by mouse movements. Listing 13-11 shows the code, and Figure 13-8 shows its output.

Listing 13-11. A demonstration of parallel transitions

```
import javafx.stage.Stage;
import javafx.scene.shape.*;
import javafx.scene.input.*;
import javafx.scene.*;
import javafx.animation.transition.*;
import javafx.scene.paint.*;

var xAxis : Integer = 0;
var yAxis : Integer = 0;
var scene : Scene ;
var grp : Group = Group{};
 var star : Path ;

var bgRect : Rectangle = Rectangle{
    width : 250
    height : 250
    focusTraversable : true
    onMouseMoved: function (e: MouseEvent): Void {
        insert star = Path{
                    elements: [
                        MoveTo {x: 24.413, y: 12.207},
                        LineTo {x: 15.979, y: 14.947},
                        LineTo {x: 15.979, y: 23.816},
                        LineTo {x: 10.766, y: 16.641},
                        LineTo {x: 2.331, y: 19.381},
                        LineTo {x: 7.544, y: 12.207},
                        LineTo {x: 2.331, y: 5.032},
                        LineTo {x: 10.766, y: 7.772},
                        LineTo {x: 15.979, y: 0.597},
                        LineTo {x: 15.979, y: 9.466},
```

```
                                    ClosePath { },
                                    MoveTo {x: 0, y: 0},
                                    MoveTo {x: 24.413, y: 24.413}
                                ]
                            translateX: bind e.x
                            translateY: bind e.y
                            strokeWidth: 1
                            fill: Color.RED
                } into grp.content;

                ParallelTransition {
                    node: star
                    content: [
                        RotateTransition { duration: 1s byAngle: 360  },
                        ScaleTransition { duration: 2s node: star byX: 2 byY: 2 },
                        FadeTransition {
                                duration: 3s fromValue: 1.0 toValue: 0.0
                                action : function(){
                                    delete star from grp.content;
                                }
                        }
                    ]
                }.play();
            }
        }

        Stage {
            title: "Rotating and fading start"
            scene: bind Scene {
                content : bind [ bgRect  , grp]
                width: 200
                height: 200
            }
        }
```

Figure 13-8. *Output of the parallel transition program*

In Listing 13-11, we are creating and adding a star-shaped path to a group when the mouse is moved within a black rectangle. At the same time, we are defining a parallel transition that rotates, scales, and fades each of the stars added to the group. Because it is a parallel transition, all the transitions happen over the same time, and when you move the mouse within the black rectangle, you will notice that the stars are being created continuously and each undergoing different transformations at different times. Some shapes will be rotating, some of them will be fading out, and some of them will be zooming. There is no dependency defined among the transitions and hence you will see stars undergoing different transitions according to the time at which they were added and the time at which their parallel transition was started.

However, if we make the container transition sequential, then the stars first all appear, then rotate, then scale to the given scale factor, and finally fade out. All the transitions do not happen in parallel; instead, one transition is a dependent on the previous one, and a new transition cannot start until the previous one is complete.

You can easily see the difference by running both Listing 13-11 and the following Listing 13-12 (Figure 13-9 shows its output) and comparing their behaviors.

Listing 13-12. *A demonstration of sequential transitions*

```
//Previous code is the same as Listing 13-11
    ...
    ...

    SequentialTransition {
        node: star
        content: [
            RotateTransition { duration: 1s byAngle: 360  },
            ScaleTransition { duration: 2s node: star byX: 2 byY: 2 },
            FadeTransition {
                    duration: 3s fromValue: 1.0 toValue: 0.0
```

```
                            action : function(){
                                delete star from grp.content;
                            }
                        }
                    ]
                }.play();
            }
        }

        //Following code is the same as Listing 13-11
        ...
        ...
```

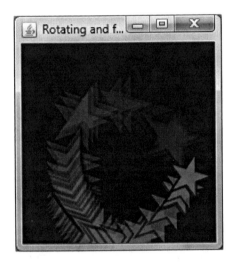

Figure 13-9. *Output of the sequential transition program*

Listing-13-12 uses the same code as that of Listing 13-11, with one difference: `ParallelTransition` is replaced by `Sequential Transition`. Again, just run the two versions and watch the difference in their behavior, and you will easily understand the difference between parallel and sequential transitions.

■ **Note** The `duration`, `repeatCount`, and `autoReverse` instance variables have no affect on these classes and are defined separately for each transition declared in the content variable.

Sequential and parallel transitions can be used in combination to create even more advanced visual effects. If a desired transformation cannot be implemented by a combination of any predefined animated transitions, you can override the `rebuildKeyFrames()` function of the `Transition` class to implement the keyframes that suit the logic of your application.

Summary

Animation can be defined as the change in a variable's value over a time period, and it is built into the JavaFX language syntax and independent of any UI library. Animation in JavaFX is defined through a set of keyframes (snapshots of the animation at specific times) and an enclosing timeline. This timeline can be played, paused, and stopped just like a movie played on your DVD player. Animation comes with its own operators that are handy in defining the value change and interpolation. Each keyframe can also have an action associated with it. You can use the elaborate or the simplified animation syntax depending on the complexity of your animation.

Animation also offers a set of predefined transitions that can be used to create transformational animations such as scaling, rotation, fading and translation. A node can be animated along the path of arbitrary shape using path transitions. Multiple transitions can be combined to create highly advanced visual effects, and the dependency between the transitions can be clearly defined using parallel or sequential transitions.

Index

Symbols

=> operator, 272

A

abstract classes
    definition of, 106
    using a JavaFX class to extend a Java abstract
        class, code listing, 151
abstract functions, 106
access specifiers, 75, 94
    abstract, 106
    accessing protected members freely within the
        same package, 126
    applying access specifiers to class definitions, 136
    base and derived classes, 124
    Car.fx script, code listing, 125
    combining primary and secondary access
        specifiers, 132
    definition of, 109
    enforced run() function requirement, 129
    honoring access specifiers for Java classes, 123
    JavaFX Script and, 110
    JavaImpl.java, code listing, 123
    Main.fx script, code listing, 123
    MediaBox.fx script, code listing, 131
    MediaPlayer.fx script, code listing, 131
    package, 76, 115, 118, 137
    protected, 76, 124, 138
    public, 76, 127, 139
    public-init, 134
    public-read, 131
    Rectangle.fx script, code listing, 128
    script-private, 111, 137
    secondary specifiers, 110
    syntax of, 110
    UIBuilder.fx script, code listing, 128
    using package access specifiers for class
        members, 121
    using secondary access specifiers with def
        declarations, 136
    using secondary access specifiers with var
        declarations, 131
    using the public access specifier with caution, 129
    Vehicle.fx script, code listing, 125
    See also data types
actual arguments, 77
Adobe Flash, 1
Adobe Flex, 1
advantages of JavaFX, 9
after keyword, 181
AJAX, 1
alpha channel, 220
animation
    => operator, 272
    animation in JavaFX, 269
    AnimationPath.createFromPath(), 287
    applying a rotation matrix to a targeted node,
        code listing, 288
    applying a scale transition, code listing, 289
    at clause, 283
    attributes for starting and stopping a timeline,
        274
    autoReverse, 273, 276
    changing the value of any attribute over a
        timeline, 269
    Circle Zoom program, code listing, 270
    combining multiple transitions to animate an
        object, code listing, 291
    creating a path transition, code listing, 284
    definiton of, 269
    FadeTransition class, 291

inbetweening, 272
interpolation, 270
javafx.animation, 270
javafx.animation.KeyFrame, 270
javafx.animation.Timeline, 270
javafx.animation.transition, 270, 283
javafx.lang.Duration, 271
javafx.scene.shape.Path, 289
javafx.scene.shape.SVGPath, 289
keyframe animation, 270
KeyFrame.action, code listing, 277
KeyFrame.canSkip, 277
KeyFrame.canSkip set to False, code listing, 280
KeyFrame.canSkip set to True, code listing, 281
KeyFrame.values, 272
LINEAR interpolation, 271
parallel transitions, code listing, 297
PathTransition class, 284
persistence of vision, 269
playFromStart(), 273
playing, pausing, and stopping an animation,
        code listing, 274
read-only variables that give the current
        animation status, 276
rebuildKeyFrames(), 300
repeatCount, 273
RotateTransition class, 291
ScaleTransition class, 289
sequential transitions, code listing, 299
simplifying the syntax of the Circle Zoom
        program, code listing, 282
state transition of a scene or node, 269
synthesizing a starting keyframe, 276
Timeline.INDEFINITE, 272, 280
Timeline.keyFrames, 272
Transition class, table of attributes, 284
transitions, using, 283
TranslateTransition class, 291
trigger clause, 282
tween operator, 272
using simplified syntax, 282
See also Duration class; KeyFrame class;
        PathTransition class; Timeline class
anonymous functions, 84
Application Execution Model, 25
AreaUtil.fx script, code listing, 117
arguments, 76
arithmetic expressions, 48
arithmetic operators
    arithmetic assignment operator, 51
    definition of, 50
    order of precedence, table of, 50

as keyword, 44
as operator
    definition of, 49
    typecasting, 49
assignment operator
    definition of, 48
    syntax of, 48
at clause, 283
autoReverse, 273, 276

B

base class, 141
before keyword, 181
bind keyword, 155
block expressions
    binding, 161
    definition of, 61
    Void, 61
Boolean, definition of, 41
bound expression, definition of, 155
bound keyword, 164
bounds
    boundsInLocal, 266
    boundsInParent, 265–267
    bounds-related attributes in the Node class, table
        of, 264
    determining the bounds calculations of a node,
        263
    javafx.geometry.Bounds, 263
    layoutBounds, 265–266
break expression, 66
browser mode, 22

C

Car.fx script, code listing, 125
cardinality, 33
charts
    creating a pie chart, code listing, 261
    types of charts supported by JavaFX, 260
classes
    abstract class, definition of, 106
    abstract functions, 106
    accessing members of a class, 95
    Account class example, complete code listing, 96
    applying access specifiers to class definitions, 136
    assigning default values to data members, 97
    base and derived classes, 92, 124
    binding with object literals, 165
    calling a Java method that is a JavaFX reserved
        word, 105

class declaration, example code listing, 94
.class files, 26
class name, 94
class-level binding, code listing, 167
colon operator, 95
creating class instances using either JavaFX style
    or Java style, 94–95
curly braces, 94
data member, definition of, 94
definition of, 91
dot operator, 95
init block, 97
initializing class attributes, 95
member function, definition of, 94
modifying class objects and data members, 99
new operator, 95
order of instance initialization, 99
package, 94, 137
parentheses, 95
postinit block, 99
protected, 94, 138
public, 94, 139
public-init, 94
public-read, 94
script-private, 137
sharing a function name between script-level and
    member functions, 104
structure of, 93
two methods for creating an instance of a class,
    94
using doubled angle brackets notation, 105
using function overloading within a class, 103
using non-member functions to access class
    objects, 101
using objects as function arguments, 100
using script-level variables and functions as static
    class members, 102
See also inheritance; object-oriented
    programming (OOP)
closure, 85
colon operator, 95
Color class, 221
comments
    comment syntax, 30
    JavaDoc Style tag, 30
    types of comments available in JavaFX, 30
common profile APIs
    alpha channel, 220
    attributes for tracking keyboard input, 231
    attributes for tracking mouse input, 232
    categories of, 203
    Color class, 221

cycleMethod, 225, 227
default values for fills and strokes, table of, 212
definition of, 203
fill, 210
how to define custom colors, 221
javafx.scene.image.Image, 238
javafx.scene.image.ImageView, 238, 244
javafx.scene.input.KeyEvent, 231
javafx.scene.input.MouseEvent, 232
javafx.scene.text.Font, 234
javafx.scene.text.Text, 234
linear gradient, 222
linear gradient REPEAT cycle, code listing, 226
linear gradient with absolute coordinates, code
    listing, 222
linear gradient with proportional coordinates,
    code listing, 224
Paint class, 220
radial gradient, 228
Shape class, 210
specifying a solid color or gradient, 210
sRGB color space, 220
stroke, 210
using a radial gradient with different focus points,
    code listing, 228
See also graphical APIs; image rendering; image
    transformations; text rendering
conditional expressions, binding, 158
continue expression, 67
coordinate system (2D), 206
coordinate system (3D), 207
curly braces, 37
CustomNode class, 251, 254
cycleMethod, 225, 227

▒ D

data abstraction, definition of, 92
data binding
    bidirectional binding, 169
    bidirectional binding with object literals, code
        listing, 170
    bidirectional binding, prohibited expressions, 171
    bidirectional multi-level binding, code listing, 171
    bind keyword, 155
    binding block expressions, 161
    binding functions, 162
    binding immutable objects, code listing, 168
    binding with conditional expressions, 158
    binding with for expressions, 159
    binding with object literals, 165
    bound block expression, code listing, 162

bound expression, definition of, 155
bound functions, 164
changing a bound expression from within a loop,
    code example, 156
class-level binding, code listing, 167
definition of, 155
eager binding, code listing, 173
eager binding, definition of, 172
implementing bidirectional binding using
    triggers, code listing, 194
implementing binding using triggers, 193
implementing hand-wired binding using triggers,
    code listing, 193
lazy binding, code listing, 173
lazy binding, definition of, 172
optimized reevaluation of a bound expression,
    code listing, 157
recalculation of bound expressions, 157
unidirectional binding, 156
using def instead of var with bound expressions,
    157
using triggers with bind, code listing, 192
with inverse keywords, 170
See also triggers
data hiding, 92, 109
data members
    assigning default values to, 97
    definition of, 94
data types, 33
    Boolean, 41
    detecting type errors at compile time, 33
    Duration, 42
    Integer, 39
    list of data types in JavaFX Script, 36
    Number, 40
    sequence, definition of, 175
    static type checkers, 33
    String, 36
    table of default values, 45
    typecasting, 43
    See also access specifiers
decimal numbers, definition of, 39
decrement operator, 53
def keyword, 34, 48
DelegateShape class, 220
delete keyword, 182
derived class, 141
designer bundle, components of, 12
desktop profile APIs
    categories of, 204
    definition of, 204
developer bundle, components of, 11

device space, 206
dot operator, 95
doubled angle brackets notation, 105
Duration class, 272
    definition of, 42
    methods of, 43
    representing indefinite time, 42
    toMillis(), 43
    toMinutes(), 43
    toSeconds(), 43
    using in a timeline, 42
    See also animation; KeyFrame class;
        PathTransition class; Timeline class

■ **E**

eager binding
    code listing, 173
    definition of, 172
Eclipse IDE, JavaFX Plug-in, 11
effects
    definition of, 263
    hardware acceleration and visual performance,
        263
    javafx.scene.effect, 263
element specifier, 33
Employee.fx script, code listing, 111
EmployeeList.fx script, code listing, 111
encapsulation, definition of, 92, 109
entry point, 27
escape sequences, table of, 38
exception handling
    throw clause, 71
    try-catch-finally block, 70
expressions
    arithmetic expressions, 48
    block expressions, 61
    break expression, 66
    continue expression, 67
    definition of, 47
    differentiating expressions, 72
    exception handling, 70
    for expression, 62
    if-else expression, 68
    looping expressions, 62
    new expression, 71
    range expressions, 59
    Void, 62
    while expression, 66
extends keyword, 141

■ F

faces, 234
FadeTransition class, node.opacity attribute, 291
false keyword, 41
fill, 210
first-class objects, 86
floating-point numbers, 40
focus, 231
focusTraversable, 231
fonts, 234
for expression, 62
    binding, 159
formal arguments, 77
from keyword, 183
functions
    access specifiers, 75–76
    actual arguments, 77
    anonymous functions, 84
    arguments, 76
    body of a function, 76
    closure, 85
    defining a function above the statement that calls it, 76
    definition of, 75
    example of how to write a function, 76
    first-class objects, 86
    formal arguments (formal parameters), 77
    function expression, 84
    function overloading, 82, 92, 103
    functions available in the JavaFX APIs, 75
    how a function works, 77
    identifier, 76
    local variables, 82
    member functions (instance functions), 75
    naming functions, 76
    parameters, 76
    polymorphism, 82
    recursive functions, 83
    run(), 86
    script-level functions, 75
    script-level variables, 81
    specifying the return type, 76
    syntax for defining a function, 75
    Void as a default return type, 76
    writing functions with arguments and a return value, 80
    writing functions with arguments but without a return value, 78
    writing functions without arguments but with a return value, 79
    writing functions without arguments or a return value, 77
    See also sequences; variables
.fx file extension, 26, 110

■ G

getArguments(), 88
glyphs, 234
graphical APIs
    alpha channel, 220
    categories of, 203
    Color class, 221
    common profile APIs, 203
    coordinate system (2D), 206
    coordinate system (3D), 207
    creating a first UI application, 212
    creating custom shapes, code listing, 218
    cycleMethod, 225, 227
    dashed stroke with auto synthesis of scene and stage, code listing, 216
    default values for fills and strokes, table of, 212
    DelegateShape class, 220
    desktop profile APIs, 204
    device space, 206
    drawing three circular rings (part 1), code listing, 212
    drawing three circular rings (part 2), code listing, 213
    drawing three circular rings (part 3), code listing, 214
    drawing three circular rings, complete code listing, 214
    drawing three circular rings, output of, 215
    fill, 210
    how to define custom colors, 221
    immediate mode rendering, 204
    javafx.scene.input.KeyEvent, 231
    javafx.scene.paint.Color, 213
    javafx.scene.Scene, 205
    javafx.scene.shape.Path, 218
    javafx.stage.Stage, 206
    linear gradient, 222
    linear gradient REPEAT cycle, code listing, 226
    linear gradient with absolute coordinates, code listing, 222
    linear gradient with proportional coordinates, code listing, 224
    morphing one shape into another, 220
    Node class, table of attributes, 209
    Paint class, 220
    radial gradient, 228

retained mode rendering, 204
scene graph data model, 204
Shape class, 210
specifying a solid color or gradient, 210
sRGB color space, 220
stroke, 210
synthesizing the scene and stage at runtime, 216
table of, 207
user space, 206
using a radial gradient with different focus points, code listing, 228
See also common profile APIs; image rendering; image transformations; text rendering

H

Hello World application
building and running from the command line, 27
deploying using NetBeans, 21
JAVA_HOME, 27
JavaFX Packager utility, 28
JAVAFX_HOME, 27
Main.fx, code listing, 19
PATH, 27
running in browser mode, 22
running in Mobile Emulator mode, 25
running in standalone mode, 21
running in standalone mode from the command line, 27
running in Web Start mode, 23
running on a browser or in Web Start from the command line, 28
storing the class files, 27
using the JavaFX Packager utility for the DESKTOP profile, 28
using the JavaFX Packager utility for the MOBILE profile, 29
writing a first JavaFX application, procedure for, 16
hexadecimal numerals, definition of, 39
history of JavaFX, 10

I

identifier, 76
if-else expression, 68
image rendering
controlling the rendering quality of a scaled image, 244
image formats supported by JavaFX, 238
javafx.scene.image.Image, 238
javafx.scene.image.ImageView, 238, 244

loading an image from a URL or a local file system, 238
loading an image in the background, code listing, 241
loading an image of a specific size, code listing, 240
loading an image, code listing, 239
placeholder images, 243
preserveRatio, 240
using a viewport, code listing, 244
See also common profile APIs; graphical APIs; image transformations; text rendering
image transformations
applying scale and shear transformations, code listing, 252
CustomNode class, 251, 254
Node.rotate attribute, 249
Node.transforms attribute, 246
rotation transformation using rotate on a custom node, code listing, 249
rotation transformation, definition of, 249
scaling transformation, definition of, 252
shearing transformation, definition of, 252
translation transformation using translateX and translateY, code listing, 247
translation transformation, definition of, 246
See also common profile APIs; graphical APIs; image rendering; text rendering
immediate mode rendering, 204
in clause, 63
inbetweening, 272
increment operator, 53
Indaba, 5
indefinite time, representing, 42
inheritance
abstract classes, 150
base and derived classes, 92, 124
base class, 141
comparing mixins in Java and JavaFX, code listing, 146
considerations when implementing inheritance in JavaFX, 145
creating a subclass extending from multiple mixin classes, code listing, 148
creating a subclass from a regular class and a mixin class, code listing, 147
definition of, 92, 141
derived class, 141
example of, 141
extends keyword, 141
implementing Java interfaces anonymously, code listing, 152

initialization order of data members, code listing, 142

instantiating a derived class that extends a mixin class, 147

java.awt.event.ActionListener, 152

mixin classes, 145

multiple inheritance, 145, 148

order of initialization in multiple inheritance, code listing, 149

override keyword, 142–143

overriding the data members or instance variables of a base class, code listing, 143

subclass, 141

super keyword, 144, 148

superclass, 141

using a JavaFX class to extend a Java abstract class, code listing, 151

See also classes; object-oriented programming (OOP)

init block, 97

input handling

attributes for tracking keyboard input, 231

attributes for tracking mouse input, 232

focus owner, 231

focusTraversable, 231

geometry-based picking versus bounds-based picking, 233

javafx.scene.input.KeyEvent, 231

javafx.scene.input.MouseEvent, 232

Node.blocksMouse, 232–233

Node.hover, 232

Node.pickOnBounds, 233

Node.pressed, 232

nodes that contain focus, 231

requestFocus(), 231

Stage.containsFocus attribute, 231

transferring focus to the next node in the focus cycle, 231

insert keyword, 181

insert statement, 64

Integer

definition of, 39

minimum and maximum values of, 39

interpolation, definition of, 270

into keyword, 181

▒ J

Java Network Launching Protocol (JNLP), 15

java.awt.event.ActionListener, 152

java.lang, 88

java.lang.Integer, 39

java.lang.Object, 42

Java.lang.String, 37

JAVA_HOME, 27

JavaFX

=> operator, 272

advantages of, 9

animation as changing the value of any attribute over a timeline, 269

animation in JavaFX, 269

at clause, 283

bind keyword, 155

checking the system and software requirements, 16

Circle Zoom program, code listing, 270

.class files, 26

combining multiple transitions to animate an object, code listing, 291

common profile APIs, 203

coordinate system (2D), 206

coordinate system (3D), 207

data binding, definition of, 155

declarative programming language, 27

designer bundle, components of, 12

desktop profile APIs, 204

developer bundle, components of, 11

device space, 206

entry point, 27

FadeTransition class, 291

.fx file extension, 26

graphical APIs, categories of, 203

graphical APIs, table of, 207

history of, 10

implementing Java interfaces anonymously, code listing, 152

inbetweening, 272

interpolation, 270

Java platform support, 9

Java Platform, Mobile Edition (Java ME), 9

Java Plug-in, 15

Java Runtime Environment (JRE), 9

Java Store, 15

Java Virtual Machine (JVM), 9

Java Web Start, 15

java.awt.event.ActionListener, 152

JavaDoc Style tag, 30

javafx, 26

JavaFX Graphics Viewer, 12

JavaFX Media Factory, 12

JavaFX Packager utility, 15, 28

JavaFX Plug-in for Eclipse IDE, 11

JavaFX Plug-in for NetBeans IDE, 11

JavaFX Production Suite, 10, 12

javafx.animation, 270
javafx.animation.KeyFrame, 270
javafx.animation.Timeline, 270
javafx.animation.transition, 270, 283
javafx.geometry.Bounds, 263
javafx.lang, 88
javafx.lang.Duration, 271
javafx.scene.Control, 255
javafx.scene.CustomNode, 251
javafx.scene.effect, 263
javafx.scene.image.Image, 238
javafx.scene.image.ImageView, 238, 244
javafx.scene.input.KeyEvent, 231
javafx.scene.input.MouseEvent, 232
javafx.scene.layout, 256
javafx.scene.Node, 208
javafx.scene.paint.Color, 213
javafx.scene.paint.Paint, 220
javafx.scene.Scene, 205
javafx.scene.Scene.stylesheets, 260
javafx.scene.shape.Path, 218, 289
javafx.scene.shape.Shape, 210
javafx.scene.shape.SVGPath, 289
javafx.scene.text.Font, 234
javafx.scene.text.Text, 234
javafx.stage.Stage, 206
javafx.util.Sequences, list of functions, 187
javafxc, 26
keyframe animation, 270
KeyFrame.action, code listing, 277
KeyFrame.values, 272
LINEAR interpolation, 271
Mobile Emulator, 11, 29
morphing one shape into another, 220
NetBeans IDE 6.7.1 for JavaFX 1.2.1, 11
Oliver, Christopher, 10
overview of the JavaFX 1.2.1 platform, 11
overview of the various platform elements, 13
parallel transitions, code listing, 297
PathTransition class, 284
playing, pausing, and stopping an animation,
    code listing, 274
plug-ins for Adobe Illustrator and Adobe
    Photoshop, 12
reusing existing Java libraries, 10
RotateTransition class, 291
ScaleTransition class, 289
scene graph data model, 204
sequential transitions, code listing, 299
simplifying the syntax of the Circle Zoom
    program, code listing, 282
standalone JavaFX 1.2.1 SDK, components of, 12

Sun Microsystems, 10
supported image formats, 238
SVG Converter, 12
Timeline.keyFrames, 272
Transition class, table of attributes, 284
TranslateTransition class, 291
tween operator, 272
tweening, 272
types of comments, 30
user space, 206
using a JavaFX class to extend a Java abstract
    class, code listing, 151
writing the Hello World application, 16
See also JavaFX Script; NetBeans IDE; Rich
    Internet Applications (RIAs)
JavaFX Mobile, overview of, 14
JavaFX Packager utility
    mandatory input parameters, list of, 28
    optional parameters, list of, 28
JavaFX Script
    abstract classes, 150
    access specifiers, 110
    accessing class variables from within a script, 113
    accessing script-private variables across multiple
        classes in a script, 114
    AreaUtil.fx script, code listing, 117
    as keyword, 44
    base class, 141
    benefits of, 10
    Boolean, 41
    calling the methods of Java's String class, 37
    cardinality, 33
    case-sensitivity of, 33
    character and string escape sequences, table of,
        38
    choosing between var and def when declaring
        variables, 34
    curly braces, 37
    data types, 33, 36
    data types, table of default values, 45
    decimal numbers, definition of, 39
    def keyword, 34, 48
    derived class, 141
    detecting type errors at compile time, 33
    Duration, 42
    element specifier, 33
    Employee.fx script, code listing, 111
    EmployeeList.fx script, code listing, 111
    expressions, 59
    extends keyword, 141
    fully qualified name of a class or script, 115–116
    functions, 75

.fx file extension, 110
hexadecimal numerals, definition of, 39
honoring access specifiers for Java classes, 123
implicit and explicit casting, 43
inheritance, definition of, 141
Integer, 39
JavaImpl.java, code listing, 123
Main.fx script, code listing, 19, 123
MediaBox.fx script, code listing, 131
MediaPlayer.fx script, code listing, 131
mixin classes, 145
multiple inheritance, 145, 148
naming variables, 34
nonstatic context, 110
Number, 40
object literals, 21
object-oriented programming (OOP), 91
octal numbers, definition of, 40
operators, 47
order of precedence for all JavaFX Script
    operators, table of, 57
override keyword, 142–143
package, definition of, 115
public-init access specifier, 134
public-read access specifier, 131
reserved keywords, table of, 35
scene, 21
script variables, importing, 117
script-private access specifier, 111
ScriptPrivateClassDef2.fx script, code listing, 113
ScriptPrivateClassDef3.fx script, code listing, 114
ScriptPrivateWithClassDef.fx script, code listing,
    113
secondary specifiers, 110
sequences, 44
ShapeBuilder.fx script, code listing, 117
single- and double-quoted text, 37
stage, 21
static context, 110
static modifier in Java, 110, 117
static type checkers, 33
statically typed language, 33, 36
String, 36–37
subclass, 141
subpackages, 115
super keyword, 144, 148
superclass, 141
syntax for declaring a variable, 35
trigger, definition of, 189
type inference, 35
typecasting, 43
understanding the script paradigm, 110

upcasting and downcasting, 43
using secondary access specifiers with def
    declarations, 136
using secondary access specifiers with var
    declarations, 131
var keyword, 34–35
variable declarations, 33
variable's type declaration, 35
See also JavaFX; NetBeans IDE; Rich Internet
    Applications (RIAs)

■ K
KeyFrame class
    attributes of, 276
    keyframe animation, definition of, 270
    KeyFrame.action, code listing, 277
    KeyFrame.canSkip, 277
    KeyFrame.canSkip set to False, code listing, 280
    KeyFrame.canSkip set to True, code listing, 281
    KeyFrame.values, 272
    synthesizing a starting keyframe, 276
    See also animation; Duration class;
        PathTransition class; Timeline class
keywords
    abstract, 106, 150
    after, 181
    as, 44
    before, 181
    bind, 155
    bound, 164
    class, 94, 150
    def, 34
    delete, 182
    extends, 141
    false, 41
    from, 183
    init, 97
    insert, 181
    into, 181
    lazy, 172
    mixin, 145
    mod, 51
    on replace, 189, 192, 197
    override, 142–143
    package, 116
    postinit, 99
    reverse, 184
    super, 144, 148
    table of reserved keywords in JavaFX Script, 35
    true, 41
    var, 34
    with inverse, 170

▓ L

lazy binding
    code listing, 173
    definition of, 172
ligatures, 234
linear gradient
    definition of, 222
    stop values, 224
    Stop#offset variable, 222
    syntax of, 222
LINEAR interpolation, 271
local variables, 82
logical operators, table of, 56
looping expressions
    break expression, 66
    continue expression, 67
    definition of, 62
    for expression, 62
    if-else expression, 68
    in clause, 63
    insert statement, 64
    null values, 65
    Void, 62
    where clause, 63
    while expression, 66

▓ M

Macromedia, 1
Main Project, 21
Main.fx script, code listing, 19, 123
Main.html, 29
Main.jad, 29
Main.jar, 28–29
Main.jnlp, 28
Main_browser.jnlp, 29
MediaBox.fx script, code listing, 131
MediaPlayer.fx script, code listing, 131
member functions, definition of, 75, 94
Microsoft Silverlight, 1
mixin classes, 145
Mobile Emulator, 11, 25, 29
modulus operator
    definition of, 51
    mod keyword, 51
Mozilla Prism, 1
multiple inheritance, 145, 148

▓ N

NetBeans IDE
    Application Execution Model, 25
    building and running applications from the command line, 27
    checking the system and software requirements, 16
    deploying the Hello World application, 21
    downloading and installing, 16
    JAVA_HOME, 27
    JavaFX Packager utility, 15, 28
    JavaFX Plug-in for NetBeans IDE, 11
    JAVAFX_HOME, 27
    Main Project, 21
    Main.fx, code listing, 19
    Main.html, 29
    Main.jad, 29
    Main.jar, 28–29
    Main.jnlp, 28
    Main_browser.jnlp, 29
    NetBeans IDE 6.7.1 for JavaFX 1.2.1, 11
    object literals, 21
    PATH, 27
    Projects tab, 21
    Run Project, 21, 24
    running applications in standalone mode from the command line, 27
    running applications on a browser or in Web Start from the command line, 28
    running in browser mode, 22
    running in Mobile Emulator mode, 25
    running in Web Start mode, 23
    scene, 21
    stage, 21
    storing the class files, 27
    updating, 16
    using the JavaFX Packager utility for the DESKTOP profile, 28
    using the JavaFX Packager utility for the MOBILE profile, 29
    writing the Hello World application using NetBeans, 16
    See also JavaFX; JavaFX Script; Rich Internet Applications (RIAs)
new expression, definition of, 71
new operator, 72, 95
Node class, table of attributes, 209
nonstatic context, 110
not operator, 55
null values, 65
Number

declaring, 41
definition of, 40
floating-point numbers, 40
range of, 41

■ O

object literals, 21
object-oriented programming (OOP)
    abstract class, definition of, 106
    access specifiers, definition of, 109
    advantages of, 91
    base and derived classes, 92, 124
    class declaration, example code listing, 94
    class, definition of, 91
    class, structure of, 93
    data abstraction, definition of, 92
    data hiding, 92, 109
    data member, definition of, 94
    encapsulation, definition of, 92, 109
    features of, 92
    function overloading, 92
    inheritance, definition of, 92
    member function, definition of, 94
    new operator, 95
    object, definition of, 92
    polymorphism, definition of, 92
    procedural programming languages and, 91
    secondary specifiers, 110
    two methods for creating an instance of a class, 94

    writing an API library, 109
    See also classes; inheritance
objects
    binding with object literals, 165
    definition of, 92
octal numbers, definition of, 40
Oliver, Christopher, 10
on replace clause, 189, 192, 197
operators
    => operator, 272
    arithmetic assignment operator, 51
    arithmetic operators, 50
    as operator, 49
    assignment operator, 48
    colon, 95
    decrement operator, 53
    definition of, 47
    dot, 95
    increment operator, 53

    logical operators, 56
    modulus (remainder) operator, 51
    new operator, 72, 95
    not operator, 55
    order of precedence, 52
    order of precedence for all JavaFX Script
        operators, table of, 57
    relational operators, 55
    reverse operator, 184
    sizeof operator, 176
    tween operator, 272
    unary - operator, 54
    unary + operator, 54
    unary operators, 52
override keyword, 142–143

■ P, Q

package, 76, 94
    definition of, 115
    organizing hierarchically, 116
    organizing source files into a single package, 116
    organizing with subpackages, 115
    package access specifier, code examples, 118
    package members, 116
    package-accessible classes, 137
    using package access specifiers for class
        members, 121
Paint class, 220
parameters, 76
parentheses, 95
PATH, 27
PathTransition class
    applying a rotation matrix to a targeted node,
        code listing, 288
    creating a path transition, code listing, 284
    See also animation; Duration class; KeyFrame
        class; Timeline class
persistence of vision, 269
placeholder images, 243
playFromStart(), 273
playing, pausing, and stopping an animation, code
    listing, 274
polymorphism, 82, 92
postfix mode, 53
postinit block, 99
prefix mode, 53
preserveRatio, 240
procedural programming languages, 91
Projects tab, 21
protected, 76, 94, 124

accessing protected members freely within the
same package, 126
Car.fx script, code listing, 125
code examples of, 125
protected classes, 138
Vehicle.fx script, code listing, 125
public, 76, 94, 127
enforced run() function requirement, 129
public classes, 139
Rectangle.fx script, code listing, 128
UIBuilder.fx script, code listing, 128
using the public access specifier with caution, 129
public-init, 94
code examples, 134
syntax of, 134
public-read, 94
code examples, 131
syntax of, 131

▨ R

radial gradient
definition of, 228
syntax of, 228
range expressions
definition of, 59
starting and ending values, 59
step value and step criteria, 59
table of, 59
rebuildKeyFrames(), 300
Rectangle.fx script, code listing, 128
recursive functions
definition of, 83
examples of, 83
relational operators
definition of, 55
table of, 55
requestFocus(), 231
reserved keywords in JavaFX Script, 35
retained mode rendering, 204
return type, 76
reverse operator, 184
Rich Internet Applications (RIAs)
Adobe Flash, 1
Adobe Flex, 1
AJAX, 1
characteristics and advantages of, 2
definition of, 1
designing a truly engaging user experience, 4
developing for a variety of devices, 4
enterprise applications, 4

example web sites, 5
exposing the pitfalls in a traditional web
application, 4
history of, 1
Indaba, 5
Macromedia, 1
Microsoft Silverlight, 1
Mozilla Prism, 1
new user interface requirements, 4
offering a solid designer-developer workflow, 3
storing data contextually, 4
See also JavaFX; JavaFX Script; NetBeans IDE
RotateTransition class, node.rotate attribute, 291
rotation transformation, definition of, 249
Run Project, 21, 24
run()
accessing command-line attributes, 87
defining with or without parameters, 87
definition of, 86
example of, 86
generating implicitly, 86
javafx executable, 86

▨ S

ScaleTransition class, 289
scaling transformation, definition of, 252
Scene class, 205
scene graph data model
definition of, 204
example of, 205
root, branch, and leaf nodes, 205
Scene class, 205
Stage class, 206
scene, definition of, 21
script-level functions, definition of, 75
script-level variables, 81
script-private access specifier, 111
script-private classes, 137
ScriptPrivateClassDef2.fx script, code listing, 113
ScriptPrivateClassDef3.fx script, code listing, 114
ScriptPrivateWithClassDef.fx script, code listing, 113
secondary specifiers, 110
sequences
accessing the elements of a sequence, 176
after keyword, 181
applying bidirectional binding between
sequences, 186
before keyword, 181
binding an element of a sequence to a variable,
186

binding sequence values to a range expression, 186

creating and initializing a sequence, 175

creating sequences using range expressions, 178

declaring, 44

definition of, 44, 175

delete keyword, 182

deleting elements from a sequence, 182

determining the number of elements, 176

differentiating sequence slicing from sequence predicates, 180

excluding the end value when using a range expression, 179

from keyword, 183

implementing a stack using a sequence, code listing, 184

insert keyword, 181

inserting elements into a sequence, 181

into keyword, 181

javafx.util.Sequences, list of functions, 187

nested sequences, 177

reverse operator, 184

reversing a sequence, 184

sequence slicing, 179

sequence triggers, 196

sequences as zero-based, 177

SequenceTriggerNewSyntax1.fx script, code listing, 198

SequenceTriggerNewSyntax2.fx script, code listing, 198

SequenceTriggerWithBind.fx script, code listing, 200

sizeof operator, 176

specifying the step value when using a range expression, 178

trigger defined on a sequence, code listing, 196

using a predicate to create a subset of a sequence, 180

using for loops and bind to create a sequence trigger, 200

using sequences as function parameters, 184

See also functions; variables

Shape class, 210

ShapeBuilder.fx script, code listing, 117

shearing transformation, definition of, 252

sizeof operator, 176

sRGB color space, 220

Stage class, 206

stage, definition of, 21

standalone mode, 21

static context, 110

static modifier (Java), 110, 117

static type checkers, 33

stop values, 224

Stop#offset variable, 222

String

calling the methods of Java's String class, 37

curly braces, 37

definition of, 36

escape sequences, table of, 38

examples of String declarations, 36

single- and double-quoted text, 37

Strings as immutable, 37

stroke, attributes of, 210

style sheets

customizing the built-in look of nodes and controls, 260

javafx.scene.Scene.stylesheets, 260

subclass, 141

subpackages, 115

Sun Microsystems and Christopher Oliver, 10

super keyword, 144, 148

superclass, 141

SVG Converter, 12

■ T

text rendering

breaking text into multiple lines, 235

demonstrating various text alignments, code listing, 236

faces, 234

font families, 234

fonts, 234

glyphs, 234

javafx.scene.text.Font, 234

javafx.scene.text.Text, 234

ligatures, 234

text node with a bound font, code listing, 234

wrappingWidth, specifying, 236

See also common profile APIs; graphical APIs; image rendering; image transformations

throw clause, 71

Timeline class

attributes for starting and stopping a timeline, 274

autoReverse, 273, 276

Duration data type, 42

playFromStart(), 273

playing, pausing, and stopping an animation, code listing, 274

read-only variables that give the current animation status, 276

repeatCount, 273

synthesizing a starting keyframe, 276
Timeline.INDEFINITE, 272, 280
See also animation; Duration class; KeyFrame
    class; PathTransition class
toMillis(), 43
toMinutes(), 43
toSeconds(), 43
Transition class
    rebuildKeyFrames(), 300
    table of attributes, 284
TranslateTransition class, 291
translation transformation, definition of, 246
trigger clause, 282
triggers
    accessing the old value of a variable, 191
    avoiding a divide-by-zero scenario using triggers,
        code listing, 195
    code examples, 189
    definition of, 189
    implementing bidirectional binding using
        triggers, code listing, 194
    implementing binding using triggers, 193
    implementing hand-wired binding using triggers,
        code listing, 193
    implementing nested triggers, code listing, 201
    on replace clause, 189, 192, 197
    sequence triggers, 196
    SequenceTriggerNewSyntax1.fx script, code
        listing, 198
    SequenceTriggerNewSyntax2.fx script, code
        listing, 198
    SequenceTriggerWithBind.fx script, code listing,
        200
    syntax of, 189
    syntax of a trigger with new clauses defined, 197
    trigger defined on a sequence, code listing, 196
    using for loops and bind to create a sequence
        trigger, 200
    using triggers as validators of data values, 195
    using triggers with bind, code listing, 192
    See also data binding
true keyword, 41
try-catch-finally block, 70
tweening
    definition of, 272
    inbetweening, 272
type inference, 35
typecasting
    as keyword, 44
    definition of, 43
    implicit and explicit casting, 43

upcasting and downcasting, 43
See also data types

■ U

UI
    controls supported as of JavaFX 1.3, list of, 255
    creating a first UI application, 212
    creating custom shapes, code listing, 218
    dashed stroke with auto synthesis of scene and
        stage, code listing, 216
    drawing three circular rings (part 1), code listing,
        212
    drawing three circular rings (part 2), code listing,
        213
    drawing three circular rings (part 3), code listing,
        214
    drawing three circular rings, complete code
        listing, 214
    drawing three circular rings, output of, 215
    javafx.scene.Control, 255
    javafx.scene.layout, 256
    login form using controls and a Panel layout,
        code listing, 256
    preview controls, list of, 256
    synthesizing the scene and stage at runtime, 216
UIBuilder.fx script, code listing, 128
unary operators
    decrement operator, 53
    definition of, 52
    increment operator, 53
    not operator, 55
    postfix mode, 53
    prefix mode, 53
    sizeof operator, 176
    unary - operator, 54
    unary + operator, 54
unidirectional binding, 156
user space, coordinate system (2D), 206

■ V

variables
    Boolean, 41
    choosing between var and def when declaring
        variables, 34
    def keyword, 34, 48
    local variables, 82
    naming variables, 34
    script-level variables, 81
    sequence, definition of, 175
    sequences, 44

syntax for declaring a variable, 35

type inference, 35

using secondary access specifiers with def declarations, 136

using secondary access specifiers with var declarations, 131

var keyword, 34–35

variable declarations, 33

variable's type declaration, 35

See also functions; sequences

Vehicle.fx script, code listing, 125

viewport, 244

Void, 61–62, 76

▓ W, X, Y, Z

Web Start mode, 23

where clause, 63

while expression, 66

wrappingWidth, 236

You Need the Companion eBook

Your purchase of this book entitles you to buy the companion PDF-version eBook for only $10. Take the weightless companion with you anywhere.

We believe this Apress title will prove so indispensable that you'll want to carry it with you everywhere, which is why we are offering the companion eBook (in PDF format) for $10 to customers who purchase this book now. Convenient and fully searchable, the PDF version of any content-rich, page-heavy Apress book makes a valuable addition to your programming library. You can easily find and copy code—or perform examples by quickly toggling between instructions and the application. Even simultaneously tackling a donut, diet soda, and complex code becomes simplified with hands-free eBooks!

Once you purchase your book, getting the $10 companion eBook is simple:

❶ Visit **www.apress.com/promo/tendollars/**.

❷ Complete a basic registration form to receive a randomly generated question about this title.

❸ Answer the question correctly in 60 seconds, and you will receive a promotional code to redeem for the $10.00 eBook.

You Need the Companion eBook

CPSIA information can be obtained at www.ICGtesting.com
Printed in the USA
243311LV00009B/35/P

9 781430 271994